SECOND EDITION

BEYOND THE NUMBERS

SECOND EDITION

BEYOND THE NUMBERS

Making Data Work for
Teachers and School Leaders

Stephen H. White

LEAD+
LEARN
PRESS

ENGLEWOOD, COLORADO

The Leadership and Learning Center
317 Inverness Way South, Suite 150
Englewood, Colorado 80112
Phone 1.866.399.6019 | Fax 303.504.9417
www.LeadandLearn.com

Published by Lead + Learn Press, a division of Houghton Mifflin Harcourt.

Library of Congress Cataloging-in-Publication Data

White, Stephen H., 1949–
   Beyond the numbers : making data work for teachers & school leaders / Stephen H. White. — 2nd ed.
     p. cm.
   Includes bibliographical references and index.
   ISBN 978-1-935588-07-8 (alk. paper)
1. Educational statistics—United States. 2. Educational indicators—United States.
3. Educational evaluation—United States. I. Title.
   LB2846.W439 2011
   379.1'58—dc22

                                                                              2011004686

ISBN 978-1-935588-07-8

Printed in the United States of America

16 15 14 13 12   04 05 06 07 08 09

Yohannon, Allan, and Carter

CONTENTS

ACKNOWLEDGMENTS

Beyond the Numbers, Second Edition, has been updated to include lessons learned and to frame this popular work in terms of emerging challenges to public education. The work is a combination of decades of public education experience and a growing belief in the collective wisdom and professional judgment of educators to make wise decisions when presented with very imperfect data.

My association with The Leadership and Learning Center has had a dramatic influence on my thinking about leadership, teaching, and learning: leadership, because the example of the Center's founder, Dr. Douglas Reeves, has been one of transparency, encouragement, and a relentless focus on building a better future; teaching, because the example of Bonnie Bishop, Tony Flach, Barb Pitchford, Laura Benson, Cathy Lassiter, Kristin Anderson, Lynn Howard, Larry Ainsworth, John Van Pelt, and dozens of others has elevated the profession to reflect the complexity, challenge, and dedication of the profession; learning, because each and every service from this extraordinary organization is designed to respect adult learners, draw out participants with lessons of research to apply their best thinking, and challenge educators everywhere to apply practical and user-friendly strategies to improve their practice individually and collectively.

My experience has blessed me with the opportunity to work with thousands of dedicated professionals at all levels who have been asked to respond to light-speed societal and political changes, dramatically improve student achievement, and generally save the world. Some of their stories are included in Beyond the Numbers, and I acknowledge their contribution and ask their forgiveness for blending stories across school systems and even across decades in the composite scenarios.

My wife Linda's ability to laugh at my foibles and encourage my best work at the same time is a gift I continue to experience and treasure.

Analysis of data is inextricably linked to accountability, assessment, and standards in the pursuit of effective means to make the promise to leave no child behind a reality, and this second edition is dedicated to make the best practices that carry that promise common practice in every school we have the opportunity to influence.

Stephen H. White, Ed.D.

Dr. Stephen White is a nationally recognized educational consultant with proven expertise in data analysis, systems, leadership assessment, program evaluation, and school improvement that is helping to change the way educators view themselves and manage data in an era of high-stakes accountability and testing.

His deep experience as a public school administrator includes 19 years of service as a superintendent, an assistant superintendent, an executive director, the CEO of a K–20 BOCES, a high school principal, and a coordinator of special education.

He is the author of several books, including *Leadership Maps* (2009), *Beyond the Numbers*, and *Show Me the Proof*, and coauthor of *School Improvement for the Next Generation* (2010). He has authored numerous articles and two invited chapters for best-selling authors, including "Data on Purpose" in *Ahead of the Curve* (2007). As a former superintendent and high school principal, Dr. White brings more than 35 years of experience at all levels. His résumé includes extensive work forging partnerships between K–12 and higher education and leadership in special education, crisis management, and technology prep. He is the primary author of the PIM™ school improvement framework and the Leadership Maps, a self-assessment instrument, and has reviewed more than 2,300 school improvement plans since 2005. He is active in his church, The Rock: Real Community, in Castle Rock, Colorado, and lives with his lovely wife, Linda, in Highlands Ranch, Colorado.

Dr. White can be reached at SWhite@LeadandLearn.com

When I began the first edition of *Beyond the Numbers*, the impact of the federal No Child Left Behind legislation was just beginning to be felt throughout the United States, and a sea change in terms of skill requirements for practicing teachers and principals was building. The field was beginning to realize that improvement was no longer optional for every child and that far fewer schools with students of color from families of poverty achieved at very high levels. In the intervening years, the conversation has shifted from the need for data-driven decision making to the need for the data to yield changes in practice that lifts achievement for all students.

Since the publication of the first edition, I have had the privilege of working in school systems that routinely break the mold, closing achievement gaps for second-language learners in Ontario, Canada, Colorado, and California; seeing individualized education plan (IEP) students compete with their peers on state assessments in Virginia, Connecticut, and Nebraska; celebrating postsecondary achievement and scholarships at elite universities by students of poverty in Denver and St. Paul; and participating in powerful interventions that succeeded in eliminating the achievement gaps for African Americans in Indiana, Minnesota, and Washington State. The discussion five years ago about whether it was possible to close achievement gaps for certain student groups has changed from a cascade of opposition to a whisper, and the need for data that I referenced as an axiom for reform in 2005 has accelerated to a call for data that is immediate and predictive. A steady drumbeat during this period has been a relentless pressure for educators to produce gains that can be sustained faster than ever before, as evidenced by the high expectations of Race to the Top, pervasiveness of value-added systems of teacher effectiveness, and an emerging expectation that teachers will be evaluated, at least in part, by the gains their students achieve.

Today, there are a number of emerging and sophisticated growth models (e.g., Tennessee, Alaska, Arizona, Delaware, 2008; Colorado Growth Model, 2009) that identify with some precision the growth trajectory for each student and the slope of the hill they must climb to catch up or keep up with their peers in terms of student proficiency. Adoption of the Common Core State Standards by more than 30 states will clearly introduce new measures of proficiency, as states and local school systems work to find the array of student assessments that most appropriately reflect the knowledge and skills students need in this current era and the measures that most accurately and fairly reflect teacher effectiveness. More than ever, educators are realizing that failure to make changes that improve student achievement as shown by specific, external measures of performance will not be tolerated. Thus, the ability to make quality decisions based on local data is a commodity that continues to be in great demand.

At Leadership and Learning Center data series seminars, thousands of participants have indicated a continued hunger for skills and understanding that go beyond the numbers. Astute educators remark, "I know how to collect the data and develop improvement plans. What I need is the ability to make sense out of data that doesn't tell me enough. I need tools that allow me to know why I'm getting the results I'm getting and what I need to do to get better results." In *Beyond the Numbers* and its handbook companion, *Show Me the Proof!*, teachers, principals, and even board members won't need a Ph.D. in educational tests and measurement to become experts in data analysis.

Beyond the Numbers describes the foundational principles for data analysis and provides the strategies necessary to turn that analysis into action. For too long, data has been associated with statistical tests, p values, and sampling error rather than professional judgment, discoveries, decisions, and innovation. It provides tools to those new to data analysis that they can use tomorrow in their schools and classrooms, and it supports savvy educators who are looking for more.

The first two chapters set the stage for a comprehensive program of data analysis, introducing readers to the rearview-mirror effect, bureaucratic creep, the importance of routine continuous improvement cycles, and the need to establish assessment calendars. Chapters 3 through 5 describe tried and true principles for effective, data-driven decision making that effectively represent the educational equivalent of due diligence to mitigate risks, ensure full disclosure, and lead from evidence rather than common myths or conventional wisdom. Chapters 6 and 7 offer powerful methods to glean insight from the events at school as they transpire, and Chapters 8 and 9 illustrate the need to gather evidence across learning conditions, professional practice, student achievement, and leadership decisions to identify what practices should be replicated to make best practices common practice. The final chapter, "The Teacher as Expert" (Chapter 10), summarizes the lessons of *Beyond the Numbers*.

Each chapter is updated to include a section about how the concepts and principles introduced can be applied to the Common Core, and this second edition also includes a number of new visuals and lessons learned in the effort to get "beyond the numbers."

Beyond the Numbers continues to use scenarios extensively with hypothetical data based on real experiences the author has encountered in more than 35 years in the field, and its message can still be summed up in the five Rs of data analysis:

- **Recognize** the influence of the rearview-mirror effect on current practices and policies and in our values about teaching and learning.
- **Realize** that data provide an opportunity that requires thoughtful analysis, infusion of our own experience and insights, and decisions that change how we practice the craft of teaching.
- **Reflect** on available data with other professionals, engaging the power of collaboration to examine student work, implement and monitor insightful changes, and improve student achievement.
- **Respond** to urgent challenges.
- **Replicate** practices that work to share the wealth of knowledge and expertise that exists in every school in the United States.

The instructional strategies that really lift performance in the twenty-first century will emerge locally, will represent replications of highly effective practices, and will come from the collective wisdom of teachers and school leaders in our schools today. The ideas in this book represent different ways to look at ourselves and our craft; they call us to get beyond the numbers to strategic and powerful analyses that result in actions that change our paradigms and make sustained differences that improve student achievement. I am convinced that the collective strengths of educators in schools and classrooms in every community are sufficient to understand where we have been, to chart a path leading to where we need to go, and to know why and how we will get there, until the promise of leaving no child behind becomes a reality.

CHAPTER

The Rearview-Mirror Effect

Most people are more comfortable with old problems
than with new solutions.

—ANONYMOUS

Data-driven decision making is widely accepted today as a necessary element of school leadership. Spurred by the movement toward standards and accountability in every state, educational systems today are under much greater pressure than ever before to produce measurable results. No fewer than 23 states have charter school takeover provisions in their accountability system, and virtually every state has some form of sanctions ranging from closure to reconstitution to charter takeovers (Steiner, 2005). States and districts themselves act much more often to intervene in low-performing schools, a shift from a prior disposition to defer to districts to handle their own affairs (Blume, 2010; Denver Public Schools, 2010; Education Week, 2010). Consequently, all across the United States, results in student achievement are driving responses by teachers and principals. Educators are realizing that failure to make changes that improve student achievement as measured by specific, external measures of performance will not be tolerated. Efforts to transform schools to comply with the No Child Left Behind Act of 2001 (P.L. 107-110) have been extended by a continuum of services referred to as "turnaround schools" (U.S. Department of Education, 2010, pp. 71–74), spurring dramatic changes in curriculum, standards, accountability, and assessment by states and local school systems. Thus, the ability to make quality decisions based on local data is a commodity in great demand.

At seminars offered by The Leadership and Learning Center, participants have indicated a hunger for skills and insights that go beyond the numbers. Savvy educators remark, "I know how to collect the data and develop improvement plans. What I need is the ability to make sense out of data that do not tell me enough. I need tools that allow me to know why I'm getting the results I'm getting and what I need to do to get better results." This book addresses those issues surrounding data analysis.

Toward that end, we begin in this chapter to examine the fundamental problem that continues to hamper efforts of dedicated public servants to achieve improvements in performance, implies the need for new methods toward discovering new solutions, and frames valuable student achievement data as necessary but insufficient. Consider the following fictional case of one such dedicated and capable public servant, someone not so different from you or me.

CASE STUDY

Superintendent Susan Ellison was not looking forward to tonight's board meeting, and for good reason. The local newspaper published the results of the statewide assessment test this morning, which revealed that the district average for achievement fell below the state average for the second consecutive year. Last year, Dr. Ellison persuaded a reluctant school board to double its investment in professional development; adopt a model computer program that provided multiple assessments for students at every grade in math, reading, and language arts; and institute a pay-for-performance system for administrators based solely on improved student achievement on the state test. It had been a bold move, but as Dr. Ellison reviewed the agenda, she knew a number of pointed and angry questions would be asked, and not a few board members looking for a scapegoat.

"Carol," Dr. Ellison said to her secretary, "please excuse yourself early tonight. I have a feeling the board meeting will go a little longer than usual. Go on home and put your feet up. We're as ready as we're going to be."

"Are you sure? I've got plenty to keep me busy. Should I call those who are presenting and remind them?"

"No thanks, Carol. We're all set. Tell John hello for me."

"Thanks, I'll be back at 6:30 to start the coffee."

Dr. Ellison smiled, then gently shut her office door behind her, clutched her coffee cup, and put her feet up herself.

"Where did I go wrong?" she asked herself, looking back over the past 18 months. "What gets measured gets done; focus on student achievement; maximize learning opportunities; accountability is about improvement."

She recalled the Center on Education Policy briefs published recently that reported slow but steady gains in closing achievement gaps (Kober, et al., 2010a, 2010b, 2010c) and highlighted research linking the use of data to the narrowing of those gaps (van Barneveld, 2008). She could see the faces of her staff, the software program salesman, the consultants; she knew the pride of staff who presented with her at the national conference she attended with three board members last year. Yet, here she was, without answers, wondering how much of all she had learned had been little more than hype. Dr. Ellison had made it a point to review school improvement plans each cabinet meeting, showcase schools that showed gains last year, and require each school to submit data by student and classroom from their online assessment program twice a month. Every principal and school improvement team designed goals, activities, and training in response to last year's scores, and Dr. Ellison provided great latitude to schools to adjust times and schedules to address skill deficits indicated by the state tests. Her curriculum director could provide data for every sub-group in math, reading, and language arts by grade level and by school without opening a file or book. She was that good, that organized, and that well informed about student achievement results. Never in the 76-year history of the district had so much data been collected by so many with as much purpose and intensity.

"For what?" she thought, closing her eyes and savoring the heat of her premeeting Starbucks.

"I should have left things the way they were," she thought briefly, realizing she was on the verge of self-pity.

She recalled the frequent attacks by the teacher's association: complaints about being overwhelmed, about how unfair the tests were, and especially about being out of the classroom for training. She remembered the comment in November that almost moved her to laughter: "We have enough trouble implementing the homework grading policy and sending out progress reports on time."

Dr. Ellison wasn't laughing tonight. She had been most certain about the positive impact of professional development. Perhaps she did move too quickly. Just then, the phone rang, and Dr. Ellison knew it was the school board president.

"Dr. Ellison, my phone's been ringing off the hook…"

Superintendent Ellison conducted herself throughout the board meeting with courage and dignity to maintain the support of the board and even support for her initiatives. She drew from a reservoir of inner strength and love of children to weather this storm, articulately describing the reality of learning as a complex and multifaceted process, the reality that state test data by grade measures location, not cohorts, and the reality that it takes time to make improvements. The meeting ended on a sober if not somber note, and although the local reporter had cooperated by pitching only softball questions, Dr. Ellison's drive home was not nearly as uplifting and positive as the carefully worded presentations of her staff would suggest. She glanced frequently out the rearview mirror tonight, trying to re-create what could have been, what should have been. The most disconcerting thought for Dr. Ellison was, however, the fact that for the first time in her professional life, she really did not know where to turn. Deep down, she was even more incensed than her lay board or the public about the results, and she feared another year of swimming against the tide would produce an all-too-similar result. She determined this would not be so, not on her watch.

Rearview-Mirror Effect

Dr. Ellison experienced the full brunt of the rearview-mirror effect, all the while not realizing she had succumbed to it. The rearview-mirror effect is defined as planning the future on the basis of past events, and it has four debilitating characteristics.

The first harmful characteristic of the rearview-mirror effect is responding to a rapidly changing reality based on past events. The rearview-mirror effect fails to anticipate urgent challenges and fails to elicit fresh feedback from students, parents, and teachers about the reality they are experiencing. A common example of the rearview-mirror effect is educators waiting for instructional practices to be verified in the educational literature before allowing changes to be introduced. How many schools or school systems insist on 80 percent faculty approval before instituting a new approach? How often are school improvement goals developed from popular conceptions rather than derived from trend data about student performance?

Like the view through the rearview mirror, we see what allowed us to get where we are today and little more. Schools commonly write improvement goals such as "80 percent of students will demonstrate one or more years' growth on the state assessment or standardized achievement test." Measurable? Yes. Realistic? Probably. Helpful? No way. This goal effectively defines success as one student in five falling further and further behind in proficiency. Rather than closing the learning gap, this plan accepts opening it wider.

A very popular superintendent in the 1990s had a long and distinguished career characterized by a refusal to adopt practices based solely on their popularity. By avoiding the fads of his day, he and the district stayed the course with instructional practices validated in the 1970s and 1980s. Schools performed at an achievement level expected for the district's demographics, and parents, teachers, and patrons were satisfied with the results. In today's environment, this wait-and-see approach will not produce the breakthrough results educators everywhere are challenged to create. It will not move educators one iota closer to meeting standards for all students, just as rearview-mirror thinking will not close the learning gap. The analogy of driving by looking out the rearview mirror illustrates the challenge all too clearly: one does not consider what is ahead when driving by looking out the rearview mirror, and anyone who drives this way for more than a split second is inviting disaster, even on the quietest country road.

The second debilitating characteristic of this effect is hesitating to act until the road reveals itself by waiting for and depending on annual assessments. Reliance on state assessment results as the single most important dimension of learning invites the very dilemma Superintendent Ellison's district experienced simply because data are examined after the fact. In many states, this rearview-mirror effect is exacerbated by a several-month wait for results that spans two different school years, a sore point to practitioners that is evident in more recent calls for Web-based assessments that render immediate results (Gewertz, 2010). In addition, a common and legitimate complaint from those held accountable for such results is that scores are compared from year to year with completely different students. This is one reason No Child Left Behind (NCLB), and several states prior to its passing, instituted annual testing to facilitate examination of test results by student cohorts. Unfortunately, even with this capacity, states continue to report scores in the most cost-efficient manner—annual test results—which explains in part the rise of growth models that help predict learning trajectories and at least document how steep the climb is for students to catch up or keep up with proficiency expectations. Annual assessments can be valuable in analysis, but reliance on them is part of the rearview-mirror effect because it creates a situation in which any response to the data is too little and too late. All too often educators chart a path of action, close their eyes, hold their nose, and jump, waiting patiently for positive results until the test scores roll in—annually. The most detailed school improvement plans periodically err in this way, glancing through a rearview mirror of data.

The third unhelpful characteristic of the rearview-mirror effect is its focus on a single dimension of the highway, a focus only on what students do. This focus is evident when educators fail to gather data on the factors that influence student achievement, limiting their analysis of "data" to measures of student achievement, behavior, or demographic characteristics. The most successful school systems understand that teacher behaviors, professional development, learning conditions, resources, teacher qualifications, curriculum alignment and development processes, assessment variety, common planning opportunities, and a host of antecedent conditions and structures influence student achievement. Teachers and administrators in these schools gather, analyze, and monitor data to determine the degree to which these practices and structures are implemented. Superintendent Ellison looked only at student achievement data, and the most reliable achievement data were gathered only annually. Is it any wonder that the important changes she initiated felt like a bold gamble? This reality is shared by schools across the country, as well-intentioned efforts to respond to lessons discerned from the data are hampered by an inability to look beyond a narrow definition of data itself. "Data" is not just numbers, and examining only student achievement data is a recipe for frustration. Proactive and safe drivers in the twenty-first century anticipate what is ahead; they attend to speed, driving conditions, the condition of the vehicle, and traffic. They pay attention to drivers in front, behind, to the right, and to the left of the vehicle. In the twenty-first century, schools that rely just on student achievement data to make decisions shortchange themselves and fail to access the expertise, wisdom, and intelligence of the faculty within them.

The fourth characteristic of the rearview-mirror effect is a wistful looking back to a prior time when "things were simpler." Few teachers and administrators would admit it, but Superintendent Ellison's reaction to less-than-favorable results was not unusual, especially with the heightened accountability that exists today. Criticism abounds about the unfairness of state assessments: "If only I could be left alone, I could go back to teaching." Our experience working with school leaders, teachers, and district administrators across the continent suggests that such responses are akin to driving via the rearview mirror with all the attendant consequences. Sustained breakthrough improvements in student achievement that exceed expectations will never occur by looking backward for answers.

We all know the adage, "If we continue doing what we have been doing, we will continue to get what we are getting." An adaptation might read, "If we do something different, we'll get something better." But there is no guarantee of the latter. Is it any wonder that the district Dr. Ellison served produced the same results from one year to the next? In fact, if her district achieved its goals in such a rearview-mirror context, that would be a real cause for wonder. What can be done to diminish the rearview-mirror effect? The answer can be summed up in five Rs to be examined in greater detail later:

- **Recognize** the influence of the rearview-mirror effect on current practices, policies, and our values about teaching and learning.
- **Realize** that data provide an opportunity that requires thoughtful analysis, infusion of our own experience and insights, and decisions that change how we practice the craft of teaching.
- **Reflect** on available data with other professionals, engaging the power of collaboration to examine student work, implement and monitor insightful changes, and improve student achievement.
- **Respond** to urgent challenges.
- **Replicate** practices that work to share the wealth of knowledge and expertise that exists in every school in the United States.

A major focus will be to eliminate as much as possible the rearview-mirror effect and equip educators to understand the reasons for the results their students achieve. Only when educators look beyond the numbers to examine the dynamics of teaching and learning will schools, systems, and states make the dramatic improvements that will need to be commonplace in the future. When professionals examine student work, they should take a close look at correlations and ask why. When the antecedents of excellence that precede improved performance are revealed and institutionalized, students will surprise us and colleagues will surprise each other. The 90/90/90 schools identified several years ago by The Leadership and Learning Center (Reeves, 2004b) continue to confound the skeptics because the results challenge the conventional wisdom about race, ethnicity, and poverty, as 90/90/90 schools are those with 90 percent of students in poverty, 90 percent of students of color, and 90 percent of students meeting state proficiency standards.

Data Everywhere, But Not a Drop to Use

Today's technology offers educators opportunities to monitor student achievement, offer quality corrective feedback, and adjust instruction to meet individual needs in ways only imagined by the previous generation of teachers. Data, like paperwork, increased exponentially prior to the accountability mandates that exist now in virtually every state, province, or national educational ministry. Our lives are inundated with data in print and electronic media, across every industry, and in every home. Surveys exist at fast-food restaurants and hospitals, and charts and graphs are much more prevalent in the daily work life of employees than ever before.

Dr. Douglas Reeves (2004a, p. 71) astutely observed that while students may be "over tested" in today's climate, they are also likely to be "under assessed." In other words, performance is rarely examined in terms of proficiency or to offer insights that can help us improve.

Test data and even more benign assessments are used to compare, rather than improve, performance. Before the reader considers such a judgment too harsh, consider whether:

- time is deliberately set aside for reflection on actual student work,
- a process exists in your school that ensures teacher reflections and insights are used to modify current practices, and
- action is taken as a result of patterns and trends that emerge from the data.

Far too often, these sources of quality analysis are overlooked or omitted. Experience at The Leadership and Learning Center indicates not so much a lack of data as an absence of analysis, and a greater absence of action driven by the data. It is not unusual for school districts to require reports for safety, attendance, behavior, demographics, budgets, school improvement, professional development, Title I designation, facility usage, parent visits, volunteers, committee meetings, staff observations, summative evaluations, activity reports, accident reports, field trip reports, immunizations, special education referrals, intervention efforts, technology purchases, e-mail usage, and the amount of copier toner used or copies made. This list, however lengthy, is not exhaustive, and readers who serve in schools today will easily identify additional reports to those listed here.

Now What Do I Do? The Dilemma of Data Collection

Few of us intentionally add superfluous data and record-keeping tasks, but doing so is an easy trap to fall into, particularly if employees in your school or district are typical of educators everywhere: dedicated, thorough, and hard-working employees committed to doing the best job they can, particularly in complying with expectations for production. The dilemma of data collection can best be illustrated by a look at the various data requirements of NCLB (Exhibit 1.1) and subsequent expectations in applications for consideration in the Race to the Top Initiative, a program developed as part of the American Recovery and Reinvestment Act of 2009.

In 2010, the Race to the Top Initiative (American Recovery and Reinvestment Act, 2009) added a number of new policy components as selection criteria, 52 percent of which require evidence of accomplishment (data), while 48 percent of the application describes a detailed and cohesive planning process. In addition to all the NCLB requirements, Race to the Top requirements involve numerous new data systems with monitoring and reporting capacity, and states across the nation have rapidly responded to that challenge. Both federal initiatives have resulted in much more granular data requirements that occur not only at the district level but also at each school and classroom. Exhibit 1.2 delineates the Race to the Top selection criteria.

These additions do not include the data requirements imposed by individual states or districts, nor do they reflect the "bureaucratic creep" so common in federal initiatives. In the U.S. form of government, separation of powers prevails among the legislative, executive, and judicial branches, and additional requirements or expectations can be anticipated at each level of implementation. Exhibit 1. 3 describes the process inherent in bureaucratic creep.

EXHIBIT **1.1 | No Child Left Behind Requirements**

Standards and Assessments

Reading standards
Mathematics standards
Science standards
Annual assessments in reading
Annual assessments in mathematics
Assessments in science
Assessment of English language proficiency
Inclusion of limited English proficiency
  (LEP) students
Inclusion of students with disabilities
Inclusion of migrant students
Disaggregation of results

NCLB School Improvement

Timely identification
Technical assistance
Public school choice
Rewards and sanctions
School recognition
School restructuring
Corrective action for local educational
  agencies (LEAs)

NCLB Safe Schools

Criteria for unsafe schools
Transfer policy for students in unsafe
  schools
Transfer policy for victims of violent crime

NCLB Accountability

Single accountability system
All schools included
Continuous growth to 100% proficiency
Annual determination of adequate yearly
  progress (AYP)
Accountability for all subgroups
Primarily based on academics
Graduation rates and additional indicator
Separate math and reading objectives
95% of students in all subgroups assessed

NCLB Report Card

State report card

NCLB Teacher Quality

Highly qualified teacher definition
Subject matter competence
Test for new elementary teachers
Highly qualified teacher in every classroom
High-quality professional development

NCLB Supplemental Services

Criteria for supplemental services
Approved supplemental services providers
Monitoring of supplemental services
  providers
Implementation of supplemental services

EXHIBIT **1.2 | Scoring Rubric for Race to the Top Initiative (2010)**

Selection Criteria	Points	%
A. State Success Factors	**125**	**25**
(A)(1) Articulating state's education reform agenda and local education agencies' (LEAs) participation in it	65	
(i) Articulating comprehensive, coherent reform agenda	*5*	
(ii) Securing LEA commitment	*45*	
(iii) Translating LEA participation into statewide impact	*15*	
(A)(2) Building strong statewide capacity to implement, scale up, and sustain proposed plans	30	
(i) Ensuring the capacity to implement	*20*	
(ii) Using broad stakeholder support	*10*	
(A)(3) Demonstrating significant progress in raising achievement and closing gaps	30	

EXHIBIT **1.2** | **Scoring Rubric for Race to the Top Initiative (2010)** (continued)

Selection Criteria	Points	%
(i) Making progress in each reform area	*5*	
(ii) Improving student outcomes	*25*	
B. Standards and Assessments	**70**	**14**
(B)(1) Developing and adopting common standards	40	
(i) Participating in consortium developing high-quality standards	*20*	
(ii) Adopting standards	*20*	
(B)(2) Developing and implementing common, high-quality assessments	10	
(B)(3) Supporting the transition to enhanced standards + high-quality assessments	20	
C. Data Systems to Support Instruction	**37**	**9**
(C)(1) Fully implementing a statewide longitudinal data system	14	
(C)(2) Accessing and using state data	5	
(C)(3) Using data to improve instruction	18	
D. Great Teachers and Leaders	**138**	**28**
Eligibility Requirements (b)	eligibility	
(D)(1) Providing high-quality pathways for aspiring teachers and principals	21	
(D)(2) Improving teacher and principal effectiveness based on performance	58	
(i) Measuring student growth	*5*	
(ii) Developing evaluation systems	*15*	
(iii) Conducting annual evaluations	*10*	
(iv) Using evaluations to inform key decisions	*28*	
(D)(3) Ensuring equitable distribution of effective teachers and principals	25	
(i) Ensuring equitable distribution in high-poverty or high-minority schools	*15*	
(ii) Ensuring equitable distribution in hard-to-staff subjects or specialty areas	*10*	
(D)(4) Improving the effectiveness of teacher and principal preparation programs	14	
(D)(5) Providing effective support to teachers and principals	20	
E. Turning Around the Lowest-Achieving Schools	**50**	**10**
(E)(1) Intervening in the lowest-achieving schools and LEAs	10	
(E)(2) Turning around the lowest-achieving schools	40	
(i) Identifying the persistently lowest-achieving schools	*5*	
(ii) Turning around the persistently lowest-achieving schools	*35*	
F. General	**55**	**11**
Eligibility Requirements (a)		
(F)(1) Making education funding a priority	10	
(F)(2) Ensuring successful conditions for high-performing charter schools/innovations	40	
(F)(3) Demonstrating other significant reform conditions	5	
Competitive Preference Priority 2: Emphasis on STEM (science, technology, engineering, and mathematics)	**15**	**3**
Total	**500**	**100%**

Source: U.S. Department of Education, *Race to the Top Application* (2010, 76).

EXHIBIT **1.3** | **Bureaucratic Creep**

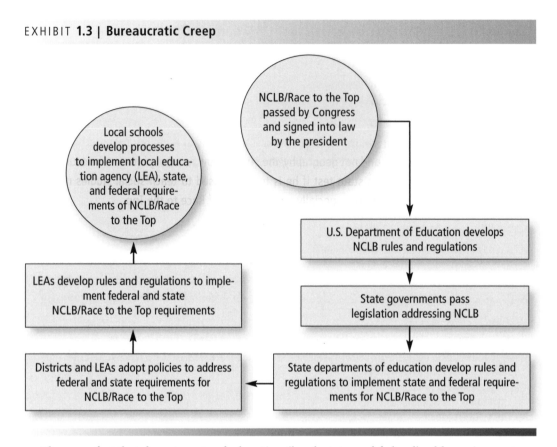

The mere fact that departments of education (local, state, and federal) add requirements does not make those requirements onerous, in and of themselves. Whether the requirements are based on local board policy or acts of Congress, an appropriate balance is needed between administering the spirit of a law and defining the process that will govern its implementation. The problem with bureaucratic creep emerges when each level, in its effort to add value, also adds complexity. What does bureaucratic creep have to do with data? Using the Race to the Top as a frame of reference, consider the following not-so-far-fetched scenario:

CASE STUDY

Mr. Hutchinson teaches seventh-grade social studies in a small, rural, Midwest community. Until three years ago, his students did not have to take a standardized measure of any kind, as the district was satisfied with screening at kindergarten; administering a norm-referenced test at grades 3, 6, and 8; and relying on ACT and SAT scores and completion rates at the high school to monitor the quality of the district's curriculum and its ability to challenge students to strive for achieving their potential. All that has changed: now an annual district writing assessment is administered and scored by all content-area teachers; the state has required a reading and math assessment at every grade; the district curriculum director has insisted that every secondary course (grades 7 through 12) administers an end-of-course (EOC) assessment with higher-order thinking items and applied demonstration of key skills; and the social studies department has elected to add constructed-response items to its multiple-choice, criterion-referenced exam as a pre- and post-test. Mr. Hutchinson believes all he does now is test students. Gone is his opportunity to delve deeply into world geography; develop student-generated units on various cultures; and take several (two per nine-week grading period) field trips into the state capital to visit museums and meet with people from a wide variety of ethnic, religious, and cultural groups from around the globe. In addition, because he had majored in psychology and not geography, the state is now requiring him to take courses in geography and pass a state test if he is to be licensed to teach social studies next fall. Mr. Hutchinson is angry, especially about NCLB and Race to the Top.

Was bureaucratic creep evident in Mr. Hutchinson's situation? Very few of these new demands were required by either NCLB or the Race to the Top Initiative. Though the use of EOC assessments helps align and focus the curriculum and ample evidence exists that a writing assessment that engages all classroom teachers is good for students and good for teaching (Reeves, 2000), neither of these innovations is actually required. What about the licensure problem? Even that requirement has some latitude, and if his state were to license teachers by a broad discipline designation (e.g., social studies), Mr. Hutchinson's psychology major could suffice. The use of standardized, norm-referenced assessments is not required, as long as the state math and reading assessment requirement is met, and Mr. Hutchinson's rich world geography units with hands-on interviews, multiple applications, and quality team learning could be incorporated into a meaningful performance assessment that aligns with standards. The example illustrates how bureaucratic creep is a natural outgrowth of the federal system of separation of powers and how easily schools and school systems respond with additional requirements that tax teachers in counterproductive ways. Bureaucratic creep, then, begs the question, "What can I get rid of? What should I stop doing, and how?" The following true story drives home the point.

CASE STUDY

A supervisor included in each payroll record for her department a form listing current department employees, their social security numbers, and their start time and end time for each day. This handwritten report was attached to time cards, which had been modified in 2009 to identify only days absent or out of the district for school business (e.g., a training seminar). After three years of this policy being in place, and 11 years of duplicating information, an inquiry was made to the supervisor and to the accounting department.

The inquiry to accounting proceeded as follows:

"Was the additional form required by accounting?"

"No, we thought the supervisor needed to submit the report for someone else."

The inquiry to the supervisor:

"Who required you to append the department list to the time cards?"

"We've done this since I arrived here 11 years ago, and I assumed accounting needed the data."

No one used the information, and no one made a decision resulting from the additional data, but the supervisor spent at least 30 minutes every two weeks and nine employees within her department spent 15 minutes each compiling details on a form whose origin no one remembered. The math would be funny, if it weren't so representative of busy school systems that do not slow down long enough to subtract unnecessary reports, paperwork, and just plain busywork. Over that 11-year period, almost 20 weeks of time were given to that activity.

Was this situation an isolated case? Do procedures or forms that duplicate current effort hang on because "We've always done it that way" in your setting? All too often, the candid response is yes. As professional educators, we cannot see the forest for the trees if we don't find ways to subtract the data we gather at least every time we add something new.

The Need for Subtraction

The need to subtract redundant practices or duplication of effort resonates with almost everyone. Most would agree that a mechanism to achieve this balance would be absolutely essential for any accountability or data-driven decision-making system. Unfortunately, subtraction within organizations bound by policies, rules, and regulations requires explicit permission to do so. The surprise for the individuals in the previous example occurred because assumptions were made and permission to stop doing something was not spelled out, or more appropriately, shouted from the rooftops. Leaders must be intentional and explicit in their communication of this principle if schools are to avoid obsolete practices that take time away from the important work of improving the achievement of students and performance of staff. Responsibility for results is meaningless without the authority to make changes. The following scenario brings the concept of subtraction back to the classroom.

CASE STUDY

Mrs. Andrew's 24 third graders were expected to score as high or higher on the state reading assessment as her previous year's class. Unfortunately, Mrs. Andrew also knew that this year's 24 students were starting at entirely different places in terms of their reading abilities than those in the previous year, when all but two students were reading at or above grade level by the end of the first nine-week period. Nonplussed, Mrs. Andrew initiated several differentiation strategies and increased the quantity and quality of writing by insisting that every culminating activity in every subject have a writing component and by using explicit analytical writing rubrics, preferably stated in terms generated by the students themselves. This approach worked well, and despite the fact that four disabled students were being served on plans in adherence to Section 504 of the Rehabilitation Act of 1973 (not eligible for special education) and three others were English language acquisition students with only minimal literacy in their first language, Mrs. Andrew was seeing progress. By the end of the second nine-week grading period, however, it was clear that the integrated curriculum strategies and differentiated instructional strategies needed more direct intervention for five of her students. Without additional time for small-group or even one-to-one instruction for these five students in the skills of reading, she was certain they would not come close to scoring proficient on the state assessment in the spring.

She approached her principal with the dilemma, but the district had a board-approved minutes schedule for elementary curriculum that prescribed minutes for art, music, health, physical education, peer mediation, and social studies to complement the areas tested by the state: language arts (including reading and a writing assessment), mathematics, and science. The principal would not allow her to deviate for these five students, citing board policy. Mrs. Andrew was responsible for improved student achievement, and she was committed to helping all her students achieve at their highest level, but she did not have commensurate authority to adjust time or content, except in terms of homework. Was she as effective as this master teacher could have been? She improvised and was resourceful but was restricted in her options.

The authority to act requires permission to subtract. Teachers and administrators, in formal and informal settings, almost universally identify the need for more time as one of the most pressing challenges today. The angst felt by Mr. Hutchinson in the example earlier was likely just as much a response to the need to reinvent how he teaches as it was to the apparent marginalizing of his craft. Both examples require teachers to change what they are doing, based on evidence of how students are achieving, and therein lies the rub. No longer is our business about "teaching." Standards have forever changed the equation, as teaching is more and more focused on what students are learning, and why. Quality data analysis can reveal insights about individual students and teaching skills that are not evident without reflecting, examining, probing, and questioning data from various perspectives. Schmoker (2006) speaks of how data, when analyzed in a collaborative way, "makes visible the invisible," leading us to make changes that improve performance. Data provide information we otherwise would not have. It behooves us to stop and reflect on what student achievement data, antecedent data, teaching data, and all kinds of data tell us. I have found the following rule of thumb to be particularly helpful in counseling schools and school districts around the country:

Data that is collected should be analyzed and used to make improvements.

The bureaucratic creep depicted in Exhibit 1.3 illustrates how easily data can be multiplied but not necessarily improved. A second reality of data systems in public schools that is unavoidable occurs when data are collected for compliance purposes. Many times, regulations for statute compliance require reporting of data that are never analyzed and never used to improve processes, let alone student achievement. Consider the following description of a state school finance requirement that has been in place for almost 20 years.

CASE STUDY

> To protect the taxpayer and ensure transparent financial management of schools, legislation was passed to provide the legislature annual fiscal reports that included each transaction for each school district. Because public kindergarten through grade 12 (hereafter referred to as K–12) education was the state's largest expenditure (all 50 states share that distinction), it was believed that a complete electronic transmission of expenditures would provide insights and potential savings that would advise future legislatures. Since that time, data have been collected but never analyzed for that purpose. The state education department implements the law, and local districts commit inordinate amounts of labor to submit and resubmit the detail. The information is used just to verify compliance.

This example is striking in its costliness to all parties. It also represents one of the worst examples of data collected just because it has to be collected. It makes the case that if data are collected, they should be analyzed and used to make improvements (or analyzed to affirm current practices and stay the course). Data should invite action. Gathering data for compliance purposes is a reality that professionals often must contend with, but all other data gathered should be scrutinized under this rule of thumb:

If the data is not being used, stop collecting it.

The Common Core State Standards and the Rearview-Mirror Effect

Adoption of the Common Core State Standards, as of the time of this writing, included well over two-thirds of the states as they moved forward to raise performance expectations and improve student performance in English language arts and mathematics. The process began long before these standards were developed or adopted, and long before NCLB became law. In fact, this recent iteration of standards was a culmination of state-by-state standards development over the past two decades that pursued clear definitions of what students should know and be able to do to succeed at school, succeed in pursuit of postsecondary options available to them, and succeed in life. The Common Core State Standards, commissioned by the National

Governors Association, represent a stellar accomplishment characterized by rigor and clarity, clear connections among grade levels, and clarity and specificity of every standard.

In English language arts, the Common Core prescribes a diverse array of classic and contemporary literature as well as challenging informational texts in a range of subjects by expecting students to build knowledge, explore possibilities, gain insights, and broaden understanding and perspective. Of particular note is a new emphasis on nonfiction writing in K–12 and across content areas, and the standards call out specific quality literature content at all levels as standards themselves, including cultural classics. Even more striking is the fact that the Common Core requires the progressive development of reading comprehension from grade level to grade level, teaching level to teaching level. Six elements of literacy (reading, writing, speaking, listening, vocabulary enhancement, and the use of media and technology to communicate) are systematically addressed in this sequence of standards, providing a comprehensive effort to lift student performance to levels needed to succeed in the current global environment. Finally, literacy is interdisciplinary, the recognition of which is an important breakthrough in both identifying authentic requirements of an educated public and creating a foundation for exceptional and engaging assessments (Common Core State Standards Initiative, 2010a).

In mathematics, the Common Core extends early forays into mathematical proficiency by insisting that each standard at every level be demonstrated through eight discrete practices that deepen understanding and application of mathematics to authentic challenges: (1) make sense of problems and persevere in solving them, (2) reason abstractly and quantitatively, (3) construct viable arguments and critique the reasoning of others, (4) model with mathematics, (5) use appropriate tools strategically, (6) attend to precision, (7) look for and make use of structures, and (8) look for and express regularity in repeated reasoning (Common Core State Standards Initiative, 2010d).

The Common Core State Standards may fall victim to a variety of rearview-mirror effects, including sole reliance on student achievement—high-stakes annual assessments—or viewing the Common Core from the experience of the past that led to multiple approaches to establishing standards across the states. An even worse effect is a proliferation of assessments without attention to the need to focus and prioritize instruction on the knowledge and skills that serve as gateways and launching pads to increased understanding, depth of skill application, and rapid assimilation of information across content areas. The good news is that the Common Core was designed to break this historical pattern by offering practitioners practical and explicit tools, content, and strategies that can augment student achievement data and more effective real-time analysis to ensure progressively more rigorous, challenging, and engaging learning by every student.

Summary

Superintendent Ellison had ample data at her fingertips, yet she knew the data were driving her and her staff, rather than improving her ability to make decisions. It is not enough to achieve results if one has no idea how to replicate them. Teaching and learning are complex endeavors that require the best thinking of practitioners, accountability that empowers, and strategic implementation of instructional approaches. We collect lots of data, sometimes using hundreds of person-hours as in the example of district budgets noted earlier, where data were collected but never analyzed or used. In an era of standards, schools are swimming, and sometimes drowning, in data, but systematic analysis is often lacking or absent.

Effective decision making driven by data requires active involvement of educators in the field. By understanding analysis as well as lesson plans, data can come alive with insights and understanding that can in turn empower educators and improve student achievement. This discussion of the rearview-mirror effect, the challenge of having too much data, and the need for subtraction provide a preview for the remainder of this book. Classroom teachers and hands-on building principals all over the nation possess the expertise to make decisions on the basis of sound data, and the Common Core State Standards offer high-quality content and structures to wisely leverage data to identify the most successful practices and translate them into common practices in the years ahead. The ensuing chapters are designed to unlock that expertise for every reader and for the students each reader serves.

Reflection

BIG IDEA: To get beyond the numbers, educators must be as intentional about analysis as they are about lesson plans.

Do you have a process in your school, classroom, department, or system for subtracting obsolete practices?

BIG IDEA: Data that are collected should be analyzed and used to make improvements.

Do you currently analyze data about teacher practices related to short-cycle achievement gains to help you avoid making rearview-mirror decisions?

What are some limitations of annual testing? School improvement planning?

Analysis: Key to Data Management and Decision Making

Men occasionally stumble over the truth, but most of them pick themselves up and hurry off as if nothing had happened.

—SIR WINSTON CHURCHILL (1874–1965)

CASE STUDY

Timberline Middle School serves a diverse student population and community, with a sufficient number of students to compare all No Child Left Behind Act (NCLB) sub-groups. Its 1,150 students in grades 6 through 8 come from middle-income working families. The school served an older inner-suburb community that has seen a dramatic change in its demographics over the past decade, as families who raised children in the 1960s have been replaced by families new to the community, including many families new to the United States.

Principal Smith is in her third year as a principal, having served in the adjacent school system as an assistant principal for the previous 18 months; she has finished her master's program. Principal Smith is acutely aware of the high stakes involved with the state accountability system, demands of NCLB, and more recent expectations that teacher effectiveness be linked to student achievement. As in other states, if her school fails to make adequate yearly progress (AYP) for five consecutive years, it will likely be reconstituted under an autonomous charter with entirely new staff and a new focus that may or may not be related to the local community. This possibility is unacceptable to Principal Smith.

Her leadership is recognized for high expectations; extensive data systems; and accountability for students, teachers, and parents. Adapting lessons from a successful inner-city academy model, Principal Smith offered after-school and Saturday opportunities for students to demonstrate proficiency, and students, teachers, and parents realize that advancement from grade to grade and into Timberline High School requires a clear demonstration of proficiency for each standard.

Data is important at Timberline Middle School, and a wide range of student assessments is administered. For example, Timberline sends home progress reports every three weeks, and parents can access data on attendance, behavior, classroom assignments, and grades online. This process has proved to be an excellent means of communication for parents whose work makes it difficult to attend the trimester parent conference meetings in the evening. Timberline's range of student assessments is presented in Exhibit 2.1.

EXHIBIT **2.1 | Hypothetical Student Assessments**

Assessment	Frequency
Skills timings (reading speed, math computation)	At least weekly in language arts and mathematics; teachers differentiate timing requirements to build skills with massed practice
Progress reports	3 per trimester
Grades	Trimester report cards
End-of-course (criterion-referenced test) multiple-choice assessments	1 per core subject per trimester
Performance assessments	1 per course per trimester, all courses
Unit tests	6 per year for core: language arts, math, science, social studies
District writing assessment	Pre/post, K–10, fall and spring testing
Statewide writing assessment	Fall, grades 3–10
Statewide academic content standards assessment	Spring, grades 3–10, math, reading, writing
Standardized norm-referenced test	Grades 2, 5, 8, 11; spring
Postsecondary assessments (SAT, ACT, and Armed Services Vocational Aptitude Battery [ASVAB] for the armed services)	Grade 11, fall and spring; grade 12 for SAT and ACT; grade 10 for ASVAB
Computerized basic skills testing in math and reading	Ongoing; students access reports in weekly computer labs after each test, and administration and teachers have desktop access to monitor progress

Principal Smith is very proud of the range of data collected, and classrooms that show the greatest improvement on writing assessments are recognized on her "data wall" outside the office. Student attendance, tardies, and school improvement targets for the statewide tests and the norm-referenced test (NRT) results are displayed in the same area, and students are expected to maintain self-assessment notebooks to chart their own progress, especially for timings, end-of-course (EOC) assessments, performance assessments, and unit tests.

She is convinced that "what gets measured, gets done," and each department is expected to be prepared to offer evidence of progress for each student, each subject, at any time. Her staff and students manage their performance with charts and graphs. Results data are disaggregated by sub-group at faculty meetings (data vary), and each department identifies students who need additional help at least monthly, submitting a report of students when data show flat or negative trends in two or more core subject areas or one state indicator.

At Timberline, students consistently outperform the district and state averages, and Ms. Smith has had no problem identifying classrooms that are showing growth or scoring well above their peer groups for recognition purposes every month and at each assembly. To her supervisor, Principal Smith is a data-driven principal. Teachers and some parents have begun to ask for data to verify policies and practices observed throughout the school.

Of late, Timberline has been vulnerable to failing to meet AYP, simply because some sub-groups have seen learning gaps widen with the overall student population. A large group of English language learners (175 students) has shown only slight improvement for three consecutive years, a trend Principal Smith attributes to an influx of students from Kazakhstan and Honduras who arrived with very limited literacy in their first language. Asian students scored at considerably higher levels on state and EOC assessments than their peers, and the learning gap between boys and girls has persisted as a concern, with boys falling far behind their female peers in all core subjects.

Principal Smith is not sure what additional action to take; she has already commissioned a school improvement team to work on goals and prepare the school improvement plan application every spring, and every department complied with the requirement for EOC and performance assessments. She has also provided training in key instructional strategies. At the same time, teachers are unabashed about the fact that they do not have time to get everything done. Veteran teachers complain about the time required to test students and maintain data records. Principal Smith had viewed this concern as typical resistance to change, but now she is beginning to wonder.

This example illustrates the need for deliberate and collaborative analysis and the need to balance the cost in time and resources to gather data with the benefits that accrue as a result of data analysis. Appendix A, "Scoring Matrix for Analysis of Data," articulates standards for six major principles of effective data analysis, which will be addressed in this and subsequent chapters: data management (this chapter), antecedents of excellence (Chapter 3), collaboration around student work (Chapter 4), accountability (Chapter 5), triangulation (Chapter 7), and replication (Chapter 9). The remainder of this chapter examines the principles of effective data management that inform decision making, introduce building blocks that allow practitioners to manage their data, and describe systems to create and maintain a balanced and effective assessment framework.

Data-Driven Decision Making: Principles That Make It a Reality

Continuous improvement is the foundation of effective data-driven decision making (DDDM). It provides a process to identify needed improvements, develop a strategy to make the improvements, make adjustments along the way, and learn lessons from the process for the next level of improvements; hence it is continuous. Data-driven decision making has been evident in some schools for decades. The school system in Brazosport, Texas, for example, was able to affect results in such a way that over a seven-year period, students in every ethnic group and from every income level showed dramatic improvement on the state assessments (Schmoker, 2001). Brazosport officials attributed their success to a continuous assessment and reteaching system known simply as the "eight-step process." Joan Richardson (2000), of the National Staff Development Council (NSDC), described a similar 10-step process for an effective data plan. The federal Race to the Top Initiative took its lead from lessons learned by the Consortium on Chicago School Research (2010), where research was designed to inform policy and influence classroom practice through explicit project management to achieve milestones as its own continuous improvement cycle. The Leadership and Learning Center developed a data-driven decision-making process that is also characterized by a continuous improvement cycle. Literally hundreds of schools and thousands of teachers have adopted this seven-step process. These four models are compared in Exhibit 2.2.

EXHIBIT **2.2 | Continuous Improvement Cycles**

	Eight-Step Process (Brazosport, TX)	10-Step Data Plan (NSDC)	Seven-Step DDDM Process (The Center)	Race to the Top Project Management
STEPS	• Test score disaggregation • Timeline development • Instructional focus • Assessment • Tutorials • Enrichment • Maintenance • Monitoring	• Collect basic information • Identify additional data • Disaggregate the data • Analyze the data • Summarize the data • Brainstorm causes • Collect more data • Analyze and summarize the data • Identify a goal • Repeat the process	• Treasure hunt • Analyze data/prioritize • Set, review, revise goals • Select instructional strategies • Determine results indicators • Evaluate lessons learned • Implement action plan (implied seventh step)	• Theory of action and logic model • Defined beginning and anticipated end date • Specific deliverables and tasks required to realize those deliverables • Specific assignment of tasks to individuals • Specific timelines

Schmoker (2006, p. 7) notes "schools can and will improve if they gear up to strive for increasingly better results by examining and refining the processes that most directly contribute to designate results," referring to improvement cycles. Doug Reeves (2004b, p. 122) recommends a feedback cycle for continuous improvement that involves formative and summative evaluations, decisions informed by that feedback, and actions taken on the basis of that feedback to make improvements and initiate new initiatives. Rick DuFour (DuFour, DuFour, & Eaker, 2008, pp. 284–288), a leader in professional learning communities, stresses the need for leaders to create a systematic process in which teachers work together to analyze and impact professional practice to improve their individual and collective results. Each model presented in Exhibit 2.2 offers systematic processes with explicit steps, and several other examples may be found in the literature (Wade, 2001; Killion & Bellamy, 2000; Shipley, 2001; Hattie, 2009). To enhance understanding of these cycles, The Leadership and Learning Center process for data-driven decision making is described below.

Step 1: The Treasure Hunt

In treasure hunts, we do not know for certain where the treasure hunt is or what we will find, but we know we must be attentive to external factors if we are to discover it, and we know it is valuable enough to pursue with our best efforts and best thinking. This is the key to data analysis, that we examine it for insights. Data-driven decision making participants are directed to examine trends by looking at data over time, preferably a series of scores or data points over a year or more. We begin by looking at Timberline Middle School's recent history on state-level assessments (Exhibit 2.3).

EXHIBIT **2.3** | **Timberline Middle School State Assessments, 2008–2010**

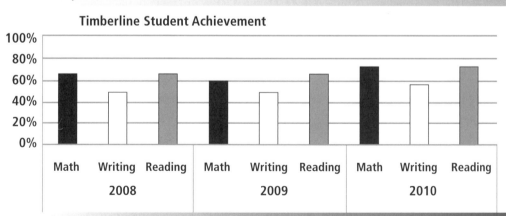

Math scores improved from 66 percent to 70 percent proficient during the period, reading increased from 67 percent to 73 percent, and writing saw improvement from 48 percent to 57 percent. Timberline appears to be making steady growth, but the data do not tell us why. Exhibit 2.4 examines teacher participation in professional development in math, reading, and writing, and incorporating high-yield instructional strategies.

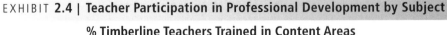

EXHIBIT **2.4** | **Teacher Participation in Professional Development by Subject**

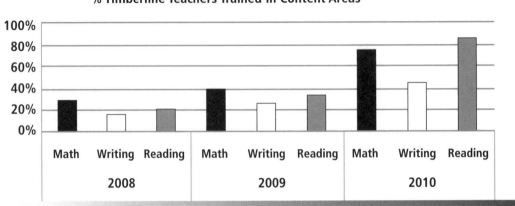

Almost 80 percent of teachers were trained in "5 Easy Steps to a Balanced Math Program," 86 percent in "Reading Strategies," and 45 percent in "The Writing Process." After three years, the school had a vast majority of classrooms with teachers trained in the same approach to reading (86 percent) and math (78 percent), with 45 percent trained in the writing process. However, Timberline gained only 8 percent more proficient students in math, with more than one in five nonproficient. The training in reading strategies was now almost universal at the school, yet only 6 percent of the students not proficient in 2008 were added to the proficient column by 2010. In writing, the school increased the number proficient by 9 percent but trained an additional 30 percent of teachers to get there. Did Timberline err in implementing such training? Perhaps. Readers will note that no data exist on the degree of implementation or adoption of the strategies and materials associated with the professional development, nor do we have information regarding coaching support. Exhibit 2.5, however, adds insight as to the effectiveness of the professional development simply by disaggregating student performance on the basis of such training. By attending to more than the obvious information, Timberline faculty were able to make an important discovery worth celebrating.

We can infer at least that the professional development had an influence on improved student achievement scores. In this brief and simplified treasure hunt, we were able to identify trends and draw some inferences by looking only at professional development in two content areas. If Timberline were to examine its rich treasure chest of student achievement data and monitor key teaching strategies, routine behaviors, conditions, and structures that influence results, the school would be well positioned to make all kinds of improvements that lead to increases in student achievement. "Wait a minute," the skeptic demands, "the percentage proficient is still under 80 percent, meaning almost one student in four is still not achieving at the desired level. How can we make the case that this strategy makes a difference?" Good question. Move to step 2, analysis.

EXHIBIT **2.5** | **Professional Development as a Factor of Student Achievement**

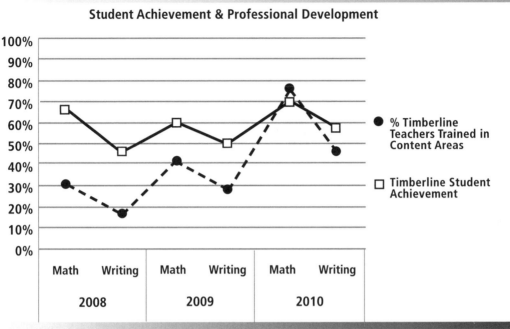

EXHIBIT **2.5** | **Professional Development as a Factor of Student Achievement**

Step 2: Analyze and Prioritize

Analysis answers two questions: What did you find out from your treasure hunt? and What can you learn from what's working? Analysis is designed to identify strengths or successes to celebrate, challenges to be met, and trends across subjects and grades. This aspect of analysis will be reviewed later in this chapter as part of a process to "unwrap" assessments to identify their strengths and weaknesses. From the data reviewed, we know that Timberline invested a lot of time, effort, and money in particular staff development programs. We know that just under 80 percent of students in classrooms where teachers were trained were proficient, and we know that the school saw an 8 percent increase in proficient students in math and gains in both reading (6 percent) and writing (9 percent) from 2008 to 2010. Is this program really working? How can we find out? Exhibit 2.6 compares performance as a function of whether teachers received professional development in math and writing.

EXHIBIT **2.6 | Student Achievement as a Function of Teacher Professional Development**

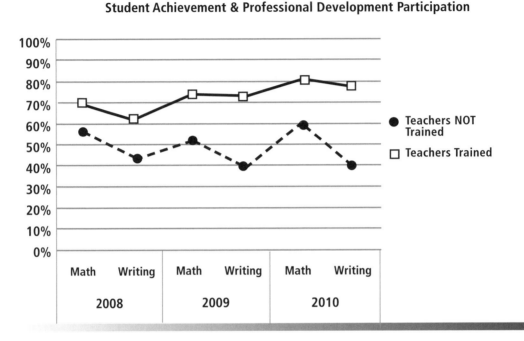

Student Achievement & Professional Development Participation

Students were much less likely to score at the proficient level in classrooms where teachers did not have training in both content areas, with variation greater than 20 percent of students enrolled. The more teachers were trained, the greater was the number of students who scored proficient or better. Absent the training, student performance stalled or declined. Note that these data do not address second-language learners, those receiving free or reduced lunch, or whether significant mobility has occurred in and out of various classrooms. What our treasure hunt does indicate is that participation in professional development in "5 Easy Steps" and "The Writing Process" was a powerful contributing influence. It served, in this case, as an antecedent or predictor of improved performance.

Data in Exhibits 2.3 through 2.6 reveal that professional development in writing and mathematics contributed to improved student achievement and that writing was the content area where the greatest opportunity for growth existed. Setting priorities is merely responding to the reality in schools that faculty cannot address every need all at once. Because each year a greater proportion of students scored proficient on the writing assessment, and because trained teachers experienced much higher student achievement levels, Timberline would be wise to prioritize improved writing performance as its primary goal in the coming year. The key to data analysis is to make the best decision based on the best information available, however limited. Never let the desire for perfection become the enemy of improvement.

Step 3: SMART Goals

The key in this step is to make sure any and all goal statements are specific, measurable, achievable, relevant, and timely (SMART). Later chapters provide a number of strategies for timely review and revision of goals to minimize the rearview-mirror effect.

Step 4: Instructional Strategies

This step corresponds to Brazosport's steps 3 through 6 by stipulating adult actions to deliver instruction related to needs and goals. The Leadership and Learning Center's data seminars adroitly distinguish strategies from activities, programs, or textbook adoptions. School improvement plans all too often identify such purchases or plans to purchase as instructional strategies. Powerful instructional strategies require training and practice by adults, and the most powerful will consistently impact student achievement when implemented well. A useful definition for an instructional strategy is a teacher-to-student interaction that requires training to acquire, requires practice with feedback to perfect, and is recognizable by discrete elements or components (e.g., reciprocal teaching is characterized by questioning, clarifying, predicting, and summarizing).

Step 5: Results Indicators

This step is a key aspect of data-driven decision making, but a difficult one because practitioners struggle to come up with measures of student achievement rather than indicators of changes in practice or behavior that portend success meeting SMART goals for achievement. Results indicators should show that the strategy is on track toward achieving the goal, and some of the best indicators are as simple as increased participation by reluctant learners in class discussion or teacher-reported changes in their questioning or feedback strategies. They represent data points that need to be verified, and the most effective are indicators that efforts are working in one of two ways: (1) Is the selected strategy/lesson being implemented as designed? and (2) Is the selected strategy/lesson having the intended effect on student learning or behavior? Results indicators are critical to extract educators from the rearview-mirror effect. They offer ongoing and interim measures that allow the education professional to make a midcourse correction and do so systematically.

Step 6: Pre-/post-assessment

This step is the simplest in the data-driven cycle but one that can be controversial, even among Data Teams whose members have worked together for some time. Many teachers prefer not to spend much time on pre-tests, particularly if the content is new, because they worry about student frustration and lost instructional time, resulting in variable practices when administered (reliability concern). Others struggle with developing an assessment of the standard or skill and whether the items are an accurate reflection of the desired learning (validity concern). A few practical tips will ensure that each pre- and post-assessment is an instrument with which team members have confidence in the results and confidence that the results represent the knowledge and skills students need to succeed.

a) Keep the assessment short and differentiated. Short-cycle assessments (less than six weeks of content) should have fewer than 10 items and require no more than 15 to 20 minutes to administer. Consider offering four or five select-response questions (multiple choice, true/false, or fill in the blank), one or two short-response items where students are asked to solve a problem and explain their findings, and one constructed-response item where students need to demonstrate their ability to think in writing. By keeping the assessment short, team members can be selective as they choose or develop the items that address the core attributes of learning.

b) Use familiar assessment items from familiar materials. If a social studies class for tenth grade chooses to pursue the Common Core State Standard for literacy #4 to use vocabulary within text to describe political or economic attributes of a particular unit, it makes little sense to ignore existing high-quality items found in unit exams or end-of-chapter review questions. Teacher teams need to confidently draw from what they know best to develop or even lift wholesale assessments from their existing battery.

c) Experiment with pre- and post-assessment formats. There is nothing sacred in administering word for word the same assessment, but it is critical that teams administer the same content assessed to demonstrate the same competencies from pre- to post-assessment. Teams often elect to repeat these four approaches by varying the items while assessing the same skill (as in math problems requiring addition and subtraction of numbers within 20 for first graders).

d) Assess simultaneously. The tendency to use pre- and post-tests only when convenient to individual teachers compromises the reliability of results, so teams need to agree on the date and time or at least days and times when they will simultaneously administer both pre- and post-assessments.

These four approaches can help teachers develop practical assessments quickly, leaving time to focus on quality strategies and lesson plans.

Step 7: Lessons Learned

Continuous improvement cycles need to be explicit and supported sufficiently by administration to ensure fidelity of implementation to meet deadlines and produce deliverables. Exhibit 2.7 illustrates the continuous improvement cycle in which lessons learned is the final step. It implies application of those lessons to the subsequent cycle. The seven steps, then, represent a single application of one continuous cycle. Improvement cycles require leadership's follow-up and relentless efforts to ensure that decisions will truly be driven by informed data.

Analysis: The "Unwrapping" of Data

The *Merriam-Webster Online* dictionary (2010) defines *analysis* as "separation of a whole into its component parts." To analyze, then, is to examine any whole by dividing it, breaking it into component parts, looking for relationships and functions. Readers familiar with the "unwrapping" process (Ainsworth, 2003, pp. 109–112) will quickly recognize that

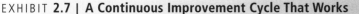

EXHIBIT **2.7 | A Continuous Improvement Cycle That Works**

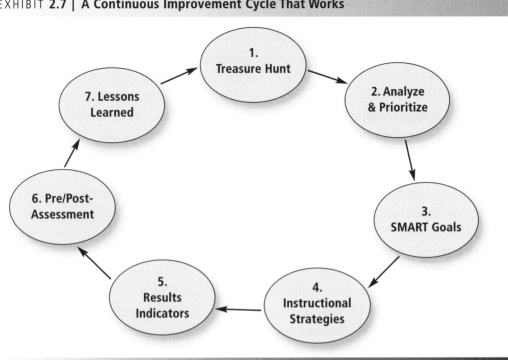

"unwrapping" of standards is really a simple and effective method of analysis. The following quote from Ainsworth succinctly defines the "unwrapping" process: "'Unwrapping' the academic content standards is a proven technique to help educators identify from the full text of the standards exactly what they need to teach their students. 'Unwrapped' standards provide clarity as to what students must know and be able to do."

This powerful technique has created literally thousands of "ah-hah" moments for teachers and administrators across the country. Its basic premise is that analysis is needed to identify the essential concepts and skills in each standard. Just as "unwrapping" offers teachers a tool to integrate the key academic content with the most powerful instructional strategy, "unwrapping" of data offers teachers a means to make visible the invisible and reveal insights on the dynamics of teaching and learning. Analysis, rather than the collection or even disaggregation, of data is the catalyst for improvement. And analysis is best when it is collaborative. This is especially true in education, a business Linda Darling-Hammond (1997) refers to as "work characterized by simultaneity, multidimensionality, and unpredictability." Statisticians consider education to be the most difficult of the social sciences in which to conduct research because of all the uncontrolled variables that impact virtually any research design (Kerlinger, 1986). Hence, elaborate efforts have been designed by statisticians to develop sophisticated statistical multivariate analyses to control for variances attributed to unknown or uncontrolled variables.

Is it possible to collect too much data? As we learned in Chapter 1, any data collected but never analyzed or acted upon represent an added burden and little more. On the other hand, it is to our advantage as educators to be able to reduce everything that happens to our schools and classrooms of any importance into meaningful information. Reliable observations of events and behaviors that affect learning can help us make improved decisions when the information is translated and analyzed for patterns, trends, or relationships. End-of-course assessments help align the curriculum and draw teachers together to collaborate on what is important in each course. Proactive performance assessments ensure that standards are addressed. Assessments that provide incremental evidence of proficiency assist teachers in minimizing the rearview-mirror effect and in making appropriate modifications for every student. Timberline Middle School used all of the above but erred by emphasizing the collection of data, and did so at the expense of helpful analysis. In schools, where the nanosecond is a reality and interruptions legendary, one can easily find ways to lose the forest for the trees. Let's reexamine Timberline's data to help the school "unwrap" required student assessments.

Function

When we look at function, we examine both the nature and purpose of assessments in terms of what they measure and what we hope to accomplish with them (validity). What do the progress reports measure? Are assessments designed to test knowledge, skills, or both? By examining the purpose of assessments, areas of redundancy are identified. What is the purpose of EOC assessments? Is it to evaluate content knowledge, achievement of standards, or application of skills? What about performance assessments? Consider the hypothetical Timberline data in Exhibit 2.8 for the entire K–12 district, included to reveal differences across grades and how quickly an assessment program can become unwieldy.

Emphasis

The greatest emphasis will always be on those assessments that take more time and effort to administer, so we "unwrap" them to know with certainty the reasons for doing so. In our Timberline example, pressure is being exerted to test all year long, with 12 assessments per trimester and six additional unit tests per year, or 14 per trimester. The result in our imaginary Timberline is a school that emphasizes so many assessments that it emphasizes none. "Unwrapping" examines assessments by month, season, trimester, and grade to provide a baseline for making changes and developing a comprehensive assessment calendar.

Relationship

This final step in "unwrapping" provides a much clearer picture of the entire assessment program in terms of alignment and the degree to which assessments complement one another, offer unnecessary redundancy, or corroborate other assessments. What is the relationship between progress reports and unit tests? Unit tests and EOCs? Do we really need all three? Understanding relationships helps us prioritize and simplify assessments.

EXHIBIT 2.8 | Timberline School District K–12 Assessment Emphasis by Grade

Assessments per Year	K1	2	3	4	5	6	7	8	9	10	11	12
Trimester Assessments												
Basic skills—weekly	30	30	30	30	30	30	30	30	30	30		
Skills timings	24	8	8	8	8	8	4	4	—	—	—	—
Progress reports	3	3	3	3	1	1	1	1	1	1	1	1
Content performance	4	4	4	4	4	4	6	6	7	7	7	7
End of Course/Semester												
Grades	2	2	2	2	2	2	2	2	2	2	2	2
EOC—core academics	4	4	4	4	4	4	4	4	4	4	4	4
All-subject unit tests	6	6	6	6	6	6	6	6	6	6	6	6
Annual Assessments												
Statewide writing—fall			1	1	1	1	1	1	1	1		
Statewide standards—spring			3	3	3	3	3	3	3	3		
NRT—spring testing		1			1			1			1	
Annual Pre-/Post-Tests												
District writing	2	2	2	2	2	2	2	2	2	2		
Postsecondary											2	1

Exhibit 2.8 illustrates how Timberline used a huge number of assessments, was top-heavy with skills timings and computerized basic skill assessments, and made little progress in delineating the nature of the assessments. And, as is so often the case, Timberline added NCLB requirements to the assessment battery with little evidence of any testing being subtracted. Further "unwrapping" by time periods for test administration would reveal test-heavy months around trimester time in the fall and in the spring, especially for NCLB adherence in grades 3 through 10. One might also surmise that so many content-level assessments could actually inhibit the presence of writing or constructed-response assessments in this school system. Does the system lend itself to quality assessments that stretch students to apply higher levels of thinking consistent with Bloom's taxonomy?

"Unwrapping" to determine assessment emphasis should create an awareness about the impact and value of current assessment practices and raise questions when adjustments are needed. An analysis of the degree to which assessments are related assists by clarifying similarities and differences between assessments, revealing areas of conflict, duplication, and areas that need to be subtracted or assessment needs that have not been addressed. One can see clearly from this hypothetical example how important it is to determine where and how to scale back.

It is just as important to "unwrap" data and assessment systems as it is to "unwrap" standards. Without analysis that emerges from "unwrapping," decision makers are just as limited as teachers and specialists who attempt to design quality instruction without a clear understanding of the requirements and expectations of various standards. Without "unwrapping," decision makers are left to assume that assessments measure what educators expect them to; that assessments are administered proportionately; that the purposes of assessment are clearly defined and complementary; and that assessments are aligned to focus instruction and generate reliable data for curriculum design, differentiation of instruction, and professional development. These assumptions are much more apt to be true after the "unwrapping" process or assessment audit has been completed.

Time for Reflection

Timberline Middle School's assessment battery was "over the top" in terms of time demands, with very little time for reflection. Unfortunately, few school systems deliberately set aside times to analyze data and then reflect on it.

When the time and resources required to administer assessments, surveys, or studies of any kind are calculated, the need to take time for reflection becomes an ethical issue about public stewardship. The earlier "unwrapping" exercise to identify Timberline's areas of concern raise questions about the scope of Timberline's data system, and focus efforts on aligning the assessments should have taken each reader no more than 10 minutes to complete. Even brief time frames of 30 minutes can initiate analyses that will make a difference (Schmoker, 2001, p. 119). Schools may consider setting aside times in department, grade, or faculty meetings as soon as possible after assessment results become available. Formal, explicit, and protected time periods to do nothing but apply the best thinking of school teams and faculties to the analysis of data is time well spent. Assessment calendars provide such a structure by establishing time for both analysis and reflection for every assessment in the district's battery.

Assessment or Data Calendars

An assessment calendar (see Exhibit 2.9) establishes time frames, accountability, and collaboration to conduct the following nine steps to quality analysis and decision making:

1. A time frame for administration (implementation of any new practice)
2. A precise and published window for collecting the data
3. A precise and published window for disaggregating the data
4. A precise and published time for analysis
5. A separate time to reflect on the data after it has been analyzed, graphed, and charted for trends and patterns
6. A precise window given to recommend changes of any kind or maintenance of the status quo

7. A specific date when decisions will be made regarding the recommendations
8. A specific time to provide a written rationale for the selected decision
9. A time when data are disseminated to stakeholders, including parents and even students, depending on the data

Assessment calendars are useful for keeping all parties focused on the real purpose of data: to provide meaningful information that "makes visible the invisible" (Schmoker, 2001) and leads to improved performance. Notice how the nine-step cycle is designed to create a culture that expects assessments to be completed at one time, analyzed at another, examined for usefulness (reflection) at another, and results and decisions published at yet another. The value of having explicit time frames and communication structures is that it invites external scrutiny and awareness while ensuring that action is taken as a result of the data. Our sample calendar provides specific dates to spread the testing battery throughout the school year. Note that the date for reflection is distinct from the analysis date, and the dates for making a decision are different from most of the recommended change dates. The reason for this framework is pragmatic: specific dates for specific purposes are scheduled well in advance to help ensure that sufficient time is given to each critical step in data analysis. This structure minimizes the likelihood that team members will have another activity competing for their time and increases the likelihood that action will follow analysis.

An effective assessment calendar will reveal redundancy and the "overtesting" represented by the hypothetical Timberline School District. Few practices are ever subtracted in education, and a calendar causes decision makers to weigh the value of assessments in this era of accountability. As you examine the recommended calendar, note the relationship between the time allocated and the types of assessments.

Did you recognize a pattern in Exhibit 2.9? The assessments closest to the classroom have the shortest time frame from administration to implementing changes. This distinction does not mean that any of the nine steps should be eliminated but simply that the cycle can be compressed and accomplished much quicker when fewer people are involved.

EXHIBIT **2.9** | **Assessment Calendar Template, Part 1**

Describe each assessment by specifying times when steps are to be accomplished. Use precise dates when available or windows of time (range of days, month).

Assessment	Administration	Collection Date/Window	Disaggregate Date/Window	Analysis	Reflection	Recommend Changes	Decision Point	Written Rationale	Disseminate to Stakeholders
NRTs									
State Assessment									
CRTs									
Writing Assessment									
EOC Assessments									
Common Assessments									
Performance Assessments									
Unit Tests									
Other									

- Scheduled times to collect, aggregate, and disaggregate data
- Required time for analysis, reflection, and recommendations for changes
- Decision points to proceed at status quo or implement change recommendations
- Written rationale for each decision
- Disseminated rationale driven by data to all affected parties

EXHIBIT 2.9 | Assessment Calendar Template, Part 2

Recommended times when steps are to be accomplished are provided. This example includes a recommended assessment to subtract from the district battery (see strikethroughs). Assessment calendars need to be tailored to the realities of external mandates and still provide time for quality data collection, analysis, reflection, recommendations, decisions, and action.

Assessment	Administration	Collection Date/Window	Disaggregate Date/Window	Analysis	Reflection	Recommend Changes	Decision Point	Written Rationale	Disseminate to Stakeholders
NRTs	Sept. 10–14	Sept. 17–21	Sept. 17–21	Sept. 24	Sept. 25	Sept. 27	Sept. 28	Oct. 3	Oct. 5
State Assessment	March 4–18	March 21–28	March 29–April 8	April 11	April 12	April 13	April 14	April 18	April 20
~~CRTs~~	~~Oct. 1–8~~ ~~May 2–4~~	~~Pretest~~ ~~May 5~~	~~Pretest~~ ~~May 6~~	~~Pretest~~ ~~May 9~~	~~Pretest~~ ~~May 10~~	~~Pretest~~ ~~May 11~~	~~Pretest~~ ~~May 12~~	~~Pretest~~ ~~May 13~~	~~Pretest~~ ~~June 10~~
Writing Assessment	Oct. 15–19 April 25–29	Pretest May 2	Pretest May 3	Pretest May 4	Pretest May 5	Pretest May 6	Pretest May 9	Pretest May 10	Pretest June 10
EOC Assessments	Jan. 21–23 May 9–11	Jan. 24 May 12	Jan. 24 May 12	Jan. 25 May 13	Jan. 25 May 16	Jan. 28 May 17	Jan. 29 May 18	Jan. 30 May 18	Feb. 5 June 10
Common Assessments	Last Friday of Sept./Nov./Feb.	1st Monday of Oct./Dec./Mar.	1st Monday of Oct./Dec./Mar.	1st Tuesday of Oct./Dec./Mar.	1st Wednesday of Oct./Dec./Mar.	1st Thursday of Oct./Dec./Mar.	1st Friday of Oct./Dec./Mar.	1st Friday of Oct./Dec./Mar.	Optional
Performance Assessments	Ongoing, at least 1/term/core subject	Ongoing, seamless	Ongoing, seamless	Ongoing, seamless	Ongoing, seamless	Ongoing, seamless	Ongoing, seamless	Ongoing, seamless	Ongoing, seamless
Unit Tests	No more than 2 Wednesdays/month	Same day	Same day	Same day	Same day	2nd day	2nd day	2nd day	Optional
Other	Teacher determined	N/A	N/A	N/A	N/A	N/A	N/A	N/A	N/A

- Scheduled times to collect, aggregate, and disaggregate data
- Required time for analysis, reflection, and recommendations for changes
- Decision points to proceed at status quo or implement change recommendations
- Written rationale for each decision
- Disseminated rationale driven by data to all affected parties

The CRT is recommended for elimination for the following reasons: (1) competition for testing windows with other assessments more aligned with standards such as EOC and writing assessments and (2) the opportunity to fold CRTs into EOC, textbook, and unit common assessments.

EXHIBIT **2.10** | **Process Map for Assessment Calendars**

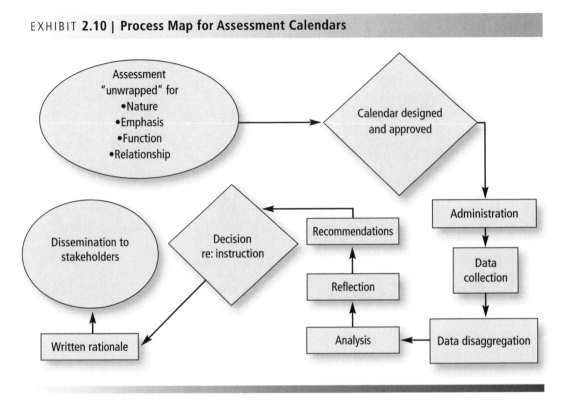

Exhibit 2.10 describes how to apply the assessment calendar through a step-by-step process map or flowchart to examine individual assessments. The process is equally applicable to data other than assessments, such as the degree to which classrooms are standards-based in their implementation (Reeves, 2002a). Steps to analyze, reflect, recommend, and decide with a written rationale have numerous applications that can assist faculty throughout a school or school system in responding to emerging challenges or refining established processes. Ovals indicate start and finish, diamonds represent decision points, and rectangles show steps in the process.

Summary

Timberline Middle School used exceptionally detailed and comprehensive data systems capable of disaggregating on the basis of all NCLB factors, and providing such information quickly to the desk of every teacher, principal, and district administrator. Absent intentional reflection periods and an effective and practical means to analyze data, however, Timberline was unable to fully benefit from the wealth of data at its staff's fingertips, and rather than gaining lessons learned and applied, data were shelved, staff and stakeholders became frustrated, and reliance on past traditions for decisions prevailed. This chapter defines analysis in the context of the "unwrapping" process, stresses the need to explicitly set aside time for reflection, and introduces the concept of assessment or data calendars. "Unwrapping" helps reveal the nature, emphasis, function, and relationship of assessments to a school's entire assessment program. The assessment calendar illustrates the importance of collaborative structures to encourage teacher judgments, team insights, and decisions driven by the data rather than implemented in spite of the data. Both "unwrapping" and data or assessment calendars set the stage to examine what works and what does not as we pursue ways to achieve success and know how to replicate that success again and again. Appendix A provides a scoring guide to self-assess one's proficiency in terms of data management. The next chapter describes the role of antecedents in data analysis and the need to measure the behavior of adults to the same extent as student achievement results are measured.

Reflection

BIG IDEA: Analysis requires time, improvement cycles, and explicit structures to leverage data into action, or

Take time to smell (analyze) the roses (data).

What inhibited Timberline Middle School from making more progress than was observed?

How does the "unwrapping" process assist educators in examining varied student assessments in your school?

What benefits can you expect from establishing an assessment or data calendar in your school or district?

CHAPTER

Antecedents of Excellence

We are free to choose our actions…but we are not
free to choose the consequences of these actions.
—STEPHEN R. COVEY

A photograph shows a young lady who lost 25 pounds. We know the result precisely, and the data are unequivocal. We even know she lost 25 pounds in three months. Should we celebrate because she reached her goal through exercise and nutrition, or should this be serious cause for alarm because the weight loss was a product of anorexia or drug abuse? Without the capacity to determine what actions resulted in the weight loss, we cannot know. The illustration makes the case for knowing the causes that produce results, for understanding the antecedents that lead to improved student achievement. Causes are routines that create specific effects or results. When a strong correlation exists between a cause and an effect—one that is strong enough to predict with some confidence—we refer to it as an antecedent. This chapter answers the question: How do I determine what to select and monitor to produce the desired effects that will ensure continuous improvement?

CASE STUDY

Dennis was a highly respected elementary school principal. A leader among his peers, he was first to pursue emerging best practices but the last to implement fads and jump on bandwagons. He viewed his teaching faculty as the most important people his students at Woodside Elementary would encounter in terms of learning, and he realized that if his efforts at this Title I school failed to excite students about learning, a majority would drop out before completing high school. Seventy-five percent of his students received free and reduced lunch, 47 percent were minority students from limited-English-speaking families, and even more students' families had members with less than a high school education. He was determined to turn the tide, and long before the term "leave no child behind" came into vogue, Dennis was committed to the concept. The number of teachers at his school with master's degrees increased from 23 percent to 57 percent in five years, and the district's first national-board-certified teachers were from Woodside. His heart was as large as his commitment, and he was collaborative in making decisions, painstakingly waiting for consensus when hiring new teachers and making sure every school improvement goal had at least 80 percent faculty support.

Woodside Elementary outperformed the other schools with its demographics so dramatically that test scores improved at grades 2, 4, and 6 in both math and reading. Woodside's third and fifth graders had the second highest percentage proficient on the district writing assessment, even though its poverty, transient, and English as a second language (ESL) populations were also second highest in town. This year a challenge was posed to every school to improve test scores, and Woodside earned $5,000, which could be spent on any expense but salaries (prohibited by the negotiated agreement). A larger-than-life facsimile check was to be presented at a school assembly. Parents would be attending, and the media would be on hand for photo opportunities and a human interest story for the 6:00 news.

In the privacy of his office, Dennis told his supervisor, "All this is very nice, and we have lots of needs for the money, but quite honestly, I don't know why our kids did so well this year. I guess we were lucky." Dennis was broadly hinting that results may be great this spring, but don't expect the same results next year. He had been around long enough to witness lots of peaks and valleys in terms of test scores, and explanations about the valleys that rarely satisfied stakeholders.

"Wait," his boss countered, "you introduced common planning periods and extensive professional development in balanced literacy, and your investment in technology and literacy coaches with discretionary Title I funds was quickly replicated by your peers. Your efforts made a difference. Take some credit for the results."

Dennis smiled, "I know, but we've been working on the same goals for years, and this is the first bump we've seen. We need to clone our sixth graders!" The assembly bell rang…

I have met leaders like Dennis in more than 35 states and provinces—principled principals, modest about their accomplishments, devoted to their staff and students. Instructional leaders, when they are as candid as Dennis, admit they just don't know what produced changes in student achievement. Kids are so complex, the argument goes, and there are so many variables. We can, nonetheless, identify factors that are highly correlated with improved performance. Schools across the United States demonstrate how common antecedents make it possible to predict with some certainty improved student achievement.

Dr. Douglas Reeves, founder of The Leadership and Learning Center, developed the Leadership and Learning (L^2) Matrix, which links understanding of antecedents of excellence with sustained results. Those who would replicate success year after year understand the conditions, structures, and strategies (antecedents) that correlate with improved student achievement and learning. Exhibit 3.1 shows the L^2 Matrix.

EXHIBIT **3.1** | **The L² Matrix**

The Leadership and Learning Matrix

Achievement of Results	*Lucky* High results, low understanding of antecedents Replication of success unlikely	*Leading* High results, high understanding of antecedents Replication of success likely
	Losing Low results, low understanding of antecedents Replication of mistakes likely	*Learning* Low results, high understanding of antecedents Replication of mistakes unlikely

Understanding of the Antecedents of Excellence

In the L² Matrix, understanding of antecedents is viewed as the distinguishing variable between leaders who experience success and those who do not. The L² Matrix suggests that those who understand the conditions and structures (antecedents) that lead to success and know how to avoid those antecedents that perpetuate mediocrity or static student performance will be able to sustain improvement year after year, despite cohort changes. This is hardly theory, as the relationship between teaching practices, leadership actions, and student achievement is well established (White, 2009; Hattie, 2009; Fullan, 2008; Marzano, 2007; Wenglinsky, 2002). It behooves us, then, to understand what antecedents are and how to distinguish between them.

Antecedents are defined as adult actions, behaviors, and decisions that precede, anticipate, or predict student performance. The most effective antecedents lead to excellence in student achievement, excellence in implementing a new program or strategy, or excellence in performing routine tasks. Dennis applied antecedents when he created common planning times, focused professional development, and devoted resources to create literacy coach positions. Antecedents are teaching strategies such as questioning, reinforcing effort, rewarding achievement, and instructing in nonlinguistic representation. Antecedents are also causal factors that correlate with effects in student behavior and achievement (results), such as classroom routines, grading procedures, and teacher-student relationships and connections. Antecedents also include conditions such as class size, technology literacy, or availability of textbooks, and structures such as requiring continuing education units (CEUs), block scheduling, Data Teams, and prescribed data reflection times. All influence achievement.

Antecedents precede something. In mathematics, antecedents are the first term of any ratio. In science, the first and conditional part of a hypothesis is the antecedent: if the sun is fixed, the earth must move. If we desire sustained improvements in student achievement, we need to determine not only what success looks like for students but also the causal factors (antecedents) that contribute to that success.

The Need for Antecedents to Get Beyond the Numbers

CASE STUDY

A large urban school system in Ontario, Canada, convened its mathematics curriculum committee for its annual review. Mathematics coordinators and teacher-leaders from 14 comprehensive secondary schools, grades 6 through 12, reviewed trends showing improved performance on the Education Quality and Accountability Office assessment (EQAO), and they reviewed an annual teacher survey that asked teachers to list the five most frequent instructional approaches they used in their classrooms. Some members felt the survey data should be excluded from the discussion because it was "soft" data that was self-reported and not verified externally. The team that gathered the data for the 800 math teachers argued that the survey should at least be reviewed, given the effort they had made to complete the survey analysis. Reluctantly, results were introduced in a PowerPoint slide:

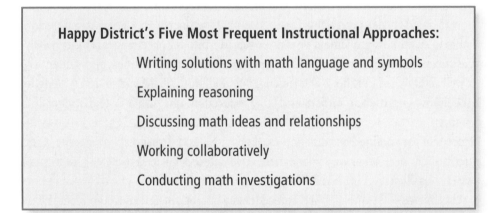

Happy District's Five Most Frequent Instructional Approaches:

Writing solutions with math language and symbols

Explaining reasoning

Discussing math ideas and relationships

Working collaboratively

Conducting math investigations

The chairperson asked, "Does anyone have questions for Mary and Bill?" Misha replied, "Which strategy was ranked highest?" Mary and Bill looked at each other, somewhat perplexed, before Bill responded, "We didn't ask teachers to prioritize." Now the mathematics supervisor's curiosity was peaked, "If we on this committee were to apply our best thinking, which of these five would we rank highest?" That question began a 45-minute discussion during which the committee determined that explaining reasoning was the most important instructional approach because explaining reasoning was implicit in the other four approaches. Before the meeting ended, the committee decided to direct the 800 mathematics teachers to gather data each week for the next school year on the frequency with which they provided opportunity for students to explain their reasoning in class. There would be no administrator involvement, other than verifying whether reports had been submitted to the committee. Some debate ensued about what the report would look like, so the committee defined the term *explaining reasoning* in this way:

1. Teachers would model explaining reasoning during class.
2. Students would be provided opportunity to explain their reasoning verbally during class (in board activities, through visuals).
3. Students would be expected to explain their reasoning in solving a math problem in writing during the class.

A brief in-service was planned in August to explain the process. To make the process easy, the committee asked teachers to submit a weekly e-mail report during the school year to their regional math coach indicating the number of days, by class section, in which all three components of the explaining reasoning strategy were present. Each week, the teacher observation data were forwarded to Misha, who agreed to aggregate them and report periodically to the committee. In June, the data were rolled up to capture the findings across the entire district. Misha presented the findings. "District-wide, the impact of explaining reasoning was not evident until we disaggregated the results by teacher use of this strategy. Our schools continue to show incremental improvement, which is a positive outcome. However, when we compare the use of the three-part explaining reasoning strategy by teachers up to two days a week with those who used it four or more days each week, the results are compelling, as exhibited in the following chart" (Exhibit 3.2).

EXHIBIT **3.2** | **Explaining Reasoning and EQAO Mathematics Results**

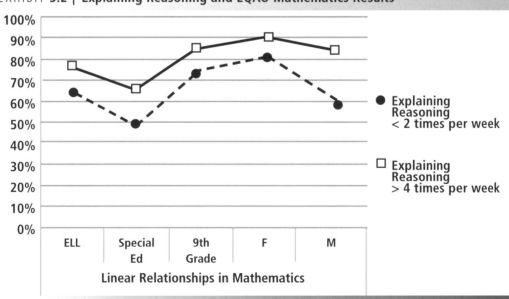

Misha continued, "For our second-language students, for our special education students, and on our ninth-grade applied exam, more frequent use of explaining reasoning had a dramatic impact, in some cases as much as 20 percent more students passing the exam."

If this were your district or school, what would be your next decision? For most of us, it would be to shift from making the use of the strategy optional to making it an expectation for all classrooms every day. This major change in policy and practice is the natural outgrowth of gathering data about professional practice and determining whether a relationship exists between that practice (antecedent action or condition) and student achievement. The ability to determine such relationships is the essential learning of this chapter.

Differentiating Antecedents as Routines, Strategies, and Conditions/Structures

Antecedents are predictors of results. Some lead to excellence, while others lead to negative achievement outcomes. A teaching strategy like explaining reasoning is much different from providing common planning time, although both may be causal factors for achievement gains. Exhibit 3.3 describes three types of antecedents that are differentiated to provide greater precision in planning changes driven by analyzed data.

EXHIBIT **3.3 | Antecedents Differentiated**

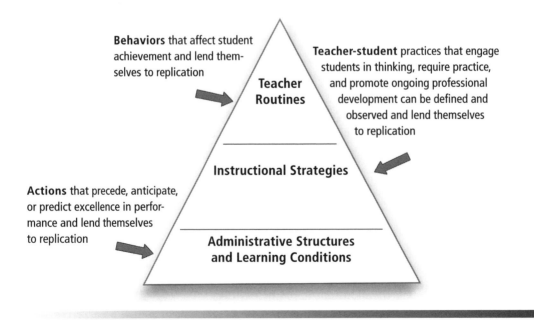

All three types of antecedents can be referred to as causes or causal factors that create specific effects or results, and all may lend themselves to replication. Every result has been caused by certain conditions, and a practical tool that helps identify causes for desired results (effects) and desirable or undesirable results is the Hishakawa fishbone. Cause data help determine what to replicate and what to subtract and reminds us that the interaction between teacher and students in the classroom holds the greatest promise for improved student achievement. Exhibit 3.4 provides examples of administrative structures and learning conditions. Note that most are typically determined by the classroom teachers, although leadership may have instituted this structure school-wide or even district-wide.

EXHIBIT **3.4 | Common Examples of Antecedent Administrative Structures and Learning Conditions**

• Transitions between activities	• Closing activities
• Routines for asking questions	• Collecting assignments
• Routine to opening every class	• How classroom rules are established
• Teaching classroom procedures	• How teams and groups are formed

These examples have been deliberately chosen to illustrate the distinction between teacher behavior and instructional strategies. They are not strategies because they do not require training for teachers to implement well, and they may or may not engage students cognitively, even though they may be excellent predictors of improved student achievement.

Instructional strategies are distinguished by the capacity to engage students in thinking and the need for training, practice, and professional development, and by the fact that the strategy can be defined by its primary elements. We want to replicate, refine, and multiply this type of antecedent to better predict improved student achievement and excellent performance. Examples include summarizing and note-taking designed to connect prior learning to new applications, or the use of corrective feedback that is meaningful, accurate, and timely. At The Leadership and Learning Center, the "Making Standards Work" seminar draws on the research regarding student engagement to include the "engaging scenario" in every performance assessment (Ainsworth, 2003). Engagement has been associated with improved student achievement at all levels (Fredricks, Blumenfeld, & Paris, 2004). When faculty understand the strategies that are most effective for specific students under specific conditions, they begin to have the ability to predict and create excellence in student performance. Exhibit 3.5 identifies instructional strategies that engage students cognitively and require training, practice, and professional development to implement well.

EXHIBIT **3.5 | Examples of Instructional Strategies**

• Written "ticket out the door" every day for every student	• Systematic use of graphic organizers for creating, planning, collaborating
• Identification of similarities and differences	• Higher-order questioning strategies
• Reciprocal teaching	• Homework for thinking with practice
• Self-assessment and reflection protocols	• Explaining reasoning
• Descriptive, corrective feedback	• "5 Easy Steps to a Balanced Math Program" *

*Five Easy Steps to a Balanced Math Program (Ainsworth & Christinson, 2000) is a complete training program with five discrete and effective strategies.

The examples listed in Exhibit 3.5 are usually more than one single cause or routine and, in all cases, produce a cognitive level of engagement from students.

The most effective instructional strategy, however, will not produce breakthrough results if it is not employed as intended. Too many dedicated educators experience confusion and frustration when they adopt a proven practice without sufficient training and skill development. When student growth fails to equal that achieved by the originators, the proven strategy is often criticized rather than analyzed to determine the degree and quality of implementation (Evans, 2001). Instructional strategies are distinguished from other antecedents by a connection to professional development and quality implementation. Data about strategies help determine whether a strategy was implemented and whether it had its desired effect. As antecedents, strategies offer practitioners the ability to identify on the front end of implementation data that will provide the most information and value rather than discover the need for different data after the strategy has been executed.

Antecedents as Conditions and Structures

One can hope that all learning conditions and administrative structures are designed and implemented as antecedents of excellence that result in improved student achievement. Unfortunately, antecedents can also institutionalize ineffectiveness. Transferring teachers or administrators who perform at marginal levels rather than assisting them to improve, counseling them to change careers, or showing them the door through dismissal is just one example. Increasing the instructional day without providing time for collaboration is another; the fictional middle school in Chapter 2 failed to accurately predict the time required to comply with reporting requirements, and that time expenditure led to reduced instructional time with students. The result was hardly an antecedent for excellence.

Many other conditions for learning and administrative structures are adopted or adapted randomly or based on tradition rather than being selected as potential antecedents of excellence. Teachers and principals often select antecedents; apply them independently; and, if successful, may see such practices replicated voluntarily by peers and colleagues. A better approach, one that advances best practices on a faster track, is to examine the research available to determine what works. Exhibit 3.6 identifies 14 practices that exemplify antecedents that align closely with standards and improved student achievement.

EXHIBIT **3.6 | Classroom Checklist for Standards Implementation**

1. Standards are highly visible in the classroom

2. Standards are expressed in student-accessible language

3. Examples of proficient and exemplary student work are displayed throughout the classroom

4. The teacher publishes in advance the explicit expectations for proficient student work

5. Student Evaluation is always done according to standards and scoring guide

6. The teacher can explain to every parent or stakeholder the specific expectations of students for the year

7. The teacher has flexibility to vary the length and quantity of curriculum content daily

8. Students can spontaneously explain what proficient means for any assignment

9. Commonly used standards are reinforced in every subject (Conventions, Organization of writing)

10. The teacher has created at least one performance assessment in the past month

11. The teacher exchanges student work with a colleague for review and collaborative evaluation at least once every two weeks

12. The teacher provides feedback to students and parents about the quality of student work compared to the standards, not in relation to a "curve"'

13. The teacher helps to build community consensus in the classroom with other stakeholders for standards and high expectations for ALL students

14. The teacher uses a variety of assessment techniques.

Source: Reeves (2004b, pp. 269–273).

These antecedents enjoy powerful support throughout the research, such as reinforcement of writing conventions, flexibility for teacher management of the curriculum, assessments, collaborative scoring, and meaningful feedback (Hattie, 2009; Marzano, 2007; Reeves, 2004a; Langer, Colton, & Goff, 2003; Reeves, 2002a; Marzano, Pickering, & Pollock, 2001a). Some items reflect best practices, alignment of effort, and even basic professional practice. Exhibit 3.7 applies what we have learned about the different types of antecedents by categorizing a sample of the antecedents described above.

The presence of highly visible standards in the classroom is an antecedent condition for learning, but whether their presence is a teacher routine or a formal instructional strategy is unclear. If the teacher refers to the displayed standards routinely, it qualifies as a teacher behavior, and if a systematic method to use the display of standards is in place to instruct students more effectively, it could qualify as an instructional strategy, but without further clarification, we know only that it is an administrative structure/condition for learning. Flexibility to vary content is also a structural and administrative antecedent, but until the teacher develops a strategy that systematically engages students, it is not an instructional strategy. Similarly, it is not a teacher routine because flexibility alone does not indicate that the teacher has applied it to the classroom, nor does its presence mean the teacher has changed his behavior to produce a specific result or effect. Flexibility in curriculum is also an administrative structure. Collaborative scoring is both an instructional strategy and an administrative structure, but it is not clear that this is a routine teaching practice. Only the feedback item meets the criteria for all three antecedent forms: it is provided to students and linked to a specific effect—work production; managing feedback requires professional development to do well; feedback engages student thinking; and provision of feedback can be mandated and instituted in a systematic way. By clearly defining the antecedents, we acquire a more explicit understanding of how the antecedent is being applied, and measurement of the antecedent will be consistent and reliable. The teacher routine demonstrates that teachers are employing the antecedent, not just being aware of its utility. The instructional strategy demonstrates that the antecedent is a function to be mastered in order to fully engage students with their best thinking, and the administrative structure ensures that the strategy and classroom application will be established to advance student learning and achievement. Antecedents offer a wealth of possibilities in data analysis unavailable to those who limit their understanding of data to achievement results. If we want improved achievement, we need to know with some precision which of the practices we employ will lead to that improvement.

EXHIBIT **3.7** | **Antecedent Matrix**

Antecedent	Replicable	Teacher Routine and Behaviors	Instructional Strategies	Administrative Structures and Conditions
1. Visibly displayed standards	✓			✓
7. Flexibility in curriculum	✓			✓
11. Collaborative scoring	✓		✓	✓
12. Feedback	✓	✓	✓	✓

Root Causes, Hunches, and Antecedents

True cause-and-effect relationships are virtually impossible to find because myriad variables are outside of our control. Antecedents can help reveal very strong correlations that help schools achieve goals, solve problems, and identify root causes (Anderson and Fagerhaug, 2000). Exhibit 3.8 provides a modified Hishakawa cause-effect fishbone, a popular tool to examine cause and effect; part 2 of the exhibit applies the fishbone to Woodside Elementary, introduced earlier in the chapter. Appendix E provides a template for readers.

EXHIBIT 3.8 | The Hishakawa Fishbone: A Cause-and-Effect Diagram, Part 1

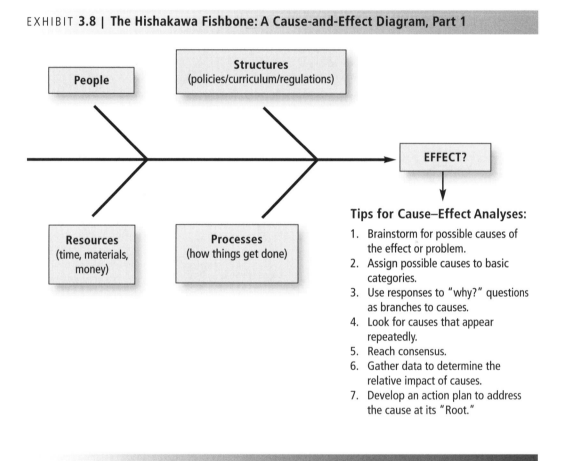

Tips for Cause–Effect Analyses:

1. Brainstorm for possible causes of the effect or problem.
2. Assign possible causes to basic categories.
3. Use responses to "why?" questions as branches to causes.
4. Look for causes that appear repeatedly.
5. Reach consensus.
6. Gather data to determine the relative impact of causes.
7. Develop an action plan to address the cause at its "Root."

Tools like the Hishakawa fishbone help make visible the invisible and provide insights that achieve goals and overcome persistent challenges. Although we do not know all the factors that contributed to success at Woodside, we can see the connections among resources, staff, policies, and processes, and we can see how Dennis's leadership marshaled those resources, created those processes, and engaged staff to make a difference.

EXHIBIT **3.8 | The Hishakawa Fishbone: A Cause-and-Effect Diagram, Part 2: Woodside Elementary School Simulation**

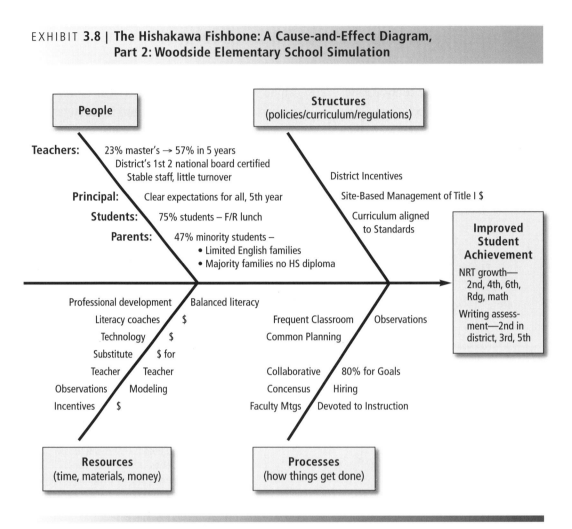

Antecedents and the Common Core State Standards

Antecedents represent all we do as professional educators to improve student achievement and ensure that every student reaches his potential and is sufficiently prepared to meet the challenges of an increasingly global economy and blending of diverse world cultures. For this reason alone, educators need to become savvy analysts of all the factors that improve student achievement, and once again, the Common Core State Standards support that mission.

Sample performance tasks are explicit, varied, and comprehensive at all grade levels, calling on students to compare and contrast a firsthand account of African American ballplayers or interpret a visual chart accompanying a text on economics and entrepreneurship (Common Core State Standards Initiative, 2010c, p. 76). These examples point educators toward instructional strategies that distinguish viewpoints, and they encourage teachers to use charts, graphs, and data across content areas in their classrooms, two powerful instructional strategies if performed correctly.

The Common Core is equally helpful in mathematics, as its nine instructional practices, such as (a) constructing viable arguments and critiquing the reasoning of others and (b) attending to precision, provide a foundation for measuring teacher practices (Common Core State Standards Initiative, 2010d, p. 14). By monitoring the frequency with which teachers attend to precision (self-reported and observed) and the opportunities provided for students to construct viable arguments, teacher teams and schools can determine which of these practices are most effective with which students. Teachers need only to become as astute observers of their own practices as they currently are of their students, and the Common Core provides a wealth of antecedent content and practices to examine professional practice, student outcomes, and the relationship between them.

Summary

The rearview-mirror effect is difficult to escape without a clear understanding and application of antecedents. The L^2 Matrix is based on the hypothesis that those who understand antecedents of excellence and apply them are better able to replicate successful practices and sustain success as cohorts of students advance to their next environment. Without that understanding, educators with only student achievement data are every bit as much at a loss as someone trying to interpret a woman's loss of 25 pounds without information as to how she lost the weight.

Antecedents were defined as strategies, teacher routines, structures, and conditions that precede, anticipate, or predict excellence in performance. We then examined the three forms of antecedents: (1) teaching routines and behaviors that lead to results, (2) instructional strategies that require mastery and engage students in thinking, and (3) administrative structures and conditions for learning. Those aspects that define a standards-based classroom were analyzed as antecedents, and a process was provided to help practitioners select antecedents capable of predicting success and preceding improvement in student achievement. The same process was used to scrutinize large-scale antecedents that teachers and school leaders make decisions about every day, and a cause-and-effect diagram was presented as a means to identify and select antecedents when faced with challenging goals that need to be realized or when persistent barriers and problems are in need of solutions.

Woodside Elementary, a fictional school, represents the experience of capable, dedicated professionals thrust into a paradigm where results and numbers seem to be all that matter. Dennis needed to understand that he was capably creating antecedents that did precede excellence and that could predict improved student achievement. Antecedent analysis offers the benefit of data describing and monitoring causes that produce results. Therein lies the hope that educators who read and apply the lessons of *Beyond the Numbers* will take the time to analyze what adults do, identify the connections with student achievement, and carefully select antecedents with the greatest capacity to engage students to think, impact their classroom performance every day, and set in motion structures and learning conditions that can be replicated widely by teachers who embrace their obligation to learn and to lead.

Reflection

BIG IDEA: For continuous improvement to occur, antecedent data must be identified, collected, analyzed, and acted upon.

What role should antecedents play in data analysis? Why isn't it sufficient to concentrate on student achievement results alone?

BIG IDEA: Determining the relationship between achievement and professional practice is the most efficient way of impacting policy and changing classroom practice.

How can early identification and monitoring of antecedents prevent unnecessary data collection?

BIG IDEA: Antecedents are the researcher's independent variable.

Describe the benefits of using a cause-effect diagram.

What distinguishes teacher behavior antecedents from instructional strategies? What distinguishes an instructional strategy from an administrative condition of learning?

CHAPTER

4

The Power of Collaboration

> Plans fail for lack of counsel, but with many advisors comes success.
>
> —PROVERBS 15:22

Educators have long been proponents of collaboration. Labor negotiations are collaborative and interest based. Education has promoted shared decision making for years, and policies across the United States have detailed descriptions of the means and format for making decisions, defining consensus, achieving parity, reaching collaborative decisions, and making executive decisions for those rare emergencies when one voice is needed. Collaboration ensures that multiple viewpoints are available and that all voices are heard, and in public education, collaboration has become as much a function of fairness and application of democratic principles as it is a practical approach to gather information and make decisions.

Collaboration is essential in data analysis if we are to get beyond the numbers. People rarely discover a blueprint for improving instruction or modifying antecedents just by examining a table, chart, or worksheet of data. The data we collect are invariably limited, as we found in Chapter 3 on antecedents. The most accurate data are even more limited if educators resort to the rearview-mirror effect. The incomplete nature of the data we have available is the very reason we need to add the human perspective, and the reason collaboration is so critical in data analysis. Surowiecki (2004, p. 41) describes this type of data as "private information," the results of interpretation, analysis, and even intuition. Tier 3 data are as critical and reliable as the numbers we crunch, and quality analysis is incomplete without the insights that emerge when teachers work together. Data of any kind are only meaningful when professionals collaboratively examine, analyze, reflect, and ultimately decide to act on data available to them. Frequent models of collaboration have been developed by well-respected scholars in the field. Surowiecki (2004) identified three conditions necessary for a "crowd," or group, to be wise: diversity, independence, and decentralization.

Diversity promotes wisdom through differing ideas and perspectives and by "making it easier for individuals to say what they really think" (Surowiecki, 2004, p. 39). Independence means relative freedom from the influence of others. It is a capacity to rely on one's own thinking, including the independence to withhold judgment and resist innovation until it resonates with one's own experience and observation. Decentralization means authority for decision making has devolved from a central authority to other units and where specialization and division of labor are prevalent. School systems possess each of these ingredients for such "wisdom," where decisions are made at various levels, specialization occurs, and the opportunity exists to benefit from diverse ideas and perspectives.

Reeves (2002b) recognizes collaboration as key to effective professional development, describing a collaborative model of professional development with the following four characteristics :

- The collaborative model depends more on teachers teaching teachers and less on outside assistance. It is primarily an internal, established process that recognizes teachers as experts.
- The collaborative model depends upon context. Integrated curriculum, standards, and leadership must all be addressed simultaneously.
- Attention to individual needs is a necessary condition of the model. Collaborative professional development is not one size fits all.
- Collaborative staff development is sustained internally.

Professional development works precisely because of collaboration in this model, which is sustained internally and relies on teacher-to-teacher instruction and practice. The model attends to the context of teaching and learning through collaborative conversations and dialogue, and it enriches understanding by capturing differences in experience, training, and perspectives of individual teachers.

Collaboration requires practice to yield the synergy and gestalt of "the whole is greater than the sum of its parts." Langer, Colton, and Goff (2003) describe the concept succinctly: "too often we expect collaborative tasks to be natural and convenient for teachers. The task may get done, but sometimes at the expense of precious time, lack of collegiality, and bad feelings." Educators will not routinely, predictably, or deliberately be able to get beyond the numbers without approaching collaboration in a systematic way.

These examples underscore the need to make sure collaboration is explicit, structured, and embedded. The same call for precision is echoed by Rick DuFour and colleagues (DuFour, DuFour, & Eaker, 2008, p. 16): "Collaboration is a systematic process in which teachers work together, interdependently, to analyze and impact professional practice in order to improve results for their students, their team, and their school." Peter Senge (2000, p. 73) adds, "At its core, team learning is a discipline of practices designed, over time, to get the people of a team thinking and acting together. The team members do not need to think alike."

Collaboration is so important that it is central to the application of analysis methods, the choice of data tools, and triangulation. Collaboration powerful enough to effect excellence in student achievement has three characteristics that form the basis for this discussion: (1) collaboration must be present from planning to execution in data-driven decision making, (2) collaboration is the means to develop team thinking and candor in data-driven decision making, and (3) collaboration needs to be integrated into every data-driven decision. We address each characteristic of effective collaboration in data-driven decision making, but first let us visit two teachers of high school science.

CASE STUDY

Mary Ann has taught chemistry at Maple High School for the past seven years, accepting a change in assignment from the biology and earth science classes she taught the previous five years to help the department. Mary Ann is an excellent teacher, loved by her students and parents and respected by her peers. Prior to coming to Maple, she taught elementary school at the primary level, rotating from kindergarten to second to first grade for 12 years, again helping whenever requested. Each of her five principals loved to observe her classroom, where every event and transition was purposeful and connected. She understood reading, and she understood children, and for most of her career she remarked, "I can't believe I get paid to do what I love." The fact that she taught high school students with the same passion, humor, and skill as demonstrated at the elementary level made Mary Ann a teacher to reckon with, especially when changes were proposed. If her principal convinced Mary Ann of the need for change, he could be assured that the other teachers would be on board as well.

Mary Ann is not pleased with the changes being implemented now, causing her to consider a change herself. She never had issues with accountability and approached every fall confident that her students would learn the material and be more than ready for the next grade or next course. She is insulted by the state assessments and No Child Left Behind Act (NCLB) requirements and believes the enrollment in her classes and feedback from students and parents are the real measures of accountability. Since she began at Maple 12 years ago, twice students have voted her to make the faculty commencement speech, and in her 24 years of teaching, she has twice been voted the teachers association's teacher of the year.

Now the district is getting in on the accountability act, and Mary Ann has had it. She tolerated the seven class periods used for state assessments, but now the district is insisting that each department create its own end-of-course (EOC) assessments based on the standards and refer to them as assessments only. "We can't call them tests anymore," she was heard complaining. The district already required teachers to collaboratively score monthly writing assessments and adhere to an instructional calendar beginning next year. An instructional calendar required departments to determine what standards would be addressed each week and to develop instructional units and performance assessments together for each course. Mary Ann really bristled at this requirement, as she long ago had developed quality units for her courses. Kids knew they were challenging, and she updated them frequently, having no problem with new textbooks, as she always served on the committees that recommended selections to the school board.

"Whatever happened to academic freedom? I am not about to take my valuable time to have to explain or justify my work to novice teachers or to spend unnecessary time always having to 'reach consensus' with teachers who are just figuring out how to manage behavior in their classrooms. It is not that I'm not willing to help," she would tell her best friend at the gym, "but I've got students who come in before and after school to see me. Do they want me to meet with some rookie instead of students? See how messed up their priorities are?"

Even worse, the "head shed," as she called the administration building, now expects faculty to evaluate the EOC assessments and review them annually for improvements.

Mary Ann told a colleague, "Now, the district expects us to do the jobs of the curriculum department. How in the world do they expect us to do anything of significance for kids when we are responsible for everything but have no authority?"

Mary Ann knew herself well enough to notice the impact of the added stress. Several times when she previously would have used humor with students, she now was abrupt, sending three of them to the principal's office this year alone, a number equal to 11 previous years combined. She didn't like the cynicism and sarcasm that she felt and expressed. Mary Ann decided that if her principal follows through on requiring departments to develop the same tests and require collaborative scoring of writing assessments each month, this year would be her last. She did not want to take early retirement, but she knew the changes planned were untenable and she could not accommodate them, even if it meant leaving the profession.

CASE STUDY

Georgia proudly received her "Maple High School Family" plaque at the end-of-year banquet, having successfully completed her third year in the district. It hadn't been easy, as she had had to take the state examination for teacher proficiency in earth and biological sciences twice. She finally passed just before the district's policy would have required her dismissal. Georgia had not been the best student. In fact, her first degree was in speech therapy, but she was unable to pass the state exam after three tries. So, because she wanted to work with kids, she went back to school long enough to take a few content requirements, complete student teaching, and earn her teaching certificate. Georgia recognized the same pattern in many of her students; they just were not good test takers, so she went out of her way to make sure they were exposed to various assessments. Georgia made it clear to all her students that they would have multiple opportunities to succeed and that she was determined that every student would be proficient, even on district and state assessments.

Every evaluation spoke of her willingness to learn, her dedication to students, and a strong work ethic. Georgia was the department's newest member, and she was like a sponge to learn from her colleagues, people she struggled to call peers because she had such respect for their knowledge, experience, and skills. Mr. Ino, the assistant principal who had observed and evaluated Georgia since day one, had assigned a great mentor/coach to help her, although Lisa was from the crosstown high school. This situation was awkward, and Georgia never really understood why her coach was from another school. The great aspect of the relationship was that Lisa helped her understand how to ask for and receive help from her colleagues, and over the three years, Georgia also received help and assistance from her department, especially by observing Mary Ann. In addition, the department chair provided lots of instructional materials and great Internet resources.

Georgia shook Mr. Ino's hand to the applause of the faculty, whispering as she crossed the banquet dais, "Mr. Ino, thanks for assigning Lisa to me. She was so helpful getting me enrolled in just the right in-services and courses. And thanks for being so encouraging while letting me know where I needed to grow!" Georgia returned to her seat as other Maple High School staff were recognized.

"This is the best job in the best school in the best district anywhere," she thought gratefully. She remembered Allen's encouragement to develop the first draft of the biology EOC assessment and the way every team member contributed great changes without putting her down. She really liked the collaborative writing requirement because she learned that she had expected too little from her students and that her own understanding of the writing process and 6+ traits was below standard and warranted additional training and support. As she looked back, she was amazed at how much she had learned. She sometimes wished her university had been so helpful, but she was confident she was becoming more proficient every day. As the last teacher accepted his plaque and everyone rose in applause for the 23 new "family" members, Georgia was moved to tears and determined right then to be the best biology teacher, maybe even better than Mary Ann.

Both of these teachers taught in the same department and same school. Both were dedicated to their craft and loved their students. Mary Ann was a talented and gifted teacher, while Georgia was learning how to become one. Mary Ann preferred her autonomy, resenting the intrusion of her colleagues, department, school, and district, and viewing the collaboration policies as an issue of academic freedom. Georgia needed assistance, knew it, and welcomed it. Their experiences form the backdrop of the discussion throughout this chapter.

Even the Lone Ranger Had Tonto

Mary Ann viewed her profession as one in which she had the obligation to independently develop her skills and content knowledge to the best of her ability and in which she had the latitude to develop her own style, set her own pace, and enrich the district's curriculum by providing in-depth units of her choice. The result: Mary Ann adhered to the "lone ranger" isolation that has characterized teaching and learning in the United States for more than a century. Teaching is an inherently lonely profession, and teachers feel isolated enough without assistance, but some very effective teachers have grown accustomed to this model and actually prefer it. And, while some may believe they have found ways to be effective within the four walls of their classroom and the limits of their respective curriculum, students are short-changed in the process. Teachers who collaborate learn from each other and support each other by bringing special talents and skills to the process. Georgia, in contrast to Mary Ann, wanted to collaborate and absorbed knowledge like a sponge when others offered assistance and feedback.

Peter Senge (2000, p. 327) refers to the "de-privatization of practice and critical review" as a characteristic of "schools that learn"—schools that have discovered ways to reduce the ability of teachers to function as lone rangers. Specialization or decentralization allows individuals to increase their expertise in certain areas because colleagues share responsibility to develop expertise in other areas.

Collaboration provides a forum to sanction or legitimize proposed changes. Collaboration is powerful because it promotes insights that individuals alone are unable to produce, and it provides an opportunity for educators to benefit from the collective wisdom of professionals and, in so doing, discover how the whole really is greater than the sum of its parts. Exhibit 4.1 depicts how collaboration in data analysis can produce high-quality insights just by teachers collaboratively examining critical incidents (see Appendix G).

The process for determining a critical incident is simple and effective: teams, which can be a

EXHIBIT 4.1 | Critical Incident Report as a Collaborative Tool

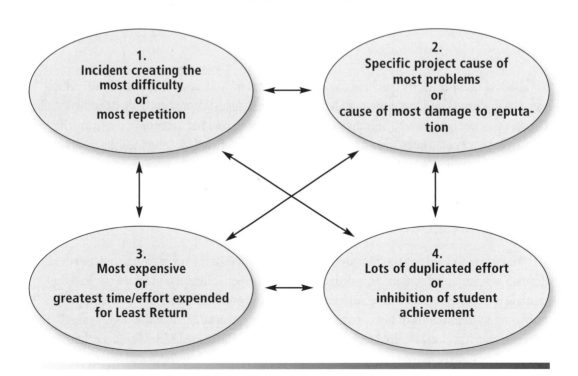

large group or as small as two people, examine each dichotomy separately, then prioritize from the four choices what is most urgent, most compelling, and most important to address first. Further analysis is likely to take place within any size organization to quantify the perceptions of the team and test their biases. The process communicates the importance of collaboration in any deliberation of data, as completion of the activity outside of a collaborative group yields merely one's individual opinion. Critical incident reviews jump-start data analysis by immediately identifying priorities from the collective wisdom of the group. Assume the following results:

1. Is most difficult: reliable scoring on 6+1 trait writing
2. Causes most damage to reputation: volleyball team suspended for drinking
3. Expends greatest time/effort for least return: homecoming parade
4. Inhibits student achievement: policy requires homework to be factored as 25 percent of all grades

Which incident needs to be addressed? Are all of the incidents sufficiently critical to require a systematic effort to prevent their recurrence? Leaders at this juncture frequently ask for student achievement data or antecedent monitoring to verify whether these anecdotal incidents were indeed critical. Even without such data, the collective wisdom of the group is its own validation for some of these issues. As a school, they experienced the damage to their reputations, they recalled the work requirements of the homecoming parade, and they labored under the prescribed homework policy, even though it was implemented with such variability as to render it meaningless in terms of proficiency. The collective and collaborative judgment (assessment) that these incidents were critical is a measure of the context within which the school operates and the "private information" each professional brings to the assignment.

The critical incident data tool offers a dramatic example of collaboration because of its ability to help professionals get to the heart of issues that impact their work lives. It also reveals how powerful collaboration is because the Lone Ranger himself could not achieve these insights independently, regardless of how skilled and talented the masked man may have been. He, or Mary Ann in our example earlier, needed the perspective of others to identify what was critical because our information is limited by our experience. The business manager might know with some certainty the program that was most expensive in a per pupil cost formula, but he would be less likely to identify what was most costly in terms of expenditure of effort by staff. The same is true for the department head, superintendent, board member, or classroom teacher. Surowiecki (2004, pp. 35–39) notes that when it comes to solving problems or identifying solutions, groups of even less informed individuals, if they are acting on their own best independent judgment and if the group represents a sufficiently diverse assemblage of thinkers, will invariably offer better solutions than the expert. But let's return to our critical incident discussion.

The high school team decides to address all four incidents simultaneously. Number 1 indicates a need for follow-up in terms of professional development to improve the quality and reliability of collaborative scoring. Number 2 indicates a need to reexamine eligibility rules, establish very clear protocols for each activity sponsor and coach, and monitor implementation of those rules to prevent a similar incident in the future. Number 3 indicates that a great deal of time and effort continues to be expended with limited perceived benefit. Perhaps a solution is to further engage the community in operating the parade or to increase the academic incentives and sanctions associated with it. Although a multifaceted problem, its introduction sets in motion actions to improve its effectiveness, clarify its relationship to student achievement, and redirect internal resources to other areas. Number 4 is viewed as a hindrance to student achievement because homework effort and cooperative behavior mask a lack of proficiency on state standards. Tackling this problem, too, puts into motion actions to correct and improve the homework process and perhaps to clarify expectations and introduce strategies and solutions that better align student and teacher efforts on the standards. In some instances, only one of these issues would be addressed, but the example is provided here to illustrate how critical incident "data" jump-start important actions to improve the climate and performance of any school or school district without examining achievement data or even numbers about antecedents. How much better informed and more reliable our decisions could be when we add meaningful quantitative student achievement data and insights from antecedents to collaborative analysis of data and events. We now turn to the need for collaboration from start to finish, planning to execution.

Collaboration: From Planning to Execution

Collaboration needs to be built into every step of data management: from data collection to action planning to implementation to monitoring to evaluation. Every step requires at least two sets of eyes, ears, brain matter, and heart. One of the most useful ways to ensure that collaboration occurs at every step is through the use of an assessment calendar like that depicted in Exhibit 2.9 or through instructional calendars whereby curriculum content is aligned with standards and addressed during a specific window of time for all teachers. Both of these approaches require teachers to work together at critical junctures in time, and both require explicit actions to take place. The assessment calendar provides a window for administration, data collection, and disaggregation of data and ensures that faculty are focused on the tasks of data management at prescribed times. Presumably, they will also adhere to similar protocols for administration and data collection and will be offered the same training and resources to disaggregate their data. That step alone brings teachers together. By setting aside specific times for analysis, administration sets an expectation that the interaction of professional experience, insights, and perspectives will produce more than what the data alone revealed. This is the essence of collaboration.

Four remaining categories in the assessment calendar establish points in time to recommend changes, make a decision, create a written rationale, and disseminate publicly decisions with rationale to affected stakeholders, including parents and students where appropriate. Each step in the assessment calendar is a collaborative process, from planning to execution, in driving decisions based on data. Recommended changes following reflection require educators to do more than see data as a report card, and to do something with the results. The point of decision should also be collaborative, where those with authority to make a decision weigh its potential benefits, barriers, costs, and training requirements to implement the recommendation. The written rationale is provided as a record of the collaborative processes and serves as a mechanism to report back to those involved at every step of the process. Should the recommendation and decision be to make no changes, a written rationale compels those involved to justify that decision on the basis of their analysis. It objectifies the process, especially if decision makers are at another organizational level, requiring communication of the process used to select the course of action. It also communicates to those involved in the tedium of collecting and disaggregating data that their work is important and that the fruit of their efforts is examined seriously. In this way, collaboration is part of all aspects of data-driven decision making, from planning to execution.

Meaningful collaboration that captures the best thinking of staff to improve student achievement can be achieved by instituting a number of antecedent structures into the daily routines in schools. Seven antecedent structures are recommended:

1) Action planning and continuous improvement cycles. The scenario at Maple High School, where Mary Ann and Georgia teach, will be used to illustrate how much more successful collaborative processes will be when a continuous improvement cycle for data-driven decision making is employed.

2) Collaborative improvements. A simple means to promote collaboration in data-driven decision making is to insist that all planned improvements, including those at the classroom level, be supported by data and one other colleague before they can be implemented. Undoubtedly, some of these data requirements will raise the ire of teachers like Mary Ann, and time and effort may be required to bring those like her along. There is a "high maintenance" aspect to building teams and professional learning communities as the friction between those desiring more collaboration and those preferring more autonomy is worked out, but if Mary Ann were convinced, her credibility would make that support a real asset for change.

3) Lesson logs. When shared and distributed by departments or grade-level teams, lesson logs create opportunities for teachers to collaborate. Given the opportunity, the vast majority of teachers are energized to model lessons or observe others, and the distribution of lesson logs provides a means for teachers to voluntarily be enriched by each other's work.

4) Common assessments. These assessments are created, evaluated, and revised by teacher teams, and they function as a catalyst antecedent for excellence. Common assessments require discussion, debate, and dialogue among peers about the heart of their business, and they serve to facilitate instituting standards-based assessments to replace less demanding multiple-choice assessments of content knowledge without the applied learning with standards.

5) Instructional calendars. Calendars represent the intent of grade-level and department teams to map out when and how standards will be demonstrated throughout the school year. Many educators are surprised to find how little their curriculum and instruction were aligned with state standards. Such calendars assist teachers to drive instruction

and apply curriculum strategically, rather than be driven by textbook sequences.

6) Program evaluation. A clearly defined process offers a means to benefit from the collective wisdom of faculty. By establishing a team of teachers who routinely examine the effect of programs and strategies implemented in the school, a culture that is open to modifications based on results emerges.

7) Data Teams. Data Teams offer schools a format to submit challenges and problems as well as insights and questions to a group of teachers who agree to monitor outlier student performance and efforts to close learning gaps in the school. This experience needs to be common to every classroom teacher, but creation of school-wide Data Teams also offers a launching point for future expansion. Data Teams are by definition collaborative, and schools may want to create systems that refer difficult data challenges to the Data Team for analysis, reflection, and recommendations. It is recommended that every teacher serve on a Data Team that examines actual work of students with real names, real faces, and real needs and that schools offer as much latitude in responding to those needs as possible.

Data Teams examine student work, develop interventions, adjust teaching strategies, and monitor results. Some are informal, others formal, and some optional. The most effective are formal enough to be scheduled and monitored but collaborative enough to identify needs, develop interventions, commit resources, monitor results, and begin the cycle again. Data Teams, professional learning communities, and whole-faculty study groups all represent teacher teams that analyze data to create interventions that improve student achievement (Leadership and Learning Center, 2010; DuFour, DuFour, & Eaker, 2008; Murphy & Lick, 2005). Because these teams represent the most granular level of collaboration, the Data Team cycle is described below. Individual teachers or principals can independently follow a continuous improvement cycle, but the power of continuous improvement is released in collaboration. Exhibit 4.2 depicts a proven Data Teams process, recalling the continuous improvement process described in Chapter 2.

The cycle implies the need to reflect on lessons learned as well as the need to select, create, and administer quality short-cycle assessments to focus on the collaborative processes teacher teams engage in. We begin with the treasure hunt.

Collaboration in the treasure hunt produces the team decision that identifies the area of instructional focus. While the team relies largely on achievement data, its decision is driven by the professional judgment of teachers as to what content area is selected, what standards and learning expectations will be critical to student success at this time, and which area teachers need to build capacity in. In this way, the treasure hunt goes beyond the numbers to select content and standards. The process may guide the team's focus for the entire school year, and the decision may be as simple as selecting the content area that aligns to the school improve-ment plan. It may, however, change during the school year as emerging challenges and needs are identified. One powerful tool that supports the treasure hunt is the critical incident tool (Exhibit 4.1).

The next part of the cycle is to analyze strengths and obstacles. The most effective teams have discovered that quality collaboration in this step will greatly enhance the value of each

EXHIBIT 4.2 | The Data Team Cycle

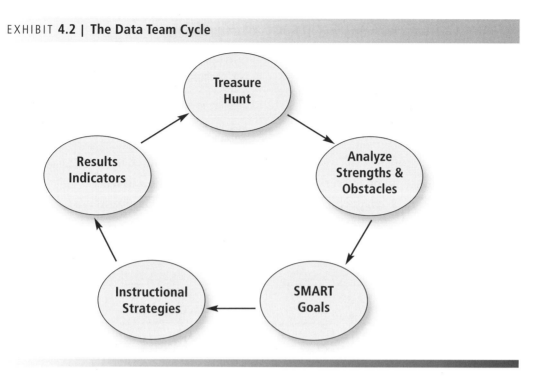

team decision. It is the "deep water" of Data Teams, where collective reflection and inquiry can yield valuable insights. The process identifies the strengths of proficient or higher student performance and identifies obstacles commonly observed when students are not yet proficient, and it invites the professional judgment of educators into the data arena (see Exhibit 4.3).

Note how this process need not provide additional data; instead, it elicits real insight from the experience and knowledge of teachers. Explicit skills are identified that are representative of students who achieve and those who struggle. While teachers may begin with the critical incident tool in the treasure hunt and offer their observations in this step, the strengths and obstacles are written in such a way as to be observable and measurable, and they track the path to increasing the strengths and minimizing the obstacles. The example astutely separates academic strengths and obstacles from behavioral strengths and obstacles to ensure that this section actually addresses the learning challenges students face. Once this brainstorming activity is complete, teams are prepared for the "deep dive" needed to craft a smart and novel instructional program for their students.

The lists in Exhibit 4.3 are instructive, and some teachers may report that they work on all of the traits in their classrooms, but a more realistic approach would be to agree about which strength represents a gateway to more consistent success for more students. The team will also need to agree on which obstacle, if removed or reduced, would allow more students to achieve proficiency than current practice does. Addressing all the traits listed in Exhibit 4.3 would be folly, but addressing one or two for the Data Team cycle is entirely possible.

In this example, the team selected the items of the exhibit shown in italics. Why these items? In the academic arena, the team recognized that the ability to draw on multiple

EXHIBIT **4.3** | **Data Team Analysis of Student Strengths and Obstacles**

Strengths of Proficient or Higher Student Performance	Obstacles of Nonproficient Student Performance
Clearly articulated steps	*Inability to organize ideas and steps*
Multiple problem-solving strategies used	Inability to write or verify choice of problem-solving strategies
Very neat work	Messy, hard-to-read work
Vocabulary/math terms concise	Lack of vocabulary/math terms
Self-edits work; recognizes errors in terms of sentence structure and conventions	Inability to complete multiple-step tasks without assistance
Uses effective reading strategies (predicting content, word attack, re-reading, use of contextual clues, etc.)	Poor sentence control (recognition of parts, punctuation omissions)
Behavioral Strengths	**Behavioral Obstacles**
Helps others without being cued	Easily distracted by sounds, visuals, others
Asks questions	*Rarely comes to class prepared*
Attention to task during lesson; asks appropriate questions, offers participating comments	Work incomplete

problem-solving strategies was a huge strength that also reflected an ability to work independently, stay on task, and complete work. When such a strength was evident, teachers reported that behavior issues were less common. At the same time, the inability to organize ideas and steps was an equally huge obstacle, requiring a lot of one-to-one time with students, frequent disruptions in class, and generally incomplete work. By removing this obstacle, the team believed it would be able to increase the number of students proficient on the standard in question, and they recognized that instruction that provides multiple problem-solving strategies to students would simultaneously help students organize their ideas into step-by-step strategies. The Data Team was strategic in selecting those items in italic, because they reinforce one another and are few enough to structure a teaching sequence around them.

Step 3 of the Data Teams process tees up the selection of the goal statement, which need not be framed just by annual state or provincial assessments. In this case, it is entirely feasible that the team would gather additional baseline data about strengths and obstacles and frame the SMART goal around those issues to address the gaps revealed initially by the data.

SMART goals are specific, measurable, achievable, relevant, and timely, an apt acronym that is better known than it is used. For example, specific goals reflect the specificity of the standard or learning expectation and of the student groups targeted in the Data Teams process. SMART goal setting is best accomplished by consulting both the treasure hunt performance data and the strengths and obstacles data to produce a blend. For example:

The number of students who demonstrate proficiency solving math problems involving the four operations given novel scenarios in content areas outside of mathematics will increase from 14 percent of third graders (17 of 121) to 63 percent (76 of 121) following the September– November 3 Data Team intervention in problem-solving strategies and organization of ideas.

This goal is specific to the content, measurable with a clear baseline and firm target for performance on a designated assessment (novel scenarios in non-math content areas), and achievable in that it will close existing achievement gaps (86 percent below proficiency to 37 percent below) by the end of the project. The relevant element of the SMART goal is evident from the use of novel scenarios (those that the students do not see until the assessment is administered) and the demonstration of math proficiency across different academic content areas. Finally, the SMART goal is timely in that an explicit date is stipulated (November 3).

Instructional strategies are identified in step 4 of the Data Teams process, but where should the team begin? If it relies solely on the treasure hunt data, the team will not benefit from the context data in the analysis of strengths and obstacles. If the team relies just on steps 1 and 2, the strategies may or may not be focused sufficiently on the desired outcome (SMART goal). However, examining all three prior steps in collaboration to understand the need, patterns, context, and target, teams are prepared to develop or select powerful strategies. Some teams routinely turn to a series of defined strategies identified by thought leaders and associated with powerful gains documented in the research (Marzano, 2007; Hattie, 2009), but unless those strategies are selected in the context of what is happening at the school, grade, or department, the process may not achieve its goal. However, if the strategy is first developed from the strengths and challenges with nuances introduced based on the experience of the teacher team that address behavioral and academic learning, the strategy will be instructional and practical from the outset. The most effective teams begin here and augment their strategy later, if needed, from the literature.

Continuing with our hypothetical example of math problem-solving strategies as our goal statement, teams may elect to adopt or adapt the use of hypothesis testing to focus student thinking and engage students as they learn multiple strategies to apply in novel settings. The team may group students in threes, differentiated by ability and practice with the problem-solving strategies, and may include movement from station to station, where each student is expected to ask for help and offer help. In this way, the selected strategies are not merely one of nine categories, or even an explicit strategy like reciprocal teaching, but rather are guided by the experience and expertise of teachers, and the Data Teams process is designed to do just that.

At this point in the process, step 5, teams are ready to launch their project as soon as they document their plan (steps 1–4) and describe how they will monitor and evaluate their results. Determining results indicators identifies what should be monitored and when, a task that many educators find awkward, as establishing a baseline, setting a goal, selecting an assessment, and specifying the timeline for completing the post-assessment would appear to complete the process. Should teams constantly assess student progress, especially considering the project is limited to only four to six weeks of instruction? The answer is no. Results indicators exist solely to monitor progress and identify a need for a midcourse correction. Rather than look to additional or incremental measures of the goal statement, collaborative teams will select true indicators that allow teams to determine whether their project is improving student performance and achieving fidelity of implementation. For student performance, readers are encouraged to revisit the strengths and obstacles to identify measures that would indicate that students are on the right track. Using our example from Exhibit 4.3, identifying the number of previously nonproficient students who are observed self-editing their work is itself a positive indicator that they are learning to apply multiple problem-solving strategies. This data-gathering process need not be difficult, as teachers need only monitor those students who historically struggle with this skill (perhaps five to seven students rather than the entire class) and can do so with a note card or record electronically from a smart phone or tablet computer. When teams convene midway through the Data Team cycle, they will share their observations on the agreed-upon indicator of student performance, self-editing. A second results indicator is recommended to measure fidelity of implementation. In our hypothetical example, we selected the use of multiple problem-solving strategies, so the team might agree to self-monitor the frequency with which problem-solving strategies are introduced in each classroom. Again, when the team convenes, it merely shares among its members the evidence they agreed to monitor and makes any changes as needed.

These five steps for Data Teams reveal just how collaborative the process should be and why collaboration is essential for any process of continuous improvement to succeed.

Collaboration in Action

Any one of the seven structures discussed in the previous section will improve the school's capacity for collaborative data analysis. It is collaboration that translates the numbers of data into actions of adults. Data cannot improve instruction; only teachers have that capacity. This caution is true for every collaborative process, as the insights that emerge from discussions, from hunches to opinions to awareness of best practices to experience, drive planned changes in curriculum, antecedent management, and instruction.

Remember how Mary Ann preferred to be a lone ranger, while Georgia was the novice who desired greater collaboration and more explicit mentoring and coaching? Let us examine Georgia's program in detail to illustrate how collaborative processes can add value, even when they are applied informally. Examine Georgia's grading system, displayed in Exhibits 4.4 and 4.5, to determine the data's relationship with the biology EOC and ascertain whether writing scores correlated with the state writing assessment.

Georgia worried about the writing assessment because her state used a holistic scoring guide for each genre and annual tests rotated from one of six genres at random. Assistant Principal Ino assured Georgia that if she could get her students to achieve proficiency in biology content and they understood the writing process and 6+ traits, even in part, they would do well. Both Mr. Ino and Lisa, Georgia's mentor/coach, encouraged Georgia to analyze

EXHIBIT **4.4** | **Biology Outcomes by Teacher G by Percentage Proficient, Maple High School, 2008–2010**

	Caucasian (%)	Hispanic (%)	African American (%)	Asian (%)
Biology EOC 2008	67	31	28	67
Biology EOC 2009	71	44	41	33
Biology EOC 2010	69	67	63	83
Department Average, 2008–2010	**75**	**55**	**43**	**81**
Biology performance assessment 2008	n/a	n/a	n/a	n/a
Biology performance assessment 2009	73	61	66.7	100
Biology performance assessment 2010	78	78	58.3	100
G district writing assessment 2008	n/a	n/a	n/a	n/a
G district writing assessment 2009	73	14	23	60
G district writing assessment 2010	53	35	39	58
District Writing Assessment, 2010	**52**	**25**	**19**	**71**
G state writing assessment 2010	33	31	36	47
State Writing Assessment, District	**45**	**19**	**17**	**53**

the data and bring her conclusions to them Friday. They would examine results for Georgia's students and develop recommendations on their own.

Georgia was overwhelmed with just about everything in year one, so there weren't many antecedent measures she could capture. Exhibit 4.5 describes the measures that Lisa helped identify and monitor during Georgia's three years of noncontinuing contracts. Georgia was shocked to hear Mr. Ino say no other teacher had monitored these outcomes. She assumed everyone would do so, especially great teachers like Mary Ann. Lisa helped Georgia secure other data from human resources and the curriculum department. Georgia was encouraged that her students outperformed the district on six of eight measures, and in 2010, her students outperformed the department on the biology EOC exam. She wondered if her input drafting that assessment would not be viewed favorably with such results, and because her first-year students struggled so, she had no idea what that might mean in terms of her contract renewal. Overall, Georgia believed the data showed she was learning and getting better at helping her students, but she worried especially about the falloff in 2009 for her Asian students and the cliff that Caucasian kids fell off in 2010. Together, the two groups comprised the vast majority of her students, and the fact that almost one-third of them were nonproficient was problematic. Georgia was also concerned that her professional development days were fewer than the district average this year, a trend that the head shed might frown on when administration was considering her contract. When Friday arrived, she was more than a little anxious, and while she knew Lisa would be supportive, she also knew Mr. Ino was accountable to others and feared he would have to deliver unpleasant news.

EXHIBIT **4.5** | **Antecedent Measures: Teacher A, Maple High School, 10th-Grade Biology**

	Teacher Attendance (%/days)	Standards-Based Classroom Components (% implemented/14)	Correlation Grades with EOC (r value)	Professional Development Days (including summer)	Graduate Credits Earned
2007–2008	99	n/a	0.06	7	3
2008–2009	97	50	0.46	11	6
2009–2010	100	79	0.39	5	3
District Average	88	n/a	0.14	5.5	1.3

Mr. Ino's task was to review Georgia's data and offer any insights he had regarding it. He knew Georgia was committed and a dedicated learner, but because she struggled during the first year and a half, the positive outcomes, especially for minority students, were surprising. The gap for Hispanic and African American students closed dramatically, and Asian and Caucasian students still met state standards. She monitored results on her performance assessments, and her commitment to professional development was extraordinary. His only concern was that her classroom management was characterized by a lax tardy policy that resulted in a disproportionate number of her students in the principal's office. He pulled the data to verify, and 17 kids last year alone were in the halls when they should have been in Georgia's class but were not counted as tardy or absent. Still, he was proud that he could encourage her, as she was becoming a fine science teacher in the tradition of the best at Maple High.

Lisa was also pleased with Georgia's work, especially regarding the progress minority students made each year. She knew the performance assessments had helped engage students to perform better on the EOC and even the writing assessments. Her one concern was that both Caucasian and Asian students seemed to have reached a plateau in their writing achievement, and she wondered whether Georgia's emphasis on a five-step writing process had become wooden and limited student performance in holistic writing by genre. Lisa felt responsible for the fact that Georgia had adopted her suggestion to require nonfiction writing every day, a goal that was achievable in biology because Georgia expected her students to react to current events related to biology and present succinct paragraphs recounting those events. Lisa wondered whether that approach had resulted in the students' written work being dominated by use of the lower levels of Bloom's taxonomy terms and whether sufficient time had been spent eliciting analysis, synthesis, and evaluation. That was also one of the criticisms and eventual revisions made of her draft EOC. Still, her students performed well and her professional development had come a long way. Whenever significant differences exist between sub-groups, it is prudent to look for patterns in those antecedents that are operating, and Georgia and Lisa found the reflection about all the data instructive.

Georgia was still a little nervous when the Friday meeting began, and she was relieved and surprised when her mentor and principal were pleased with the student achievement scores in every area. For her part, Lisa was surprised when Mr. Ino made no mention of the static growth in writing for Caucasian and Asian students. Both veterans brought a different perspective and experiences, and each perspective was helpful to the other in understanding the data. They added the "data in their heads" to the discussion, and after 45 minutes, they decided to make a serious effort to replicate Georgia's performance assessments in other departments and to survey students to determine what assessments were most useful to them. They also decided to interview students who had achieved the most growth and students who had yet to achieve proficiency, applying the following rule of thumb:

Examine outlier data whenever sub-group
differences are evident.

Finally, Lisa agreed to interview a dozen students at random over the summer for suggestions on how Georgia's class could be improved. The conference ended, with Georgia ecstatic at the praise and encouragement provided and excited to receive the data from Lisa when she returned in the fall.

This story illustrates the power of collaboration when professionals gather around student work. Lisa, Mr. Ino, and Georgia viewed the same data and were able to reach consensus on key elements. However, until they participated together in the analysis of those results, their perspectives were very different, and no action had been initiated. Furthermore, the actions they later planned were not among those any of them had previously considered. Collaboration around data should result in action that clarifies understanding, replicates successes, and responds to remaining needs, critical outcomes of the collaborative process that Georgia, Mr. Ino, and Lisa accomplished without any formal structure. Of course, the next time this team or an expanded group looks at data, they may neglect to apply the rules of thumb that were helpful the first time. They may be tired, they may have conflicting priorities, or someone may say something that is taken as an insult or a put-down rather than the constructive criticism it was meant to convey. In this second instance, because the collaboration may not be explicit, required, and recognized for its power to produce quality change through shared accountability, the group could miss opportunities to improve instruction, not only for Georgia's students but also for the rest of the school, despite the thoroughness of the analysis or the personal benefit of collaboration that was achieved.

Collaboration to Develop Team Thinking and Candor

Deliberate efforts to facilitate team thinking and candor in interactions around data, learning, and teaching are necessary to realize the true benefit of collaboration in schools. Collegiality and learning how to respect one another and work cooperatively should be the baseline for collaboration in our schools, not the end product. I have observed many leaders who genuinely promote and proclaim candor, but because of a natural reluctance among staff to be candid, it only takes a few instances of candor being discouraged to shut it down completely within any organization. For candor to be present in the discussion about results and the causes that precede them, a culture of no blame and no excuses must be modeled, communicated, celebrated, and explicitly promoted. Jim Collins, author of *Good to Great* (2001), found that this characteristic was more important than vision in distinguishing great organizations from good ones, and he devoted considerable time and effort to what he called "confronting the brutal facts." In a tangible way, candor in confronting the brutal facts is personal humility extended to the work of groups, teams, and organizations. Confronting the brutal facts does not happen in isolation; it happens in a collaborative context. Collaboration is the "naked truth" level that leaders hope functional teams strive for. How do we get where we all know we should be but where we all recognize we are not? One suggestion is to establish norms.

Langer, Colton, and Goff (2003, pp. 47–49) suggest that a culture of collaboration requires norms that help participants function collaboratively and use communication skills that promote inquiry and reflection. This approach can go a long way toward establishing trust, but setting the norms only puts in place a potential for candor. It is the testing of the norms that will establish them, so leaders and facilitators may even need to create situations to test the norms. Norms for data may include an expectation that group members ask for evidence to support any opinions or declarations made at meetings, or that meetings always have a defined purpose, recommended process, and desired results published in advance. Another norm might be that participants are expected to request clarification whenever someone's meaning is not clear and to do so by paraphrasing back to that colleague your current understanding. Other norms include fostering a diversity of ideas, being prepared to teach every day, assigning roles to elicit honest dialogue, letting the data reveal hunches, referring a set of data tools, and publishing meeting results. The following paragraphs discuss these norms in more detail.

Ensure a diversity of ideas: don't meet without them. Structure meetings to elicit differences, not similarities, in thinking. In *The Wisdom of Crowds*, James Surowiecki (2004, pp. 28–39) discusses the power of cognitive diversity, a conscious effort to bring together individuals with diverse experience and perspectives who are encouraged to consider speculative ideas and function freely enough to choose good solutions over bad. The business of education is a nurturing profession, one that is positive and one in which educators seldom confront one another. The stakes are much too high to confront a colleague about data, especially when the data appear to be lacking in terms of advising teachers about their craft. For this reason alone, we need to structure meetings to elicit those differences we do have and to encourage more diversity in ideas and interpretations before rushing to consensus. A "data" norm related to promoting idea diversity might be to identify and express different viewpoints, then examine and discuss them prior to making any recommendation or decision. Such a process would invite alternative viewpoints and communicate the value to all team members in stretching for differences.

Do your "homework": come prepared to teach. This is a particularly effective norm for data analysis whereby participants are encouraged to know their data so well that they can explain patterns and trends and address antecedents that impact the results. Meetings of busy professionals seldom extend beyond an hour. It is not too much to expect each participant to come prepared, especially when the decisions the team makes could impact a large number of students who are in real need of interventions that work.

Assign roles to elicit candor: make sure no stone (gem) is left unturned. This may be the most effective strategy to elicit candor. By assigning different roles to participants and rotating them from meeting to meeting, members learn to assist the group in various distinctive ways. The following roles are helpful examples in producing candor: skeptic, proponent, analyst, change agent, and endgame champion. The skeptic is responsible for challenging the team to make a persuasive argument (based on the data) that proposed changes will offer better results than the current state; he protects the status quo. The proponent makes the case for changes, describing anticipated benefits and reasons to support the proposed hypothesis. The analyst constantly reminds participants to ask themselves, "Where is the evidence to support that viewpoint?" The change agent facilitates the group to make decisions and take action on the basis of the data. The endgame champion promotes the desired results by insisting on a measurement that accurately reflects the end desired. By rotating the roles in a formal fashion, Data Team meetings have a greater likelihood of being productive and engaging in real candor that leaves no stone unturned.

Allow the numbers to yield hunches: don't leave meetings without one. This operational norm invites participants to take a chance, to link their own experience with the data presented, and to venture out on a limb to suggest what the data may mean. This norm is as important as those discussed to this point, as our profession is reluctant to interpret data and offer hypotheses with peers. If the meeting is important enough to take professional time to examine data, analysis and reflection should offer insights and hunches, if not recommendations.

Refer to a set of data tools to use. This norm establishes a set of data tools, several of which are introduced throughout this book. The companion handbook to *Beyond the Numbers*, *Show Me the Proof!* (White, 2005), provides a detailed set of graphic organizers, analysis methods, and data analysis tools designed specifically for educators. Data Teams should be fluent in the use of such collaborative tools, be willing to develop new tools that promote analysis, and come prepared to every meeting to apply them. Effective Data Teams collaborate often to develop new graphic organizers and data tools.

Publish and disseminate meeting results. Sharing results of meetings with those affected by them ensures quality attentiveness to discussions and adherence to operating norms of all kinds. While maintaining student confidentiality is a priority, expectations regarding adult confidentiality have no room in Data Team or data-driven meetings. Other process norms can facilitate candor, such as guidelines for conflict management and ways to celebrate success or provide feedback.

These guidelines both value and celebrate diversity of ideas, bringing the suggested norms full circle to this overarching concept. When team thinking and candor produce solutions that are valued by others, especially those generated from within one's immediate professional support group, effective collaboration is evident. When team members proactively analyze data for discussion in advance of meetings, and when team processes routinely identify improvements that result in gains in the classroom and in student achievement, effective collaboration is evident. Collaboration will become part of the culture when training is pursued, provided, and encouraged in mental models, team learning, and cognitive coaching and when teams are provided periodic training updates in data analysis tools (see appendices).

The concept of cognitive coaching (Costa & Garmston, 1997) reminds us of the need for metacognition and the ability to suspend judgment while weighing the merits of ideas and proposals. Cognitive coaching has made good use of graphic organizers to guide student and adult thinking, and nonlinguistic representations promoted by Costa and Garmston are supported in the literature as powerful instructional strategies and tools for students and adult learners, as well (Marzano, Pickering, & Pollock, 2001a).

Collaboration Is Integrated into Every Data Decision

Like the other principles of data-driven decision making, collaboration needs to be integrated into every data-driven decision. We have reviewed how assessment or data calendars ensure collaborative analysis, and our discussion of Georgia's experience at Maple High School illustrates how important collaboration is at every step of the improvement cycle. In the case study, considerable excitement was voiced about the positive achievement results in Georgia's classes, but because those working with Georgia did not have a systematic data-gathering and assessment process in place, they missed a number of opportunities to make the data Georgia collected work for her and for her school, or to suggest ways to ensure the process is collaborative. How can data be managed within your school or system to integrate collaboration into every data-driven decision you make? Consider the possibilities shown in Exhibit 4.6 and discussed in the paragraphs that follow.

EXHIBIT **4.6** | **Methods to Integrate Collaboration into Data Systems**

Integrating Collaboration into Data Systems	Additional Ways to Integrate Collaboration
1. Recommendations are reviewed only when submitted with peers.	1.
2. Collaborative schedules provide common planning, teaming.	2.
3. Teacher teams examine student work; leader requests analysis/recommendations for specific students.	3.
4. Assessment calendars establish times for collaboration in analysis, reflection, action planning, and implementation.	4.
5. Early release times are designated for collaboration around student work.	5.
6. Time and effort are reallocated to respond to urgent challenges through collaboration that develops powerful instructional strategies.	6.
7. A data analysis road map is in place.	7.
8. Interim school improvement reports provide interim, midcourse data.	8.
9. Professional development is driven by data regarding student performance and teaching quality.	9.

Team Recommendations for Change

The plan to review recommendations only when accompanied by support from a peer facilitates dialogue and discussion among faculty, providing a crack in the structure that has created teacher isolation and a tendency toward rampant private practice. Support from a peer for a recommendation presumes thoughtful dialogue between them and perhaps among faculty and staff. It communicates volumes about the importance of sharing practices, debating strategies, and employing only the most powerful interventions available to the entire faculty. As noted earlier, education is extremely complex and multifaceted. As teachers, we all need the collective wisdom of our peers, and the skills and talents outstanding teachers possess need to become the skills and talents all teachers can acquire and master. Gaining a recommendation from two staff members is a simple intervention that moves us in that direction.

Collaborative Schedules

Schedules that provide common planning and teaming times have become widespread in recent years, as school leaders recognize the value of collaboration. These investments of time can be made even more valuable by establishing expectations for sharing strategies, analyzing data, and designing and refining classroom assessments. Many teachers will choose to collaborate during these times if it is optional; many more will do so if it is expected and its importance communicated with a compelling rationale.

Assessment Calendars

We have discussed in detail the value of assessment or data calendars. They ensure that time is set aside for collaboration and that accountability structures are created to make sure that, when we take the time to gather and analyze data, we also take the time to respond with actions driven by that data.

Early Release

Early release has become commonplace in recent years to provide sustained professional development opportunities for collaboration. Without explicit expectations and guidelines, however, this valuable resource can be muted by the rampant private practice exercised by Mary Ann at Maple High and by continued wide variation in student achievement.

Time and Effort Reallocation

When time and resources are allocated to data-driven decision making, the administration sends a strong signal that collaboration around the difficult issues of data analysis and decision making has been established. The ability to commit resources is integral to the notion of accountability, to be discussed in Chapter 5.

Interim School Improvement Reports

Interim school improvement reports are not unlike progress reports that offer parents and students interim data. Interim school improvement updates offer teachers the same opportunities to make midcourse corrections. No barriers preclude schools from providing interim updates today, but as of this writing, they are as rare as early release programs were 15 years ago.

Professional Development

More and more school systems recognize the importance of investing in professional development, but many continue to make those investments on the basis of teacher choice alone, rather than a combination of district and school goals, teacher choice, and lessons from student achievement data. The most effective professional development programs examine antecedent data to determine why, what, when, where, and how professional development will be delivered, as recommended by the National Staff Development Council (*NSDC's Standards*, 2001). Collaboration increases the adoption of best practices by increasing the likelihood that teaching practices will be shared at all.

Collaboration and the Common Core State Standards

Much of this chapter has focused on the need to respect and acknowledge the professional judgment of educators who collaboratively examine student work and professional practice. Reliance on professional judgment is a central tenet of the Common Core State Standards, as the approach to text complexity anticipates that educators will contribute ideas and perspective across dimensions of quality; quantity in terms of length, cohesion, and difficulty; and reader and task considerations. While it is an elaborate and explicit framework that specifies high-quality works and high-level concepts, the Common Core anticipates local discussion and collective wisdom in determining its timing, introduction, and application within public schools.

Summary

Collaboration is more than a means to improve professional practice and student achievement where it occurs. Dr. Reeves (2002a, p. 179) described the craft of teaching in these terms:

> Ours is an inherently collaborative profession, and my respect for individual creativity does not reduce my demand for consensus on the essentials. Indeed, my commitment to fairness for students requires that educational opportunities, teacher expectations, and classroom assessment practices are never a matter of luck but a matter of right.

We know that teaching practices are even more powerful than content preparation or professional development (Wenglinsky, 2002), and it has been well established that teacher quality has a direct relationship to a student's achievement for multiple years beyond that interaction (Sanders, 1998). We need to see the opportunity to benefit from great teaching as a gain for all of our students, delivered by all of our teachers, as a result of their collaborative efforts to improve. That effort will require collaboration in earnest.

Collaborative analysis is imperative as a matter of fairness and equity. It is the forum for examining student results and antecedents affecting those results, and collaboration puts in motion changes in expectations, educational opportunities, and assessment practices that emerge best in a collaborative context. It makes it easier for a group to make decisions based on facts and expands the set of possible solutions when a problem is present. Finally, collaboration introduces a new dynamic to data analysis where the interaction between participants reveals solutions and strategies that could not be evident without diverse perspective. Appendix A provides a scoring guide for self-assessment by leaders in collaboration. Chapter 5 examines accountability as the third principle of data-driven decision making.

Reflection

BIG IDEA: Collaboration is the platform that translates data into decisions.

What is meant by the "power of collaboration"? Why should it be considered a principle of data-driven decision making?

What did Georgia; her mentor, Lisa; and her principal, Mr. Ino, fail to do in their analysis of Georgia's classroom and personal data?

How does collaboration enrich analysis of data?

CHAPTER

5

Accountability

Accountability for quality belongs to top management.
It cannot be delegated.

—W. EDWARDS DEMING

Top management in the schools includes teachers, who by their presence, expectations, and clarity of communication let every student of every age know quickly where the line for acceptable quality stands. Accountability and data are often used in the same breath, and because the terms *data* and *accountability* are so inextricably linked in educational circles, a fair question to ask is "Why?" Is it because accountability systems in all 50 states, the District of Columbia, and all U.S. territories use student achievement results data as measures of effectiveness? Is accountability a report card for adults and educational organizations? For the purposes of data analysis, accountability needs to become much more.

Accountability is taking responsibility to act on the basis of what data tell us. The medical analogy is a powerful one, with profound implications for schools. When a child has a temperature of 103 degrees Fahrenheit, few parents will wait until the next morning, let alone the next week, to take action. To even consider waiting until next semester to act on data would be unconscionable, yet schools routinely make such decisions. When the restaurant we frequent is visited by the city health department and cited for unsafe food storage procedures, we would be foolish to continue to dine there in the near future. In schools, however, the rearview-mirror effect is pervasive, as the data shout "Intervene, take action!" but we respond by noting that we tried that before, or we are planning to adopt a new math textbook later this year. Accountability regarding data analysis means, first and foremost, taking action on the basis of what the data tell us and acting quickly on the diagnosis rather than allowing it to fester.

Accountability is also student centered (Reeves, 2004a), meaning that it relies on measures of both student achievement results and antecedents of excellence. Accountability for data analysis in this context means that teachers provide leadership in the analysis process and that such leadership is fundamentally collaborative in its application. We define it this way:

Accountability is authority to commit resources (*to take action*), responsibility to demonstrate improvement (*results*), and permission to adjust time and opportunity (*permission to subtract*) so that all students achieve beyond their expectations and the expectations of adults committed to their achievement (parents, teachers, other educators).

A rule-of-thumb definition of accountability for data analysis is simply:

Authority to act, permission to subtract, and responsibility for results

---

This chapter discusses the authority to take action and the structures needed to ensure that accountability is proactive about improved performance and quality. We begin by describing a composite fictional school system constructed from real observations made over the past 15 years in public education across the United States.

No Blame, No Excuses

CASE STUDY

Colson Independent School District (ISD) was a comprehensive pre-K–12 school system serving 23,415 students as of October 1 of last year. The district had been growing steadily for the past 15 years, in large part as the result of suburban residential growth and the emergence of high-tech, clean industries that multiplied with every innovation in technology. Even the recent economic downturn failed to slow the area's growth, as Colson was developing a reputation as a high-quality school district. Though demographics were changing from an upper middle class and white school system to one more representative of the ethnic and racial makeup of the nation, achievement results continued to outperform the state average at all grades, and more than 85 percent of students pursued a four-year college education upon graduation. Two elementary schools in Colson qualified for Title I free and reduced lunch programs in 1990, and one other school has qualified since that time, an older suburban school of 430 students.

The No Child Left Behind Act (NCLB) mandates and the state accountability system are not popular at Colson ISD. The relatively high performance the district has achieved, with 72 percent of the student body scoring above the 50th percentile on the Iowa Tests of Basic Skills (ITBS) and 67 percent passing the state assessment in reading and language arts last year, no longer garners the praise and awards the school district once did. This year, the local newspaper headlines identified seven schools that failed to show improvement and referenced the learning gap for African American students and the high dropout rate for Hispanic students. Five schools were in danger of being placed on adequate yearly progress (AYP) probation, and board members, the superintendent, and every principal were getting calls from real estate agents and other business leaders demanding an explanation as to why their customers were showing less inclination to live and shop in Colson. The heat was definitely turned up this summer, as constituents and even the district's most supportive parents were watching the actions of school district leaders like never before.

The board initiated improvement efforts by passing a resolution requiring schools to collect and report student achievement data at least four times during the school year. This mandate required schools to develop common assessments within their schools that could be reported; were aligned with state standards; and reflected the rigor and high expectations of the state assessments, which were reported annually by the state and included in each school's report card. The superintendent was also directed to create an accountability system that made administrator compensation contingent on improved test scores at each school, and the system had to accommodate tracking student achievement at least quarterly for the board of education. Educators were on notice that they needed to improve student achievement scores again and again over time.

Principals, particularly those in the seven schools facing AYP sanctions, collectively decided to publish student achievement results more frequently and to hold their teachers accountable by monitoring grades and other classroom assessments routinely. Principals shared strategies to monitor student performance in each teacher's class; conduct daily walk-throughs; perform desktop audits of grades and other assessments; and post student results by teacher, department, and grade on their data walls. Agreement was reached that these strategies were the best ways to make the data work for them and share the accountability with teachers that principals had been experiencing for some time. One self-appointed leader proclaimed, "Teachers need to understand every bit as much as we do what is at stake, and we won't be here in three years unless we start seeing significant gains by sub-group."

Teachers were equally concerned with achievement results but viewed the demands for more data, and more publicly displayed data, as insulting and intrusive. "The real issue is the need for support from parents and from administration to hold these kids accountable," said one teacher in frustration. "If students don't show up, wake up, or shape up, we get blamed." Teachers knew that those students who were in attendance every day and who were motivated just enough to do what was expected of them performed well, regardless of sub-group. "It isn't as simple as test scores, and this new NCLB system that expects 100 percent of students to be proficient is humanly and statistically impossible."

The group of seven principals decided to develop common end-of-year and back-to-school agendas to set the tone with staff and to avoid the fallout from faculties that might follow if one principal were more accommodating in his approach or showed less urgency to get the scores up. The initial presentation would be to show the "brutal facts" of their situation: Scores are way too low, they are even affecting homeowner choices, and the gaps among sub-groups is widening. If these trends continue, we will find ourselves positioned to be "reconstituted" in three years, even if the neighborhood community objects. Each principal would illustrate this reality with the same type of chart, tailored to their individual school, although very little difference existed among the schools. Then, the principals would present evidence of other schools in the state with equivalent free and reduced lunch numbers and comparable second-language and minority populations that had closed the gap and shown improvement for a number of years. At this point, principals would attempt to rally the troops by declaring "X Elementary School is better than that, and if Y Elementary upstate can do it, we can, too." Each principal would then break his school's staff into small groups and invite faculty to identify the school's strengths and strategies that could make a difference with the same resources available as last year. This exercise was to take 30 minutes of the final day, including time to report out ideas. Care was taken to make sure suggestions completed the following stems: X Elementary will close the gap by _____, or X Elementary will increase student achievement school-wide by _____. Principals would then devote the rest of the meeting to securing volunteers for subcommittees, which would come back in August with concrete changes that could make their suggestions a reality. The leaders felt pretty good about their initial salvo and knew in their hearts that their respective staffs would respond with enthusiasm and common purpose.

The result, however, was anything but enthusiastic. Comments from every school returned to the need for time, resources, and reduced class size. Suggestions almost universally called for greater autonomy, more time to work independently, and time to increase the rigor of course content. Principals facilitated the meeting as productively as possible, however, closing with a reminder that next year must show improvement, that data would drive decisions, and that principals would be much more visible than ever before.

In August, five schools brought in motivational speakers from private industry unions or leadership consultants to stress the need to "work smarter, not harder" and to refine their vision with greater emphasis on continuous improvement. The remaining schools gathered input from teams for improving student achievement and closing the gap. They initiated after-school tutoring and committed to using the five professional development days for common training in differentiated instruction, data-driven decision making, and effective teaching strategies. All seven schools ended their opening day with remarks about how data would drive every decision and that everyone involved needed to pull together to make a difference this year.

As principals posted data and conferred with faculty about what the teachers would be doing to increase student achievement for specific sub-groups or the entire student body, most of the effort was devoted to increased parent involvement and providing rapid notification of absences and tardies. Teachers were also expected to develop charts and graphs that tracked student progress on standards. By the end of the first term, teachers were exhausted and behind in their reporting. Principal data walls were interpreted as "America's Most Wanted" rather than indications of growth and areas of celebration. Board members and central office staff who had previously graced the doors of these schools once every decade now visited all the time, and staff were on notice to be "on" at all times. Students wondered what all the charts were for, and periodically staff arrived in the morning to see graffiti had appeared on the charts, even though students created and updated these visuals themselves. By semester's end, fewer students were earning Fs and attendance was up in these targeted schools, from 91 percent to 94.7 percent. Teachers were much more aware of the standards addressed in various chapters and units, and the desktop audits did increase the alignment of lesson plans to standards. The tension was palpable, however, and even though teachers knew their students and their standards like never before, few were comfortable that all of this activity would produce the desired changes.

While principals did initiate some new procedures, the new responsibilities combined with ongoing demands on their time made it difficult for them to visit every classroom daily, and those visits that did take place were walk-throughs in a literal sense. By March, almost no dialogue or interaction was seen with students or teachers in that process. Faculty were resentful of the lack of integrity in these processes, which were hailed as so critical and so important to improvement, and the data itself seemed to take away from instruction more every day. The central office "upped the ante" by requiring two administrator meetings monthly as well as scheduled visits to all 28 schools each year, with a two-visit minimum to the seven targeted schools and quarterly goal meetings for each of the seven target-school principals during a scheduled cabinet meeting. This activity required receiving schools to host eight formal visits annually, which typically took 90 minutes or more. The added meetings found principals away from their buildings an additional 10½ days for administrator meetings and approximately two hours for each quarterly meeting, not to mention the preparation required for them or the follow-up to comply with requests from the superintendent and her cabinet.

Authority to Act

In the above scenario, faculties were given the authority to react, not to make instructional adjustments. Colson ISD's situation is a classic example of bureaucratic creep (Chapter 1), one played out across the nation on far too many occasions. We have seen how easy it is to collect data and how unlikely it is that schools act on the lessons of that data. The emphasis at Colson was on producing data that showed improvement rather than instructing how to show improvement. Even when schools adequately measure the antecedents and the results, if insights recognized and programs implemented fail to change classroom practice, educators can be assured that student achievement will not improve measurably, and most definitely will not improve over time. The authority to take action is central to accountability and ethical considerations. Collecting, disaggregating, analyzing, and reflecting are important elements in the process of data analysis, but failure to take action and make necessary changes based on that analysis is unethical in that it requires students and staff to behave as if action would be taken based on the test data when, in fact, the data may be collected and shelved, or analyzed just for the sake of analysis. As an administrator for 18 years, I would not infrequently hear parents counseled with the following: "We plan to change that [practice or procedure] next year" or "It will take us some time to make that change, but it will be in place for our incoming seventh graders." Does it really take a year to ensure that instruction is purposeful and aligned to standards? Is it too much to ask that grades have a relationship with proficiency, or that work completed by students be returned with feedback that is corrective and instructive? One can only wonder how many administrators and teachers face parents who ask for changes that are entirely reasonable yet find a way to avoid making changes because they do not fit into the current systems.

In Chapter 4, we discussed the notion that wide variances in teaching ability and skill are an example of unequal educational opportunity. As the craft of teaching and learning becomes more defined, and the connections and correlations become more established between improved achievement and its antecedents, acceptance of such inequality as chance or "luck" in terms of teacher assignment may even be actionable in a court of law. A recent, and serious, proposal was made to revamp how educators measure teacher effectiveness. By issuing each teacher a unique identification number and gathering the right data, states can assess the link between teacher performance and student outcomes over the course of many years (Raymond, 2003). The idea extends Sanders' (1998) seminal work in Tennessee on "value-added" instruction, and it may be the future for educators everywhere. Exhibit 5.1 describes opportunities for leaders of teachers and teachers of students to gain the authority to act, and act now.

In practice, Exhibit 5.1 demonstrates a scenario in which teachers and principals are given authority to change the time allotted for students to reach proficiency, adding time for those who need additional instruction or practice and redirecting time for those who quickly demonstrate proficiency on a particular standard. For primary students learning to read, this authority might mean giving those who have demonstrated the mechanics of reading the opportunity to read text with a higher grade level or to apply their skill acquiring content understanding in material that challenges them. For teachers in search of quality results indicators, it means the authority to collaborate in creating, implementing, and evaluating assessments. It means teachers and principals have sufficient resource capacity to make commitments for tutoring services or self-assessment software to respond to individual student needs. It means they have sufficient trust and safety to speak freely, provide peers and supervisors with quality corrective feedback, and create a classroom climate in which students are safe to speak freely, with candor, as well. Accountability also means teachers have the capacity to develop and test their "hunches" (hypotheses) about teaching and learning. All of these capacities hinge not so much on greater resources as on a sufficiently agile work environment that relies on the expertise of teachers to respond to the needs of students as revealed by data.

EXHIBIT **5.1** | **Ten Actions of Accountability**

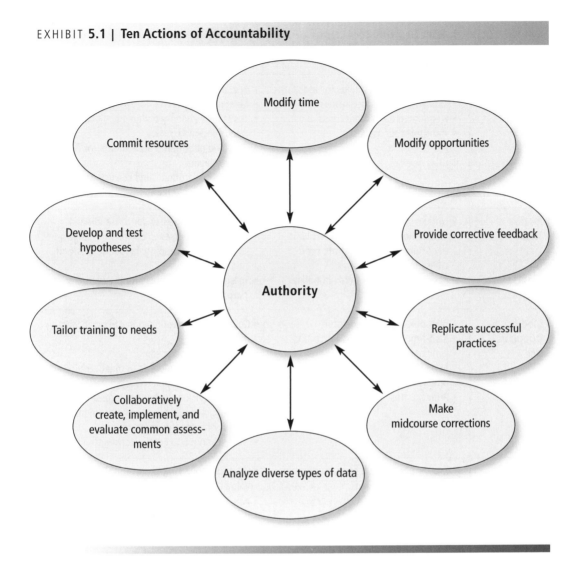

Why haven't educators been provided this authority to become accountable? The answer, in part, is that educators do not maintain sufficiently informative data to warrant granting of authority to others or even to justify their recommendations. Without data, one's desire to test a hypothesis will appear frivolous, even if the hypothesis has the capacity to dramatically improve public education across the school, district, or nation. It is entirely reasonable to expect those who have the authority to commit resources to be reluctant to delegate that authority, unless data support a strong basis for recommendations. When data are available to support recommendations, most leaders are much more likely to delegate authority to act, and when a framework exists to test hypotheses and when measures are available to provide baseline data, the opportunity for action research and innovations is also increased. Exhibit 5.2 identifies common barriers to accountability and provides possible remedies that ensure educators have the authority needed for true accountability.

EXHIBIT **5.2** | **Barriers to the 10 Actions of Accountability**

	Barriers	Remedies
Commit Resources	• One-size work schedules for assistants • Limited school or department budgets • Negotiated agreement limits • Transportation issues	• Allocate assistant time based on data trends for service needs • Insist discretionary dollars be allocated to needs verified by data • Examine negotiated agreements for flexibility or waivers • Reschedule student time consistent with transportation obligations
Modify Time	• Uniform class periods • Graduation requirements that limit opportunity to demonstrate proficiency in core standards • Required time allotments in policy	• Construct dual classes for those in need • Count dual courses in core competencies (math, English/reading, language arts/writing, science) • Integrate content areas for instructional purposes
Modify Opportunities	• Textbook-driven instruction • Seat-time requirements for credits • Limited course offerings or great variation in courses for same graduation requirement • Prerequisites	• Collaborative identification of Power Standards • Standards-based grading • Proficiency on standards to meet requirements for graduation • Opt-in provision for honors, international baccalaureate, or advanced placement programs with greater levels of rigor • Policy changes to open electives to all
Provide Corrective Feedback	• Fear or observation of retribution for speaking one's mind • Culture of collegiality over collaboration • Expectation of exemplary performance in all evaluations • Candor viewed as threatening, an invitation of grievances	• Establish operating norms for all teams that value candor, collaboration, diversity of ideas, corrective feedback • Require data to support positions, recommendations • Institute role-play format for team thinking • Dialogue with association to set guidelines
Replicate Successful Practices	• Watered-down replication • Path of least resistance • Underestimation of training required • Competing priorities that need to be subtracted • Push-back from unspoken and unwritten cultural expectations	• Replicate only when data warrant, provide in-depth training and modeling, and monitor quality indicators • Consider context of replication in terms of work habits and processes, and identify what will be subtracted before adding a new innovation • Establish clear norms for replication/ innovation

EXHIBIT **5.2** | **Barriers to the 10 Actions of Accountability** (continued)

	Barriers	Remedies
Make Midcourse Corrections	• Unrealistic curriculum coverage expectations • Single means to proficiency, such as written final exam • Non-standards-based grade expectations • Traditions	• Align curriculum/instruction to standards • Identify Power Standards that prioritize content • Develop scoring guides with multiple paths to proficiency • Align grades to standards • Gather data to verify traditional practices
Analyze Diverse Types of Data	• Existing data limited to student achievement • Teacher isolation and limited discussion of teaching strategies • Ignorance of power of classroom practices • Annual examination of data or prevalent rearview-mirror effect	• Provide staff development in data analysis with privileged choices to those who justify requests with diverse data • Have Data Teams examine and respond to actual student work • Discuss local strategies with the expectation that staff will become fluent in effective teaching strategies • Create structures to examine data routinely, at least two per month
Collaboratively Create, Implement, and Evaluate Common Assessments	• Assessments limited to district requirements • Lack of common planning time • Professional development days committed to outside seminars unrelated to local needs driven by data • Reluctance to accept collective wisdom of peers for individual classroom application	• Create collaboration, common planning, early release • Introduce collaboration at every faculty meeting • Align professional development to National Council of Staff Development standards, student achievement gaps, and faculty needs to improve achievement • Build data system for teaching, curriculum, leadership, variety of student result measures • Train in group processes
Tailor Training to Needs	• Optional training unrelated to vision, goals, student needs • Training unrelated to evaluation process • Data rarely disaggregated by antecedent strategies, structures, or teacher behaviors	• Establish collaborative professional development • Have teachers teach teachers • Review context/integration: curriculum, standards, leadership • Attend to individual needs • Sustain training, monitored internally
Develop and Test Hypotheses	• Lack of incentives to innovate • Reliance on path of least resistance • No format for action research • Opinions and "private information" not valued	• Promote pursuit of "hunches" through data systems • Provide access to simplified action research • Structure reflection time • Recognize and value risk taking and "private information" in written norms or policies

Permission to Subtract

In Chapter 1, the concept of permission to subtract was introduced as a key to effective data analysis. It is integral to accountability because the authority to stop doing something, to stop doing anything, in public education is elusive for many. Lists of innovations introduced in public education that are never officially discontinued have become commodities in schools. Programs fall into benign neglect, with remnants of the program evident sometimes years after its demise. Why? The majority of innovations that reach prominence in public education are based on sound pedagogy, are validated in research settings, and offer powerful new strategies to improve student achievement. Hence, even when implementation is hasty, partial, or watered down, educational innovations add value. In fact, those who are most adept at implementing such reforms and innovations are more apt to realize the value of those reforms and more reluctant to drop them altogether than are those who resisted such innovations or were indifferent to them. Without explicit structures that empower people to make needed changes, including subtraction of obsolete practices, many educators continue to adhere to past expectations.

We assume that people know when they have permission to make changes, but can you identify any teachers you know who have authority (permission) to make the following decisions?
- Permission to vary the time given to curriculum content
- Permission to modify or accelerate curriculum based on individual student needs, including permission for students to test out of various units or sections
- Permission to replace grades with scoring guides describing proficiency
- Permission to provide to students multiple opportunities to demonstrate proficiency as opposed to one attempt on key tests and assessments
- Permission to integrate assessments across curriculum areas
- Permission to team up to teach rather than deliver instruction independent of one's peers

And this assumption of authority is as true for administrators as it is for teachers. Do administrators in schools with which you are familiar have authority (permission) to make the following decisions?
- Permission to reassign staff midyear
- Permission to hire staff from those who meet all district criteria
- Permission to change teacher assignments based on student achievement data
- Permission to require side-by-side analyses of standards, assessments, curriculum, and lesson plans
- Permission to direct resources to create additional time and opportunity
- Permission to replace textbooks with laptop computers or to use textbooks as supplemental material, relying primarily on standards-based performance assessments

These examples illustrate that often educators have limited authority or permission to subtract ineffective practices. This is especially true if the innovation was widely adopted throughout the school or district. If a significant investment was made in the program, the program will not likely be dismissed as being of little value. To do so would be to dismiss those who bought into the program as having made a grave error in judgment, a reputation educators avoid at great cost. Exhibit 5.3 delineates questions to help determine whether and when to subtract obsolete or ineffective practices.

EXHIBIT **5.3** | **Subtracting Obsolete or Ineffective Practices**

Subtraction

	Yes	No
1. Does the practice/resource yield data about teaching or learning?	Yes	No
2. Does the practice/resource address specific content standards?	Yes	No
3. Does the practice/resource provide diagnostic data about student achievement?	Yes	No
4. Does the practice invite collaboration with colleagues?	Yes	No
5. Are data available to support the need for or value of the practice/resource to achievement in my classroom?	Yes	No
6. Is a corresponding or competing practice/resource available that accomplishes the same end/result?	Yes	No

Yes to three or fewer questions: the practice or resource should be subtracted in some measure.

Yes to four or more questions: the practice or resource should be retained or possibly replicated.

Replacement

	Yes	No
7. Can the same practice/resource be accomplished through other means such as improved technology?	Yes	No
8. Can the practice/resource be omitted and still achieve the same result?	Yes	No
9. Can the same result be accomplished in less instructional time?	Yes	No
10. Can the same result be accomplished in less preparation time?	Yes	No
11. Can the same result be accomplished with less expense, talent, and resources?	Yes	No

Yes to three or fewer questions: the practice or resource should be replaced at some time.

Yes to four or more questions: the practice or resource should be replaced as soon as possible.

A profession committed to encouraging, developing, and nurturing finds it much easier to choose the path of least resistance than to "confront the brutal facts" about past decisions. Yet, Jim Collins (2001, p. 69), in his best seller *Good to Great*, describes the ability of people in an organization to "confront the brutal facts" as a major characteristic of greatness. Collins views this inherent humility as the ingredient that allows people within any organization to learn from the successes of others and from their own mistakes. Unfortunately, schools, as collegial institutions, are often more concerned about avoiding offense than becoming collaborative and committed to improving student achievement. In Chapter 4, we defined collaboration in terms of improving student achievement and offered suggestions to increase our capacity to express diverse opinions and ideas without giving or taking offense. Subtraction requires an ability to confront the brutal facts and the humility to learn as much from our poor decisions as from our successful ones.

In the midst of Colson ISD's effort to embrace the appearance and trappings of data-driven decision making, were any activities subtracted? The superintendent, school board, principals, and teachers all fell victim to bureaucratic creep, adding activities, meetings, and methods to gather data that increased demands on their workload. Principals were unable to meet their obligation to visit classrooms, and the district spent inordinate amounts of time collecting data but very little time adjusting instruction to improve student achievement. The result, in a high-stakes and tension-filled atmosphere, was a demoralized and exhausted workforce. Rather than creating a culture of learning without blame or excuses, Colson ISD, without any formal communication or intent, created a culture of no excuses but lots of blame.

For accountability in data analysis to work, permission to subtract practices and redirect resources, time, and energy must be given to schools and classroom teachers. Without this authority, data will not drive real-time responses to needs in the classrooms but instead will be relegated to annual modifications of plans that have little impact on what happens every day in the classrooms. Knowing what to subtract requires an ability to examine data to determine what works and what does not. It requires identifying and monitoring daily routines and behaviors, the work habits of change.

Work Habits and Change

Colson ISD's teachers, principals, central administrators, and school board meant well. All applied themselves diligently to the changes with the intent to improve student achievement, and their behavior and strategies represent responses to accountability that are observed in districts and schools across the country. Yet, their approach was doomed to failure from the outset. Rather than focus on antecedents of excellence, the district pursued greater parent involvement, more data collection, increased "accountability" in terms of responsibility for results, and lots and lots of monitoring. Little, if any, attention was given to effective teaching strategies or to research about collaboration, and no effort was made to understand how things get done at Colson, or more accurately, how things fail to get done. The seven schools on probation for AYP would have to be characterized on the Leadership and Learning Matrix, introduced in Chapter 3, as "losing" because there was no apparent understanding of what factors produced low student achievement or the school's inability to close the gap for identified sub-groups. Faculty looked to deficits in students and their parents, factors that have some influence on student achievement, while neglecting factors that have much greater influence. A powerful study by Howard Wenglinsky (2002) found that professional development, teacher qualifications and content preparation, and classroom practices all have dramatic effects on student achievement. In fact, he found that classroom practices had a greater impact than did professional development or teacher quality, and classroom practices (teaching practices) carried a greater effect size than did any demographic variables such as race, income, or educational level of parents. The primary influence on student achievement is classroom practices or work habits that describe how things get done.

The process for accomplishing tasks, procedures, and daily routines are all work habits. One teacher's "bell to bell" process to optimize on-task time, another teacher's transition from language arts to science, or a kindergarten teacher's process to open every school day by checking for understanding is a work habit. Work habits define the conditions, structures, and strategies employed to effect learning. Because work habits are routine components of each job description, they are easily monitored quantitatively as counts or percentages, or monitored qualitatively as measures of completion, implementation, or adoption of a specific process. Exhibit 5.4 provides examples from various job descriptions.

EXHIBIT **5.4 | Sample Work Habits**

Teacher	Principal	Specialist	Central Administrator
• **Develops** lesson plans • **Designs** unit assessment • **Establishes** learning groups • **Collaborates** around student work • **Analyzes** data	• **Creates** master schedule • **Monitors** curriculum alignment • **Observes** teaching strategies • **Develops** feedback systems for students, parents, teachers	• **Aligns** curriculum with standards • **Monitors** textbook adoptions • **Designs** professional development based on student achievement results	• **Communicates** vision • **Establishes** accountability system • **Sets** direction with goals and vision • **Implements** policies • **Reports** assessment results • **Establishes, implements, evaluates** budgets

The most effective way to measure a work habit is to determine its primary function and measure that function's essential parts. Developing lesson plans is not nearly as important as making sure the capacity of lesson plans addresses content standards, engages students, facilitates higher-order thinking, and provides evidence of learning. Measuring the number of lesson plans developed has little value, but monitoring the degree to which they engaged students cognitively with quality work products has great value. Teacher teams can observe and monitor implementation, share and model strategies and applications, and modify lesson plans to reflect best practice. More importantly, they can measure that quality both qualitatively and quantitatively.

The value of work habits is equally applicable for the central office administrator who identifies the steps taken to communicate the goals and vision of the entire district. Work habits are key antecedents, and our understanding of what we do every day allows us to change, sometimes incrementally, the actions we take to improve student achievement. Exhibit 5.5 depicts a student-developed work habit that became the standard for every project at a large and comprehensive technical school in San Fernando, California.

EXHIBIT **5.5 | Project Management for Students**

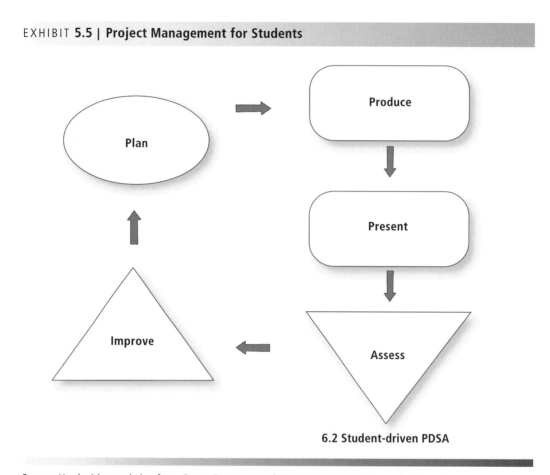

6.2 Student-driven PDSA

Source: Used with permission from Geena Espenoza and Marcos Torres, San Fernando Education Technology Team, San Fernando High School, Los Angeles Unified School District (personal communication, August 14, 2004).

Students employed this simple but powerful process at San Fernando High School in Los Angeles Unified School District, one of the largest urban high schools in the nation and one with a large English language learner student body. The process was first employed within the San Fernando Education Technology Team and was eventually extended to all students. The work habit required a public presentation, which featured skills that every student would benefit from. The process assumed an embedded and authentic assessment would be provided, and every student would be able to identify how each project could be improved. As a result of this single work habit innovation, standards and expectations were clarified, and the connection to employment opportunities and real life was a motivating factor for students within the 500-student Technology Team. Following implementation of this process, graduation rates and placements from career and technical programs into employment have more than doubled. By including the essentials of key work habits as part of the data system, we can determine the interaction and effect of that work habit on student achievement.

The Common Core State Standards and Accountability

The Common Core is all about accountability, as it defines, in many ways for the first time, a set of standards that have been almost universally accepted by the 48 states that have, at the time of this writing, adopted this elaborate and explicit set of learning expectations. In English language arts, detailed standards for college and career readiness, literature, informational text, foundation skills, writing, speaking and listening, and progressive language skills are expertly aligned within and between grades and are articulated from K–1 through grade 12. We have framed accountability in this chapter to mean transparency before the public, responsibility for results, alignment of effort, and follow-through to completion, expectations that the Common Core will facilitate at every level. By publicizing discrete and explicit standards across content areas and articulating the percentage of literature, informational passages, and communicative standards by purpose (to persuade, explain, and convey experience), the Common Core has set a high bar that is nonetheless achievable by educators willing to be held accountable to its standards.

Summary

The authority to act, permission to subtract, and responsibility for results are presented as the underlying elements of accountability, especially in regard to accountability in data analysis. Accountability is not merely collecting and reporting student achievement results; it is taking action based on those results and understanding those factors that affect the results. This view of accountability means that every professional educator needs to have sufficient authority to commit resources to intervene on behalf of students, whether they are students who need to be challenged to achieve exemplary status on assessments or students who need to close the learning gap between themselves and their peers. We also examine the notion of being able to subtract, discontinue, or de-emphasize certain practices that are no longer productive or have proven ineffective. This level of authority is equally essential to achieving real accountability. We examine work habits as those routine daily procedures and protocols that impact instruction and discuss ways to begin to gather data without overwhelming oneself in that data. In all of these applications, we again stressed the need for collaboration and the need to maintain data on those antecedents that are perceived to have the greatest impact. Educators can take responsibility for student achievement results when they have sufficient data on both antecedents and results if they collectively apply the wisdom discovered through analysis and take decisive action.

Reflection

BIG IDEA: Accountability determines our ability to deliver quality to those we serve.

Why is the authority to act so important to accountability, to taking responsibility for results? Describe areas in your work situation where that authority needs to be given or clarified.

Do you or your colleagues have sufficient authority (permission) to subtract obsolete practices? Can you identify one such practice that needs to be discontinued or de-emphasized?

Have the most important work habits in your position been reduced to a flowchart or sequence of steps? Identify one that should be reduced to writing.

What did Colson ISD fail to do in its attempt to improve student achievement and close the gap for students?

Canaries in the Coal Mine:
Get There before the Results Do

Canaries have been used for centuries to serve as early warning signals of gas leaks in underground mines. If the canaries stopped singing, miners knew it was time to get out. What "canaries" do schools and teachers need to make adjustments quickly and respond with agility based on student needs? Data Teams provide a framework by which to probe and monitor student performance in ways that facilitate a rapid and focused response. Performance assessments that rely on scoring guides as blueprints to achieve proficiency inform teachers, students, and even parents of a student's progress along the way. Performance assessments that are designed to include interim "performance tasks," as presented through Leadership and Learning Center seminars, provide even more certain canaries that allow educators to respond to student needs. Incorporating routine, corrective, and instructive feedback as a work habit assists teachers to make adjustments almost immediately, and liberal use of self-assessment offers yet another approach for the professional educator to make midcourse corrections. Let us examine several canaries applicable to schools today.

The idea of interim assessments is nothing new. Grading systems over the past 15 years have increasingly relied on progress reports distributed every three weeks to parents and students. Unit tests long ago took away the sting of historical reliance on end-of-course "final" exams for the bulk of one's grades. The difference in the current era of standards is the expectation that all students, or at least the vast majority, would demonstrate proficiency on rigorous standards that add to content knowledge the ability to apply that knowledge through discrete skills in various applications. Technology has enhanced our ability to communicate data to all stakeholders, and it is becoming common for schools to have a student data management system in place whereby parents and teachers can communicate 24/7 about individual student grades, assignments, discipline referrals, and attendance. A society that expects everything to be available instantly, or at least quickly, also expects its schools to make modifications quickly and routinely.

Recent efforts to identify predictors of future success have focused on student achievement measures. Montgomery County (Maryland) Public Schools' *Seven Keys to College Readiness* is an example, where measures of eighth-grade algebra and above-grade-level reading for kindergartners help predict success in later grades (Montgomery County Schools, 2010). Denver Public Schools (2010) recently began a similar process to identify student milestones that predict future success, such as above-grade-level reading for kindergartners, first graders, and second graders as predictors of success on state assessments in third and eighth grade, and enrollment in geometry rather than algebra in ninth grade. Allensworth and Easton (2007) found that fall semester attendance for ninth graders was one of the strongest predictors of on-track graduation in Chicago. All of these findings are instructive to educators: the early academic performance leads schools to raise expectations for reading achievement in kindergarten and adjust curriculum accordingly as well as target professional development, while the secondary predictors of postsecondary readiness lead schools to adjust course sequences, revise placement practices, and recruit a more diverse teaching workforce. These types of reforms are occurring more frequently as schools seek answers from a much broader understanding of the antecedents that influence student achievement. The trend, however, is first to keep the focus on early student achievement outcomes as predictors of later achievement outcomes and then to revise and modify antecedent strategies, structures, and conditions. This chapter offers a series of early warning or early success indicators by beginning with antecedent structures, conditions, strategies, and teacher behaviors to proactively determine what is working and what is not. The antecedents discussed in the following paragraphs are examples of professional practice that represent today's equivalent of the canary in the coal mine —early warning or early success indicators each school and classroom should require.

Data Teams

Most improvement efforts in education assume that changes in student performance take time, and lots of it, to effect and sustain accompanying changes in practice. Data Teams use collaborative, structured, and scheduled team meetings that focus on teaching and learning (Leadership and Learning Center, 2010). They bring together the components of a professional learning community (Hord, 1997) to answer practical questions such as, "Which students are reading and comprehending at grade-level proficiency?" or "Which students will need additional assistance to perform the skills in the next unit of study?" Data Teams can be entire faculties but are more apt to be small grade-level or department teams that can examine individual student work, analyze antecedent data, and drill data down to the classroom level. Teachers participating in Data Teams bring specific student data to each meeting. They serve as a powerful tool, as a persistent problem for one student is frequently similar to that experienced by several other students, and by assisting a colleague to address the problem identified, teachers help themselves address the needs of other students. The Data Teams structure adheres to a continuous improvement cycle similar to those reviewed in Exhibit 2.2; examines patterns and trends; and sets forth specific timelines, roles, and responsibilities to facilitate analysis that results in action.

An essential component of any comprehensive accountability plan, effective Data Teams serve as a practical canary in the coal mine because of the frequency of meetings, use of mini-lessons, and focus on actual students with names and faces. Data Teams allow teachers to take collective responsibility for student achievement results; communicate simple, clear, and useful meeting guidelines; and offer a proven method for improvement. The Leadership and Learning Center seminar on Data Teams (2010) provides an excellent three-part format for Data Team meetings, distinguishing the purpose for meetings prior to making instructional modifications, during the instructional intervention, and following intervention to review the success of any changes made. The first meeting examines student work and assessments to plan mini-lessons and changes that will be implemented immediately. An important product of this process is the examination of student work and assessments and evidence of teaching. Teams identify exactly what teaching strategies have been employed to equip students whose work is being reviewed to demonstrate proficiency on standards. The Data Team also examines obstacles, challenges, and misconceptions about curriculum, instruction, and student behavior. The second meeting in the midst of mini-lessons and planned interventions occurs to determine how well the process is unfolding and to examine unforeseen changes that have occurred. A third determines whether the team was successful in achieving its goal, the next essential standard for a new group of students, or what needs to be done differently if the goal has not been reached. This cycle typically occurs in bimonthly meetings, meaning that the goals and interventions are scheduled to occur within four to five weeks. The process will work with monthly meetings as well, and in both cases, action that produces changes and facilitates improved student achievement occurs much quicker than the average referral process for services for students at risk, let alone interventions to help them in the classroom. Exhibit 6.1 combines the well-known strengths, weaknesses, opportunities, and threats (SWOT) analysis framework with the Data Team emphasis on student performance and evidence of teaching as an example of data needed for first the Data Team meeting.

Examination of both student performance and evidence of teaching enriches the data available to teachers by measuring student behaviors, teacher routines, and strategies that address specific needs of students. Mini-lessons from Data Team decisions are excellent examples of embedded interventions and the use of data to drive classroom decisions.

Scoring Guides

Scoring guides also provide early warning to students, teachers, and parents by informing all involved of what is expected to demonstrate proficiency. They describe not only the desired outcome but also the pathway to that outcome through the level descriptions: not meeting standards, progressing, proficient, and advanced. Student-generated scoring guides add another dimension by asking students to describe the levels of proficiency in their own terms. When students have the ability to self-assess progress, they not only understand knowledge and skill requirements but also measure performance as they demonstrate it, making adjustments as they pursue proficiency.

EXHIBIT **6.1** | **SWOT Analysis for Data Teams**

	Strengths	Weaknesses	Opportunities	Threats
Student Performance	Students grasp concept of biosphere per quizzes 85%+; classification, vocabulary demonstrated	Unit test failure 62% average; problem solving, inventing, and determining cause-effect relationships regarding biosphere; weak performance on extended response assessments; yet to demonstrate writing with problem-solving strategies	Projects that call for higher-level operations regarding Bloom's taxonomy; explicit problem-solving strategies; more writing opportunities; unit lends itself to activities, wide range of projects	Time is limited before state assessment (90 days); sense of efficacy weak; history of poor academic performance; struggle with activity transitions; easily distracted by noise, social opportunity
Evidence of Teaching	Ticket-out-the-door writing activity (daily); characteristics, types of living organisms, and interaction in biospheres introduced with vocabulary	Essential questions and planned transitions not observed; questioning is primarily single response, yes-no, true-false	Introduce unit and essential questions; establish cooperative learning groups; Cornell Notes to summarize daily lessons; open-ended questions	Number of students at risk in classrooms; difficulty finding time to collaborate with and observe colleagues; training in Bloom's not scheduled until fall

Performance Assessments

Quality performance assessments address big ideas, essential questions, Power Standards, the "unwrapping" or analysis of those standards, engaging scenarios, scoring guides, and well-designed culminating assessments that include multiple interim performance indicators or performance tasks. In this way, performance assessments use at least two major canaries: scoring guides that inform instruction and learning, and interim performance tasks that indicate a progressive acquisition of proficiency through increasingly rigorous and challenging performance tasks. Exhibit 6.2 illustrates this concept.

Corrective Feedback

Early warning, or early "affirming," indicators of performance need not be limited to formal structures such as those suggested so far. Individual teachers who are proficient at providing feedback to students that is accurate, timely, and corrective are able to describe individual students' level of proficiency at any given time. Students are also aware of their level of proficiency because they are given useful feedback from their instructor before they apply faulty reasoning to their tasks. In short, corrective, timely, and accurate feedback is the essence of early warning systems. Corrective feedback has been viewed for years as critical in terms of acquiring a second language (Lyster, 1998; Mackey, Gass, & McDonough, 2000). It also has been identified as "the most powerful single modification that enhances achievement" (Marzano, Pickering, & Pollock, 2001b, p. 96). Corrective feedback, by definition, serves as a canary in a coal mine.

EXHIBIT **6.2 | High School Literature Performance Task Scoring Guide**

Exemplary	Proficient	Progressing	Not Yet Meeting
All proficiency criteria met PLUS: • Classifications include methods not discussed in class lecture • T-bars show unique thought when generating pros/cons • Graphic organizer branches and leaves reflect depth and breadth of knowledge of literature and cultural history of the 1990s • Other:	• Journal entry style of writing is used • Writing reflects standard English conventions including spelling, grammar, punctuation, and mechanics • At least 10 methods of classification • T-bars are included for four classification methods • T-bars accurately reflect pros/cons for classification • Chosen method for project is reasoned and appropriate • Graphic organizer is included for the chosen classification method • Chosen graphic organizer is appropriate to the classification • Graphic organizer includes at least 5 branches and 3 leaves for each branch	• Standard English conventions are applied inconsistently • Fewer than 10 but more than 6 methods of classification are included • T-bars are included for 2 or 3 methods • T-bar pros and cons are not accurately classified • Chosen method for project is limited or inappropriate • Graphic organizer is not appropriate to classification method • Graphic organizer includes fewer than 5 branches and 3 leaves for each branch	• Fewer than 6 methods of classification included • Only 1 T-bar included • Graphic organizer not included • Other:

Source: Used with permission from Laurie Graack, Righetti High School, Santa Maria (CA) Joint Union High School District.

Data in a Day

"Data in a day" is a collaborative approach to data analysis developed by Education Northwest, where teams of educators and students select a data focus area, collect and analyze the data, and present findings with recommendations within 24 hours (Hinkle, Hinkle, & Monetti, 2009). This approach uses available data to identify a problem, craft a solution, and put in motion actions that change the learning dynamic to make a difference in a short period of time. Data in a day could be used as an extension of the critical incident data analysis tool introduced in Exhibit 4.1; Exhibit 6.3 illustrates the application of observation, analysis, and implementing to make improvements.

The success of data in a day hinges on a clear understanding of the three principles of data-driven decision making reviewed in the last three chapters: antecedents, collaboration, and accountability. It requires a team of educators to understand the different types of antecedents and have the authority to act on the lessons of the data available to them. As discussed in Chapter 5, this authority to act also includes the permission to subtract practices and redirect resources when the data indicate a need for a change. Lastly, data in a day requires teams to understand their responsibility in the learning process and their capacity to improve achievement results for all their students. The public nature of the process invites students and the public as partners in making improvements and helps build a culture that embraces accountability in action, whereby a team is empowered by data, authorized to commit resources, and implements changes, and the team shares responsibility to effect results and improve student achievement. The process is similar to instructional rounds for administrators (City, et al., 2009).

EXHIBIT **6.3 | Data in a Day**

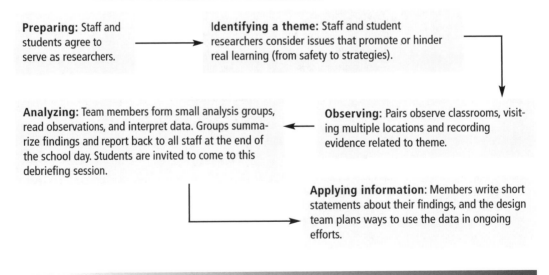

Preparing: Staff and students agree to serve as researchers.

Identifying a theme: Staff and student researchers consider issues that promote or hinder real learning (from safety to strategies).

Analyzing: Team members form small analysis groups, read observations, and interpret data. Groups summarize findings and report back to all staff at the end of the school day. Students are invited to come to this debriefing session.

Observing: Pairs observe classrooms, visiting multiple locations and recording evidence related to theme.

Applying information: Members write short statements about their findings, and the design team plans ways to use the data in ongoing efforts.

The Common Core and Canaries in the Schoolhouse

The Common Core State Standards do not provide early warning indicators explicitly, but the breadth of the standards, recommended readings, and clearly delineated and leveled materials provide educators with a wealth of content to identify the "gateway" skills that predict improved student achievement. The fact that the Common Core explicitly describes college and career readiness "anchor standards" for writing, reading, speaking and listening, and mathematics and then provides exemplars across content areas and grades speaks volumes about the intent of the Common Core to inform educators when students meet the rigorous standards needed to launch them to the next level, beginning in kindergarten. In one sense, readers could accurately view the Common Core as a set of "canary" standards that predict future success and, when proficiency is not on track by grade level, to view that occurrence as its own set of early warning indicators.

Summary

The concept of "canaries in a coal mine" as applied to education includes five strategies for developing early warning indicators that contribute to a data-driven culture where evidence is valued and where professional educators recognize their importance and capacity to make a difference quickly. The strategies of Data Teams; the use of scoring guides, powerful performance assessments, and embedded and corrective feedback; and the rapid-response nature of data in a day bring to mind analogies of medical teams of experts in hospital intensive care units: relentless about the data, securing solutions, establishing candor, and advocating for the patient, intensive care teams are just the type of structure we need in order to use the data available to us in schools today. The medical model offers numerous analogies and applications, none of which has to do with the craft of how we teach or even how students learn. Educators are the experts at education, not legislators, not skilled physicians, and not even concerned parents. The public may know what it expects and be able to establish a threshold for what it requires of us, but only educators can determine the solutions to challenges faced by students. If we allow the medical model to instruct us on how to use data effectively, infusing the power of collaboration and sense of urgency, we will not only be accountable but also achieve extraordinary results.

Reflection

BIG IDEA: Data is only as valuable as our ability to respond to the needs it reveals.

Discuss the benefits of using Data Teams and why they qualify as canaries in the coal mine.

BIG IDEA: Early warning indicators are the only means by which to respond in a timely fashion to educational needs of children.

What is meant by "canaries in the coal mine"? Reflect on those canaries in place at your workplace, and identify one area in which your work team needs its own canary.

How does corrective feedback in the classroom serve as an early warning system? What does feedback help prevent?

What would need to be in place in your setting to implement the data in a day method? Discuss with a colleague whether it is worth the investment of time and effort.

Triangulation

> We can't solve problems by using the same kind of think-
> ing we used when we created them.
>
> —ALBERT EINSTEIN (1879–1955)

This chapter introduces the reader to triangulation. In this context, triangulation is an approach that ensures the principles of collaboration, antecedent identification and monitoring, and accountability are addressed in data analysis. It draws extensively on various data analysis tools but ultimately relies on the judgment of professionals to make their best decision given limited data. Triangulation is critical to using data to make visible the invisible, and it is necessary for educators to benefit fully from the methods and tools of data analysis discussed in the following chapters.

The Mariner and Surveyor

Triangulation is well known to architects, engineers, and surveyors as a simple tool, used widely for centuries. For the architect, to triangulate means to discern with precision key load factors and points in space and time from other reliable and predictable data; for the engineer and surveyor, to triangulate means to calibrate unknown points with precision in space and time on the basis of existing data and irregularly distributed samples of data. For both professions, triangulation uses a variety of forms of existing data to calibrate the desired and unknown reference point, and the more the better. When the surveyor needs to estimate the height of a point on the land surface, he uses soil composition, density variation, contours, weather patterns, and a host of other data forms. A form of triangulation was also used by mariners; the sextant allowed explorers to plot the globe by triangulating the stars with each other and the horizon to ascertain longitude and latitude at sea.

Thus, triangulation is a means of determining precise targets with limited information. Do educators need tools to read the horizon, determine their location, and chart their path from limited information? Certainly. In broad terms, triangulation is a method of extrapolating meaning from raw data—a way to find the critical information, see the big picture, and identify key components (angles). In education, triangulation describes efforts to determine needs or targets from diverse types of data. Such efforts may include data gathering from focus groups, surveys, site visits, and one-to-one interviews as experienced by the Commonwealth of Virginia (2003) and Miami Public Schools (Grissom & Loeb, 2009). In both of these cases, data from three different ways to assess perceptions were examined (triangulated) to discover similarities that advocated for reform.

In Chapter 2, our fictional Timberline Middle School appeared to experience incremental gains in achievement until we examined that achievement in the light of professional development and found that student achievement varied dramatically as a function of the professional development provided. In that instance, the antecedent was the provision of a resource: professional development in math and writing. Determining the antecedent was the first step in triangulating data around student achievement, and the result reinforces the need to examine the myriad contributing factors (antecedents) that impact student achievement. What antecedents should we examine? Which antecedents allow us to triangulate successfully to identify what is working in our classrooms and what is not? Given dozens of possible sources of learning data available, how does one select the most meaningful and informative data to triangulate? A common framework to minimize risks in arenas outside of education is offered here, one that every teacher, every teacher team, and every administrator can logically apply to the growing range of data available to them. This framework is based on due diligence, the process of scrutinizing important information before key decisions of long-term consequence are made. Educators take care to conduct due diligence when building a new school, adopting a new information system, or selecting a new curriculum product. We need to do the same in data analysis.

Due Diligence and Data Analysis: Triangulation That Counts

As defined earlier, triangulation is a means of determining precise targets with limited information about data. When achievement scores are released, then, a reasonable process to interpret those results is to triangulate them around key antecedent factors. Three types of antecedents—high-yield instructional strategies, collaboration, and accountability—have been selected because of the wealth of research suggesting that, when they are applied strategically and systematically, student achievement gains occur (Hattie, 2009; DuFour, DuFour, & Eaker, 2008; Marzano, 2007; Reeves, 2004b). Triangulating achievement data across these constructs ensures that data analysis is guided by both research and the best practices of a standards-based framework.

Instructional strategies include provocative writing prompts, cogently used metaphors and similes, multistep problem solving with the scientific method, or mathematical analysis of relationships in time and space. Measures include the type of instructional strategy employed, degree to which protocols are implemented (e.g., days during which protocols are implemented with fidelity, mean percentage of protocol components demonstrated), and evidence in student work (e.g., higher-order questions volunteered by students).

Collaboration structures elicit team thinking and candor, ensure transparent meeting processes, and designate distinct times for reflection and analysis (Lencioni, 2004; White, 2007). Collaboration measures include the frequency of collaboration, time devoted to examining student work, and adherence to norms regarding candor and team thinking.

Accountability is the sum of follow-through, feedback, rewards, transparency, and even sanctions. Measures include the proportion of schools and classrooms that display data through data walls, how frequently action steps or implementation protocols are monitored, and how consistently feedback is provided through the supervision process.

The instructional strategy at Timberline (refer to Chapter 2) differed by grade level, as the fourth-grade team selected reciprocal teaching; fifth-grade teachers selected the basic teacher interaction of modeling, guided practice, and independent practice as a lesson template; and the sixth-grade team agreed to elaborate their questioning to improve inferencing and vocabulary selection. All teams viewed Data Team meetings as a good metric of collaboration measuring the percentage of weekly meetings where they collaborated on these strategies. Finally, the entire school was aware of its need for feedback from the principal and literacy coach for the classroom walk-throughs (CWTs) that occurred for each teacher three times each grading period, the measurement selected for accountability. This feedback element represented the level of accountability by grade level in terms of the frequency and extent of CWTs. Exhibit 7.1 depicts hypothetical data for the first nine-week grading period, with accountability ranging from 100 percent of teachers received feedback three times during the grading period to grade levels where only 58 percent of teachers received feedback at that level. Similarly, the percentage of grade-level meetings where collaboration took place around instructional strategies varied from 100 percent to 25 percent.

EXHIBIT **7.1** | **Antecedent Data for Due Diligence**

				Math/Reading Unit Tests	
	Instructional Strategy	Collaboration (%)	Accountability (%)	% Gains Proficient	Post-test % Proficient
4th Grade	Reciprocal teaching— 62%	100	100	23	65
5th Grade	Teaching interaction—58%	75	58	9	59
6th Grade	Elaboration of information— 62%	25	67	2	62

Exhibit 7.2 triangulates the data on these dimensions graphically to examine the factors simultaneously.

EXHIBIT **7.2 | Triangulation Data for Fourth, Fifth, and Sixth Grades**

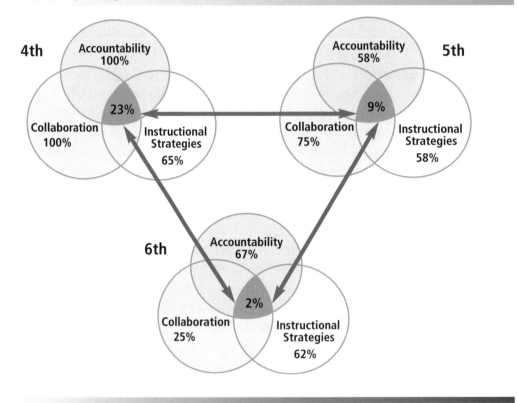

Each grade level was deliberate in agreeing to use a common instructional strategy, and each team honestly self-reported its level of implementation and time spent in collaboration. The accountability measure simply tracked the level of support provided by the literacy coach and principal, but the data help determine what is working and what is not. At this point, it is important to note that there is no one definitive answer when due diligence is exercised as in this example. However, the data are certainly more instructive than the absence of antecedent data, where all three grades scored within a narrow band of proficiency (59–65 percent). What can be learned from this example of triangulation?

1) The grade level (four) that had the most consistent level of administrative feedback (accountability) and most consistent level of collaboration outperformed classrooms in which less evidence of accountability and collaboration was seen.

2) All three grade levels struggled to implement with fidelity, suggesting room for improvement and that they selected relatively effective instructional strategies.

3) While feedback from CWTs may be a contributing factor to the level of gains experienced, a strong correlation exists between collaboration and achievement.

The result of this simple triangulation should indicate a greater emphasis on collaboration around instructional strategies than was previously shown and at least a more concerted effort than exhibited before to increase the fidelity of strategy implementation the teams agree to employ. From this triangulation, the greatest gains did not occur because of the selected instructional strategy (virtually no difference across grades); they occurred when the fourth-grade team demonstrated high levels of collaboration and accountability, practices that grades 5 and 6 practiced in a much more sporadic fashion. The triangulation reveals a wide variation in how CWTs are administered, as there appears to be a skewed level of support provided based on grade levels, where all fourth-grade teachers were observed and provided feedback from CWTs, while fifth- and sixth-grade teachers received less support (58 percent and 67 percent, respectively). If the only data inspected were the achievement results without considering collaboration and accountability, teams could erroneously conclude that the difference in gains was attributed to the selected strategy when, in fact, the distinguishing factor was the degree to which all three factors interacted for the fourth-grade team. Readers will observe the value of professional judgment for a thorough analysis to take place, especially with limited data.

Let us consider the limits of the example data. Only one measure of student achievement (math/reading) is provided in Exhibit 7.1, and that measure is a combined unit assessment. Yet, with information about antecedent factors such as accountability, strategies, and collaboration, practitioners can glean insights not available when there are several measures of student achievement to examine. James Popham (2003, p. 83), a highly respected educational statistician and expert on assessment, stresses the importance of professional judgment when he notes, "What teachers and administrators need to know about testing, at least for purposes of educational accountability, relies on common sense more than statistical exotica." By triangulating the data to examine antecedent causal factors, readers are provided much more context about the teaching-learning interaction and, hence, greater insight about how factors can most effectively interact to improve student achievement.

Triangulation does not answer all the questions we as educators will have, but it does answer some we would otherwise not address. Consider a scenario in which the same achievement gains were found, but the only distinguishing factor was the instructional strategy. In that case, the school would adopt the strategy that produced the greatest gains without any need to wait for the publication of a research article in a journal to encourage a greater use of that strategy. If consistent attention is paid to the three elements of due process (strategies, accountability, and collaboration), each iteration will provide more precise findings that inform our decisions and improve our practice.

Can we glean any concrete guidance from this exercise? One can surmise that it is not enough to implement quality instructional changes (antecedents) unless a corresponding quality change in collaboration occurs around the data and unless all faculty members are sufficiently accountable to align their efforts toward achieving desired results.

The triangulation would be strengthened with the insights and perspective of teams. Groups of readers will identify recommendations and discover meaning that individual readers will not be able to discern. While these take-aways are not necessarily concrete, this simple example of triangulation leads us to dig deeper inside the data to see how students in classes of teachers with the authority to be accountable performed on the state assessment. If they outperformed those who lacked such authority, we will have revealed a valuable finding. Furthermore, the quick application of triangulation can provide direction for further data analysis. In Exhibit 7.3, the same data are presented across four teams at the school, offering a different slice of data to triangulate. Complete the exercise by recording one insight you observe and one recommendation for the future when these data are added to those depicted in Exhibit 7.2.

EXHIBIT **7.3 | Triangulation of Data by Teams**

	Team A	Team B	Team C	Teacher D
% proficient, state math assessment	60	20	40	16
Data Team meetings per semester	17	5	13	2
Expository writing required daily	Yes	No	Yes	No
Assessments developed collaboratively	Yes	No	No	No
Assessment calendars applied to assessments	80%	No	No	No
Teachers have authority to be accountable	Yes	No	No	No

Observation from Exhibit 7.2: _____

_____

Recommendation: _____

_____

One may reach a number of conclusions from the example provided in Exhibit 7.3 to improve performance of teams B and C, and especially individual D. Even though data seldom provide such direct and powerful correlations, triangulation can help you examine data that are unrelated statistically but nonetheless valuable in identifying practices that work and those that do not. Triangulation extrapolates meaning from raw data, and as useful as it is to triangulate student achievement data with evidence about strategies or administrative structures, collaboration, and accountability, triangulation need not be limited to three types of data.

Returning to data from Timberline Middle School shown in Exhibit 7.3, we do not find stellar results in student achievement data, making it difficult to discern the factors contributing to those modest gains. However, by triangulating the data around collaborative design of assessments and expository writing, we discover that students in certain classrooms outperformed their peers dramatically. The data were sufficiently compelling to at least warrant placing greater emphasis on Data Teams; collaborative assessment design; and consistent, universal, and daily expository writing. Let us see whether a three-way intersection or triangulation adds value in any way.

Victoria Bernhardt (2000) referred to a similar process as "intersecting of data," recommending dual measure intersection, three-way intersection, and four-way intersection. This approach not only looks at the full range of antecedents, from end-of-course (EOC) assessments to instructional strategies, but also triangulates data by framing questions that represent a variety of hypotheses. Intersecting questions from practitioners with analysis across principles of data analysis helps everyone better understand the results students achieve. Exhibit 7.4 provides examples of data intersection by two-, three-, and four-way intersections, sorting them by the three principles of due diligence in data analysis.

EXHIBIT **7.4** | **Intersection of Data**

	Antecedents (professional decisions/ practices)	Collaboration	Accountability
Two-Way Intersection			
• Do students in activities perform better on state assessments?	√		√
• Do students with better grades also perform better on writing assessments?	√√		
• Do students of teachers who collaboratively design, implement, and evaluate EOCs perform better on EOCs than students of teachers who do not?		√	√
Three-Way Intersection			
• Do Asian students who participate in activities perform better on state assessments than Asian students who do not participate in activities, and do their grades correlate with activities or state assessments?	√√		√
• What teaching strategy has the greatest effect on EOC assessments for students with >15% learning gap, and what sub-group (ethnic/gender) has shown the greatest progress on EOC assessments?	√√		√
Four-Way Intersection			
• Do students who participate in activities perform better on state assessments than nonparticipants in activities? Do grades correlate with activities or state assessments? How do sub-groups differ in correlations with grades, state assessments, and activity participation?	√√		√√

Each added intersection digs deeper in the analysis process, providing more precise information. Monitoring the two-way example may establish a relationship between improved achievement and collaboration of teachers on EOCs, while the three-way or four-way example may determine the relationship of activity participation to achievement. The three-way intersections dig deeper by examining the impact of teaching strategies on the EOCs for all students while drilling deeper still to determine which sub-group benefits the most from such strategies and by examining whether activities apply to sub-groups with historically high performance. The four-way intersection digs deeper still by examining the relationship of grades to both assessments and activity participation. At this point, we have revealed important insights about collaboration of teachers, impact of instructional strategies, and accountability with much more precision than mere examination of student achievement data could offer. A valuable aspect of triangulation is the way it sets the stage for each teacher and administrator to check our assumptions at the door when it comes to data analysis.

The Myth of Apples and Oranges

Statisticians go to great lengths to convince laypeople of the errors of mixing and matching data types and the need to avoid compromising sampling and test designs to ensure reliability and validity; in other words, we are frequently warned, do not mix apples and oranges. Triangulation, however, necessitates discovery of insights from often unrelated data, so we must apply this process to educational data that is often varied, unrelated, and collected in different time frames for different purposes. But can we mix parametric and nonparametric data? How can we use classroom assessment data when sufficient rigor has not been applied to test design and item analysis? The problem regarding data in the public schools, and probably in any application other than wheat yields, is that the data available are seldom ideal for achieving straightforward analysis. Triangulation has been employed for centuries for that very purpose—to glean meaning from imperfect and incomplete data. While instances certainly arise in which data should not be compared in a statistical sense, the complexity of education compels us to look for patterns and trends in a practical sense that lead us to make decisions that improve student achievement, regardless of the type of data.

Triangulation requires teams to make assumptions, draw inferences, and come to conclusions without knowing with certainty that they are correct. When data are triangulated, each point serves as a check on the other dimension, with the desired outcome being the realization of new insights from the various data points (and types) that are not available from examining one type of data (e.g., achievement) or one perspective. The following exercise reexamines Timberline Middle School, a school with a reputation for high performance and excellence that finds itself caught in a vise between changing demographics and what seems to be an onslaught of accountability to the state, federal government, and public. Exhibit 7.5 offers insights that may be gleaned from triangulation about the experience at Timberline, which is categorized by administrative structures/learning conditions, teacher behaviors, and achievement results. After examining the exhibit for patterns, complete the reflection questions that follow.

EXHIBIT 7.5 | Triangulation for Timberline Middle School

Administrative Structures/Learning Conditions 2008–2010

- Faculty meetings devoted to data analysis
- 100% of courses have EOC assessments
- 90 class periods interrupted for some testing requirements annually
- Excelling classrooms are recognized monthly (assessment data)
- Writing improvement recognized on principal's data wall
- EOC assessments designed by volunteer teachers:
  6th grade—25%, 7th grade—100%, 8th grade—0%
- Students falling behind monitored with report sent to principal

Teacher Behaviors/Demographic Data 2008–2010

- All teachers use letter or % grades; no evidence of rubrics
- 86% volunteered for powerful teaching strategies training
- Teachers using 2+ performance assessments by grade:
  6th grade—25%, 7th grade—0 %, 8th grade—33%
- Teacher experience and proficiency with instructional strategies:

0–5 years	6–10 years	11+ years
67%	100%	8%

Student Achievement Trends 2008–2010

- English language learner gaps doubled from –15% to –30%
- Gap narrowed for Hispanic students each year, all subjects
- African American boys' gap opened from –25% to –35%

	Reading (%)	Writing (%)	Math (%)
2008	67	48	62
2009	63	49	67
2010	72	57	70
Change	+5%	+9%	+8%

Reflect about insights you discovered and list recommendations you might provide the principal at Timberline as a result of this triangulation exercise:

1. _____

2. _____

3. _____

4. _____

What do the differences in the design of EOC assessments by grade level tell us, or the distinction between those who took advantage of strategy training and those who did not? What if you knew which teachers applied what strategies or which teachers relied on rubrics or scoring guides? Even without additional data, triangulation focuses analysis to help us discover serious gaps in teacher practices and structural antecedents. While the data do not indicate what factors are contributing to growing achievement gaps, readers should see the immediate benefit of triangulation, one that multiplies when professionals triangulate through a collaborative process. Finally, it does not matter whether the data are parametric or nonparametric. You can mix and match all types of data, even observations and opinions. Use the process to verify those opinions and hunches with direct and indirect indicators.

The Wagon Wheel

This section introduces a data analysis tool to enable teachers and principals to conduct multivariate analyses without having to be an expert in statistical analysis. Modern statistics relies on the "bread and butter" multivariate methods such as multiple regression, analysis of variance, and analysis of covariance. Each statistical method allows the researcher to control for variability, enabling him to determine the relative effects of variables as they interact with and counteract each other. Undoubtedly, these methods provide the most precise means of ascertaining cause and effect in the complex study of human beings. Similarly, the wagon wheel is the most precise of the triangulation processes, comparing multiple variables at once to determine with confidence which variables have the most impact on student achievement. The wagon wheel allows practitioners to compare differences between schools, classrooms, or teachers and differences within each instructional level. Exhibit 7.6 depicts the wagon wheel and the process for employing it.

To illustrate the capacity of this helpful triangulation tool, eight different variables have been selected (see the numbered list below), and we will compare three classrooms on each variable by following the steps discussed below. A wagon wheel can have more spokes, but higher volume makes understanding difficult beyond the example. The 10 concentric circles in Exhibit 7.6 allow comparison of metric scales such as percentages or currency. The beauty of the wagon wheel, also called a spider chart, is that one can use different scales and still retain the integrity of the analysis.

Step 1: Assign Key Variables to Each Spoke on the Wheel

The wagon wheel is a graphic representation that facilitates comparison of several variables and several entities. Analysis may examine classrooms, students, and the entire school on the same wagon wheel. The tool might be used to analyze assessment results with textbook purchases and collaborative planning. It might examine professional development and its impact on student achievement, as we did with Timberline's data, or it might examine the degree to which a teacher adheres to a defined teaching process used in a specific lesson plan. Some have used the wagon wheel to monitor progress against performance standards for

EXHIBIT **7.6** | **The Wagon Wheel Data Analysis Tool and Graphic Organizer**

Steps in Using Wagon Wheels

1. Assign key variables to each spoke on the wheel (8).

2. Collect data across key variables.

3. Establish a scale for each spoke, with the highest performance on the outer rim of the circle. Label individual spokes with their own scale.

4. Plot performance data along spokes, color coding to distinguish units being compared (classrooms, schools, departments, grade levels, budgets, even certification areas).

5. Connect lines for each unit if comparisons are made between units.

6. Identify the pattern of performance against selected performance standards.

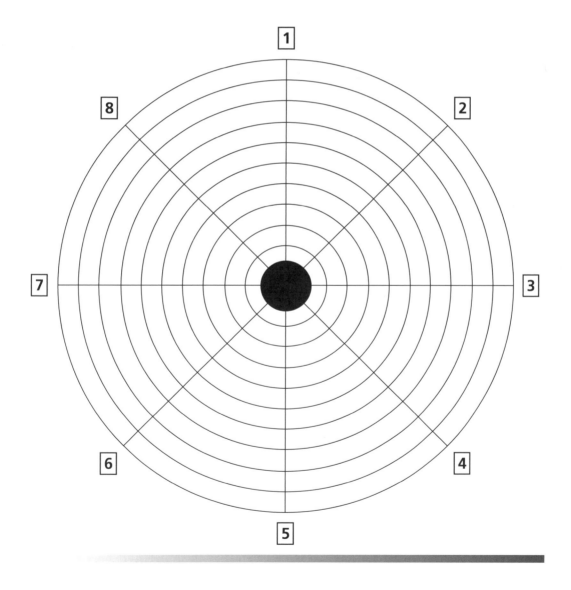

individual personnel evaluations or improvement goals. To illustrate the robust capacity of this simple tool, the following diverse variables have been selected for wagon wheel spokes:

1. Budget projections. Comparison of budgeted to actual expenditures reveals the degree of precision and accuracy for administrators, with 100 percent being the standard for excellence.
2. Use of technology. This spoke measures the degree of variability within entities in terms of fluency and application of end-user technologies, such as software applications. Measurement is based on the percentage of seven Microsoft Office Suite applications (e.g., Word, Excel, Publisher) used proficiently.
3. Percentage of total student assessments subject to assessment calendars at school.
4. Reduction of classroom interruptions (e.g., intercom announcements per day). Interruptions are measured in raw numbers ranging from 0 to 10.
5. Classroom checklist for standards implementation (see Exhibit 3.6). This variable is measured in terms of percentage of 14 items monitored by the teacher.
6. Percentage of students who score proficient on the state writing assessment.
7. Teacher absence rates. Rates are measured by the average number of days out of classroom per teacher for any reason for the previous 12-month period.
8. Time lag between special education referral and delivery of specialized instructional services. Time lag is measured by total referrals divided by the number of school days between referral and first day of service, ranging from 1 to 100.

Step 2: Collect Data

The wagon wheel's versatility is evident in step 2, as professionals can either create the wagon wheel after measures have been documented or respond to triangulation activities by creating wagon wheels to address the issues raised. The benefit of front-end planning ensures that the data are available, thorough, and accurate. Still, teams can benefit from the wagon wheel tool by simply identifying criteria important to those engaging in analysis and re-creating the data as accurately as possible, or setting in motion a wagon wheel for future review. Administrators have astutely used all eight or ten spokes as elements of evaluation criteria delineated in quality scoring guide rubrics.

Step 3: Establish Scale

Establish a scale for each spoke, with highest performance on the outer rim of the circle. This step provides the visual understanding of which entities (schools, teachers, districts, departments) are most consistently performing at or near the desired standards. Teams may want to use the "bull's eye" as the targeted performance level as an individual preference, but the important factor is that the standard is obvious, uniform, and consistent across variables being measured.

Step 4: Plot Performance

Plot performance data along spokes, color coding to distinguish units being compared (classrooms, schools, departments, grade levels, budgets, even certification areas). An alternative to color coding is to use black and white geometric shapes and patterns to distinguish units. This step advocates for a manageable number of variables and units (spokes and entities being compared).

Step 5: Make Connections

Connect lines for each unit if comparisons are made between units.

Step 6: Identify Patterns

Identify the patterns of performance against selected performance standards. This final step is really the beginning of analysis. The wagon wheel is a form of triangulation, although the data for each variable are quantitative rather than completely unknown. It is the interaction of the data that produces the "ah-has" associated with triangulation, and for that reason, the tool has been included here.

Exhibit 7.7 illustrates the visual power of the wagon wheel to reveal discrepancies, strengths, and weaknesses. For simplicity, three classrooms have been selected as units of comparison, even though spokes 1, 7, and perhaps 8 are administrative indicators that are unlikely selections as variables by teachers. The other variables, however, provide both administrators and teachers valuable information that can help them set priorities, identify antecedents, and initiate improvements.

The wagon wheel data reveal areas of strength and weakness for all three classrooms. In terms of budget projections, all three classrooms ranged from 80 percent to 95 percent, usually a positive indicator of planning and care with expenditures. Also seen was very little variation in terms of lag time (variable 8) between referral to special education and services delivered. This finding is probably attributable to district procedures to comply with federal law, but the range from 20 to 40 days is not unusual. Considerable discrepancy in standards was found, however, as classroom C performed much closer to standard in proficiency on the writing assessment, antecedents for a standards-based classroom, and adherence to an assessment calendar for almost all of its assessments. Classroom B was furthest away from the desired performance on all but teacher absences and had the lowest percentage proficient on the state writing assessment. Classroom B was also the furthest from standards in terms of technology literacy, and while there is room for all classrooms to improve, classroom B needs immediate assistance to reach the desired levels. This example intentionally included measures that counted both from the bulls' eye out and the outer rim in (time lag for services [variable 8], intercom interruptions [variable 4], and teacher absences [variable 7]) because the outer rim was the performance standard, illustrating how even the scales can be varied to provide the most complete picture of proficiency or achievement of desired targets. Schools, departments, teams, and dimensions can be compared in this way, and the possibilities to triangulate data are unlimited and user friendly. Appendix D provides a template for the wagon wheel data analysis tool.

EXHIBIT **7.7 | Wagon Wheel Illustrated**

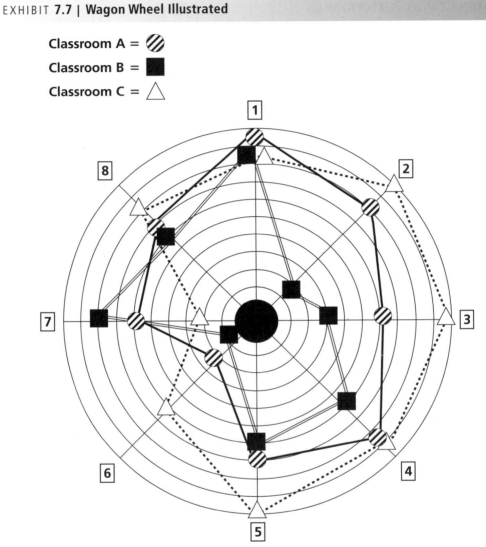

1. Budget projections
2. Use of technology
3. Percentage of total student assessments subject to assessment calendars at school
4. Intercom interruptions per day (range 0–10)

5. Classroom checklist for standards implementation
6. Percentage proficient on state writing assessment
7. Teacher absences
8. Time lag between referral and specialized services (range 1–100)

The Common Core State Standards and Triangulation

Triangulation is a process that allows educators to look behind the "curtain," to probe beyond the numbers to identify those factors that have the greatest impact on student achievement. Frequently, those factors do not operate in isolation but in concert with a number of other variables. Triangulation equips the educator to determine the right recipe of ingredients to move achievement for different groups of students. Throughout this volume, we have celebrated the capacity of the Common Core State Standards to support such analysis, whether the reference has been to the nine mathematical practices or the fine-grain distinctions of text complexity in English language arts.

The Common Core offers the practitioner a universe of content that reflects the context of learning, and in so doing supports the kinds of multifactorial analyses that triangulation is capable of. For example, the Common Core is designed to enable students to respond to the varying demands of audience, task, purpose, and content discipline and to critique evidence and assess its value. Each of these elements could be the data set for a thorough wagon wheel analysis, or a due diligence triangulation could be designed to determine the impact of technology and digital media (administrative structures and conditions of learning); the use of instructional strategies to help students construct effective arguments (instructional strategy); the methods Data Teams or professional learning communities use to help students communicate across a number of venues and engage others in the process (collaboration); and the degree to which systems are in place to ensure students have the ability to plan, revise, edit, and publish quality work products on time at high standards (accountability). Virtually every Common Core standard will require a team of teachers to strategically position resources, integrate content, and deliver engaging instructional strategies to ensure that each student demonstrates proficiency. The world may appear to be flat, but education challenges are hardly linear, and the ability to integrate, synthesize, and draw inferences from widely divergent content will require data analysis that is capable of examining multiple variables at once, leading to better decision making. Triangulation is one important tool in that journey, and the Common Core demonstrates that the time is now for the profession to embrace it.

Summary

Triangulation is a process of discovering the unknown by looking at data points from different angles. It necessitates diversity of ideas, experiences, and perspectives and therefore requires a healthy dose of collaboration. It also requires solid data points to triangulate from, whether the data describe results in student achievement, compliance with policies and procedures, or the quality and degree with which proven instructional strategies are deployed. Thus, it requires a healthy dose of accountability, where people are empowered to take responsibility not only for their actions but also for results. Accountability requires authority to take action on the basis of data and permission to sweep away obsolete and counterproductive practices and programs when needed. Triangulation reveals understanding that data standing alone cannot, as we see in the wagon wheel exercise. As educators, we must be prepared to respond to such discoveries as a moral imperative to make a difference for the students we serve. That preparation requires leadership and accountability, and the capacity to create a sense of urgency when the data indicate the need for decisive and courageous actions. Triangulation also allows the introduction of antecedents of all kinds into the analysis of data, as we did when unit test scores were examined in light of instructional strategies, Data Team participation, and classroom walk-through feedback in Exhibit 7.1. Triangulation requires a healthy dose of antecedents and a willingness to recognize their influence.

The remaining chapters assist us in getting beyond the numbers to make a difference in our schools, leveraging the principle of subtraction, and establishing a thorough process to gather information and insights from systems and a changing environment. We develop ways to replicate those brilliant teacher practices that are so often relegated to a single teacher rather than shared with the field, then we close with Chapter 10, "The Teacher as Expert." Triangulation is the fuel to move into that arena, where the expertise of the profession is applied to data analysis to create solutions beyond the numbers.

Reflection

BIG IDEA: Triangulation identifies possibilities beyond the numbers.

Describe a principle of triangulation as it relates to mixing apples and oranges.

What is the relationship between triangulation and accountability in data analysis?
Collaboration?

BIG IDEA: Due diligence in data analysis requires triangulation of key antecedent practices and decisions.

What is the benefit of developing triangulations to examine effects data in light of collaborative efforts, evidence of accountability, and teacher routines or strategies?

Consider designing your own wagon wheel with another colleague familiar with your school or position. Collaborate to identify those variables most important to your work.

The Environmental Scan

You cannot depend on your eyes when your imagination
is out of focus.

—MARK TWAIN (1835–1910)

We have seen how triangulation helps extrapolate meaning from raw data and how it can be an effective means to find the critical information and see the big picture when we have limited information. In the same way, an environmental scan helps us extrapolate meaning from the changes occurring in our classrooms, schools, systems, and communities. The best environmental scans require us to examine areas we otherwise would ignore or avoid. It is an important component of the "treasure hunt" because it ensures that we include changes in data analysis to avoid the scenario of Apple Blossom Unified School District (USD).

CASE STUDY

Apple Blossom USD prided itself for being on the cutting edge of curriculum design, professional development, and instructional technology. The community it served was a reflection of that pride: well educated, affluent, and a large proportion of the community working in networking, Internet, or wireless technologies. As a result, when the school rolled out its bold move to make Apple Blossom the first district in the state to install fiber-optic cable throughout its facilities, the school board and advisory councils were excited and the local press viewed Apple Blossom as the darling of public education. Apple Blossom had a history of achieving commendable test scores, and from real estate agencies to parents selecting prime neighborhoods to raise children, Apple Blossom was the place to live and work. Because average test scores ranged between the 70th and 90th percentile on the norm referenced test (NRT), following a consistent pattern over the last 20 years, there was considerable pride in the curriculum and in the ability of the high schools to offer a broad range of courses. Some teachers periodically questioned the range of course offerings that qualified for the same credit and, ultimately, the same diploma. Other staff, supported by a growing number of parents, inquired about starting a school of choice but were summarily dismissed by a reference to "our fine schools being the envy of the state." During the campaign for fiber optics, the district's graduation rate was reported as 95 percent, another attractive feature, so when the mill levy passed to build the fiber-optic network, it appeared that the sky was the limit, and the district had nowhere to go but up.

Within a year, the investment in fiber optics came to be seen as ill considered, the curriculum was being lambasted in the press for not being aligned to the new and challenging state standards, parents had picketed the school board for being unresponsive to student needs and subscribing to a "one size fits all" mentality, and various advocacy groups targeted Apple Blossom as a district that had misled the public and failed through indifference and prejudice to address the needs of students characterized as transient, low-income students, and students of color. What happened in that one year to make such a difference?

Apple Blossom had rested on its laurels and made a number of strategic errors, not the least of which was its failure to have quality listening systems in place. Listening systems would have revealed that an investment in fiber optics was premature in light of the move toward DSL solutions, high-speed cable, and Web-based information management through the Internet. Listening systems would also have allowed the school district to anticipate the movement toward standards and accountability that had been building for years, as well as the movement toward school choice and charter options. The district's data analysis was fixated on the use of averages, which masked serious problems for a minority of its students, and the reporting system for graduation rate was calibrated on an annual basis, reporting 95 percent graduation, instead of the more accurate 76 percent when those enrolled as fall semester freshmen are compared with those listed in the graduation program four years later. Some of these issues continue to be common in schools across the United States today, while other issues have been addressed in the requirements for No Child Left Behind (NCLB) legislation and state accountability mandates. Almost overnight, Apple Blossom saw its reputation plummet from the "darling" and "visionary" school system to at best a run-of-the-mill organization that had to react to change rather than lead it. Apple Blossom USD could indeed have benefited greatly from an environmental scan.

An environmental scan is a process to examine changes affecting an institution. These include mandatory changes like those proscribed by NCLB, optional shifts such as building a fiber-optic system, and external changes such as the movement toward "choice" that has taken flight with charter school legislation being passed in more than 40 states by 2005. Apple Blossom does not entirely represent a fantasy situation, because each component is an illustration of actual events that have stopped well-intentioned and dedicated educators in their tracks. Completion of an environmental scan will facilitate a more thorough understanding of change factors and resource needs.

Environmental scans examine seven characteristics of organizations—changes in leadership, planning strategies, quality of listening systems, information and data, work environment, work habits, and results pursued—that are equally present whether the organization is effective or ineffective. A scan can be employed by a classroom teacher, a principal and her faculty, or a school system. It is based on systems analysis, a process designed to clarify the purpose, parts, and functions of an organization to reveal its degree of interdependence and to discover any unintended consequences that occur. Recalling the information presented for Timberline Middle School in Chapter 2, one can safely conjecture that its emphasis on collecting data produced a reaction from staff against data and against data analysis that was not intended. The same is true with Apple Blossom USD; its administrators had no idea the effect reporting a 95 percent graduation rate would have on the district's reputation, even though the state probably employed the same faulty methodology. Principal Dennis, profiled in Chapter 3, did not see how his leadership in creating collaborative opportunities and aligning effort to promote literacy influenced student achievement, but it did, and Superintendent Ellison's attempt to implement too many initiatives at once and her reliance on the past to predict the future, presented in Chapter 1, also had unintended consequences that distracted efforts to improve teaching and learning, an outcome that was clearly unintentional.

A scan of the environment will examine two types of changes across three dimensions: external and internal changes across programmatic, instructional, and organizational dimensions. External changes are those that occur outside of one's control. To state officials, accommodating the demands of the Race to the Top Initiative is an external change, and while it will affect both the organization and instruction, it is a programmatic change. To a school system, legislative action that requires an individual learning plan for every student who is not proficient is also an external programmatic change, as is growth or decline in enrollment. To the school, receiving notice that it has five years to meet adequate yearly progress for all subgroups or face the possibility of reconstitution as a charter school is an external change facing schools right now in all 50 states and the U.S. territories. This change will require a response across all three dimensions. Finally, the requirement that every teacher be prepared to articulate, on demand, each student's level of proficiency on key standards, also an external requirement, will necessitate an instructional response. Colorado has even added the requirement that 50 percent of a teacher's evaluation be based on student achievement gains (Concerning Ensuring Quality, 2010). None of these is a particularly pleasant challenge facing educators at any of these levels; all are realities, and they can only be ignored at one's professional peril.

The first area to be scanned is for changes in leadership. Changes in leadership include personnel changes, changes affecting accountability issues like the authority to act or permission to subtract, and the leadership impact of collaborative structures such as Data Teams. An external change would be assignment of a new administrator; an internal change would be involvement in the selection of that new administrator. An organizational change would be reconstitution, significant changes in policy, a change in superintendent, or a shift in the makeup and philosophy of the board of education. A programmatic change that is also a leadership change would be the creation of Data Teams with authority to commit resources for materials, teacher training, or additional time and opportunity to assist certain students to close their learning gap. An instructional change regarding leadership could be a change in the actions of leadership by teachers within the classroom: How are performances monitored, expectations communicated, feedback provided, feedback elicited, and decisions made? While seldom associated with leadership in the classroom, these actions of teachers are demonstrations of leadership, and lesson planning provides a framework to intentionally respond to changes (external) or initiate changes (internal) to improve student achievement.

The second area in the environmental scan is planning strategies. Strategies have been discussed almost exclusively in terms of classroom teaching strategies, but planning certainly extends to program and organization strategies as well. One example of an external planning strategy is a teacher's response to a principal's requirement to demonstrate how each lesson relates to specific content standards. The method for creating an effective response to that requirement would be the teacher's planning strategy, such as backward curriculum mapping that leads to an effective instructional calendar. An internal planning strategy for the principal might be his approach to planning an increase in the quality of a note-taking and summarizing strategy in all classrooms. That planning process might include a compelling argument from the research, common pitfalls, and ready-to-use suggestions for teachers. It might include a planned modeling of lessons by the principal or an accomplished teacher in note-taking and summarizing. The planning process might stipulate how teams are expected to work together and produce a model, with timelines and accountability expectations delineated. Finally, an effective planning strategy would complete the cycle by monitoring implementation and providing a method to evaluate the strategy's success. The example provided addresses instructional issues (note-taking) and programmatic issues (modeling, teamwork, monitoring, and evaluation). An obvious example of an organizational planning strategy would be the approach an organization takes to face the challenge to develop an improvement plan that achieves dramatic results. Principals, teachers, central office administrators, and specialists would consider what works well in their environment and intentionally plan strategies to make a difference. Appendix H describes a data road map to initiate needed changes revealed by a thorough environmental scan.

The third area of the scan is an effort to determine the quality and effectiveness of existing listening systems. This area includes administering surveys, eliciting stakeholder feedback, addressing complaints, and collecting input from the community in a way that does not stop at the activity of the survey or completion of a focus group. Listening systems need to be pervasive, ongoing, embedded, and accountable enough to produce action that improves student achievement. External listening systems would include ways to communicate and listen to patrons and parents in the community. Internal listening systems ensure that we hear from staff and students. Data in a day, developed by Education Northwest and discussed in Chapter 6, is an example of a listening system component.

The fourth element of a comprehensive environmental scan is information and data. Not only should we gather and analyze data on each component of the environmental scan, but we also need to understand how well our data system works and what actions external and internal changes advise us to make in terms of our data system. Timberline Middle School was a system that prided itself on its range of student assessments, yet its data and information system failed to help people manage information well enough to make informed decisions. An internal data scan would examine the work habits associated with analysis, perhaps revealing that the collection system is cumbersome and uneven, that assessments lack consistency and reliability, or that end-of-course (EOC) assessments are needed for every course and grade.

Prior to the external state accountability systems, NCLB, and Race to the Top, many teachers deemed classroom-developed internal assessments, and perhaps one NRT assessment administered every three years, sufficient to determine proficiency. If a school had been using the environmental scan wisely, it would have recognized that accountability systems were coming; even the mandates of NCLB were known in detail at least a year before the requirements were instituted. Schools and districts that recognized the importance of content standards early are now glad they did. Today's challenge will be to design the right body of evidence that includes teacher-developed assessments, online assessments, interim or benchmark assessments for within-district progress monitoring, local school performance frameworks for internal school accreditation, and external statewide assessments for district accreditation.

The fifth area of the scan is the work environment, where one district would examine the impact those districts that pay higher salaries have on its ability to recruit and retain the best teachers possible. Other factors may differentiate schools as well, making one school (school A) a more desirable place to work than school B. School B's environmental scan should attempt to reveal those characteristics that make school A more desirable so school B can adopt those attributes in its effort to retain and recruit teachers. Many factors address the work environment, from common planning to facilities to resources to quality and availability of meeting rooms, to salaries and insurance packages to size of classrooms, and a high-quality scan will examine all changes that impact those working in that environment.

Work habits, introduced in earlier chapters as antecedents that describe how things get done, are the sixth area to be considered in an environmental scan. External changes frequently include additional paperwork and compliance requirements, while internal changes may be new systems to monitor performance or introduce lessons or a procedure whereby students are asked to take greater responsibility for assessing and monitoring their own performance in the classroom. Including work habits in a comprehensive environmental scan allows you to determine what is done now, what needs to be done, and what improvements will achieve greater efficiency and effectiveness.

The final component of an environmental scan is consideration of the results that are being pursued. Again, external changes may require a different reporting system or inclusion of new sub-groups. A thorough environmental scan will help establish the format for reporting, aggregating, and presenting results that provide meaningful information on an ongoing basis.

KWL as a Filter for Environmental Scans

KWL is a popular approach familiar to educators as a reading strategy for effective summarizing (Carr & Ogle, 1987) that has been associated with nonfiction reading comprehension, with wide application to classroom instruction across content areas and grade levels. Its simplicity accounts for its widespread adoption and adaptation: the K represents, "What do I know about _____ ?" the W represents, "What do I **w**ant to learn about _____?" and the L represents, "What have I **l**earned about _____ ?" It is recommended here as a filter to answer the questions regarding each component of the environmental scan. For example, what do I know about leadership? What do I want to learn about planning strategies? What have I learned about work environments? When these questions are posed to educators, particularly in a collaborative setting, much important data is gleaned that can inform planning and help teams proactively prepare for the future. The process also enables educators to better understand all the influences impacting their school, classroom, or district. Exhibit 8.1 provides a template for a thorough environmental scan, capturing programmatic, instructional, and organizational factors, addressing external and internal changes, and applying the KWL filter to increase understanding of existing data at all levels. The environmental scan combines the systems approach across seven organizational variables with the KWL filter to deepen the ability to examine the impact of changes, both mandatory (e.g., NCLB) and voluntary (e.g., Making Standards Work certification).

The template provides no fewer than 21 possible ways to scan the learning and organizational environment for a classroom, school, or district (see the checkmarks in the exhibit). Each area is then scrutinized to determine what we now know about that organizational component, what the organization wants or needs to find out, and what the organization anticipates might be learned from the data analysis. Exhibit 8.2 provides a sample completed environmental scan that demonstrates how a simple KWL method can secure answers to persistent and challenging questions, not only about student achievement but also about the health of the organization.

EXHIBIT **8.1** | **Environmental Scan Template**

Changes Initiated	Leadership	Planning Strategies	Listening Systems	Info and Data	Work Environment	Work Habits	Results in Performance and Process
Programmatic	✓	✓	✓	✓	✓	✓	✓
Know							
Want							
Learn							
Instructional	✓	✓	✓	✓	✓	✓	✓
Know							
Want							
Learn							
Organizational	✓	✓	✓	✓	✓	✓	✓
Know							
Want							
Learn							

EXHIBIT **8.2** | Environmental Scan for Data Analysis

	Leadership	Planning Strategies	Listening Systems	Information and Data	Work Environment	Work Habits	Results in Process and Performance
Programmatic	Reading recovery	School improvement plan	Satisfaction surveys	Data—student achievement tracking	Negotiated work day/hours	Barriers to professional development to improve instruction	State assessment adequate yearly progress and EOC requirements
Know (current knowledge)	1.0 full-time equivalent staff assigned to each school	Requirements, expectations, and deadlines	Data are inconclusive	Expectation to report results to community	Policies and terms of negotiated agreement	Programs, policies, traditions	Trends and patterns with dates when sub-group gaps must be closed
Want (to know)	Program effectiveness?	Possibility of midyear changes and process to add antecedent data indicators?	What do students, parents, teachers really think?	How to include qualitative and antecedents to student achievement data	How much latitude to accommodate with flexible hours, waivers, compensation?	What is needed to align with standards, increase agility, and improve instruction?	Impact of investment in professional development, curriculum alignment with standards, and triangulation of data?
Learn (evidence)	% proficient in reading within 6-month discontinued-cost/benefit $	Specific process for midcourse changes and use of antecedents	Creation of alternate data collection systems	Evidence of gaps in achievement closing, obsolete subtracted	Areas where principals can leverage incentives to achieve results	Specify policies, traditions, and barriers; actions needed when?	What is working, actions to replicate practices that work, and existing barriers
Instructional	Expectations regarding standards and assessments	Effective teaching strategies (ETS)	Student view of classroom instruction	Data—tracking of local practices to replicate	Ability—grouping, secondary; elementary departmentalization	Opening classroom activities	Cohort improvement by sub-group and gaps, opening or closing
Know	Standards are aligned with daily lessons	Teachers employ 1 or more daily	Students have no means to register concerns	No system is in place currently	Wide variation; little training; no clear expectations	Wide variation; little training; no clear expectations	3 years of cohort data by sub-group on state assessments only

CHANGES INITIATED

EXHIBIT **8.2** | **Environmental Scan for Data Analysis** (Continued)

	Leadership	Planning Strategies	Listening Systems	Information and Data	Work Environment	Work Habits	Results in Process and Performance
Want	Quality of implementation?	Which strategies, and why chosen?	What are student preferences for teaching?	How to recognize replicable practices early?	Impact on student achievement by sub-groups?	Openings promote engagement or reduce disruption?	Early-warning EOC and performance indicators (canaries)?
Learn	Gap between observed and declared lesson plans	ETS integrated, teacher declared and observed by others	Strategies, antecedents that will engage kids	Correlation between teachers and achievement	What works for all students, and what groupings close gap	Need for training, cost, anticipated student gains	Where resources and opportunities need to be created, and when?
Organizational	Site-based management	Policies promoting ETS	Community aware—standards?	Need—assessment calendar mandate	Relation—experience to achievement	Duplication of effort, related cost	Accountability and authority to act
Know	District policy that decisions made at sites	Policies exist, and principals to monitor ETS use	Accountability new to schools—misinformation	Lots of data never analyzed properly at all levels, sites	Historically positive correlation, no data since 1990	Budgets tighter every year; some processes lengthy	All staff have limitations on authority to act
Want	Discretion for staff transfers, budget carryover?	Degree monitored, when, how, data?	Need for process to communicate standards?	Correlation of achievement to testing calendars?	What is relationship between experience and achievement?	How to streamline for efficiency and effectiveness?	What artificial barriers inhibit bold, effective leadership?
Learn	Link all decisions to school goals	To disaggregate by ETS usage	Type/frequency of communication	Need for training, time, requirement	Importance of teacher longevity	Value of speed to responsiveness	How to promote creativity, risk taking

Seeing the Forest for the Trees

Throughout this book, we have stressed the need to simplify approaches and concepts, to reflect on what we do well and what we need to do better, and the need for teachers to trust their "collective wisdom." Despite dramatic improvements in recent years, education is still characterized by bureaucratic structures (Elmore, 2007). The typical response when challenges go unmet in bureaucratic organizations is to "create new offices, job titles, and programs that seek to compensate for the effects of an ill-defined system" (Darling-Hammond, 1997, p. 202). Once again, the experience of most educators will ring true with this observation, even in an era of tight budgets and increased scrutiny and accountability. The standards movement and the accountability of NCLB and Race to the Top have created positions like assessment coordinator, director of research and evaluation, executive director for learning services, instructional data manager, and assistant for assessment and continuous improvement. We do not argue that those job functions are not necessary but that our profession struggles to find alternate ways to respond to challenges. This section briefly addresses the need to keep things simple. Society has platitudes in the twenty-first century that were not common a generation ago: "Work smarter, not harder"; "Less is more"; and, of course, the definition of insanity attributed to Albert Einstein, "doing the same thing over and over again and expecting different results." Exhibit 8.3 provides an opportunity to identify all the kinds of data collected in your work situation, reports you must file, information you must process. Check "yes" for data that are *routinely* analyzed for improvement, and "never" for data never analyzed. If you are uncertain, check "no," and make a commitment to yourself to find out what happens to the information.

Confer with a colleague about your discoveries in Exhibit 8.3, and if you do not have the authority to subtract, escalate the issue to those who can give it to you and obtain it. Few can argue with a request to stop doing something that is producing no value, and everyone will be relieved to find out that such a radical idea is even possible.

Systems Analysis

Systems analysis is a method of analyzing data that is focused on two outcomes only: revealing areas of interdependence and discovering unintended consequences. When we conduct a thorough environmental scan, we need to look for these characteristics of systems. Our scenarios throughout this book have depicted smart, dedicated professionals who were all intent on improving student performance. While Dennis was successful and did not know why, Dr. Ellison, the staff at Timberline Middle School, the teachers at Maple High School, and those at Colson Independent School District shared in common a proclivity to make things worse in their efforts to make things better. How did that happen? They all failed to recognize the fundamental laws of systems: they exist whether we create them or not, they are by definition connected and interdependent, and a change in one area will most certainly affect another area whether intended or not. That is why an environmental scan is so important, and why the seven components are so universal. Leadership is a factor in any organization, whether present

EXHIBIT **8.3** | **Data, Reports, and Information at Work**

Data Source	Analyzed		
	Yes	Never	No
1.			
2.			
3.			
4.			
5.			
6.			
7.			
8.			
9.			
10.			
11.			
12.			
13.			
14.			
15.			

or absent, and every classroom in the United States has leaders who set the standard for quality and have enormous influence. Most classroom leaders are also teachers, but unless we recognize how an action in one aspect of an environment will affect another, we will not be as effective in data analysis as we would otherwise become. Classrooms have information and data, and they have a work environment for teachers and for students. They also have numerous work habits that, collectively and individually, have a dramatic impact on student achievement. Systems are not just about districts, states, and nations. They are present in families and in classrooms.

Listening Data

Listening data have been referenced several times, most prominently as a component of a high-quality environmental scan. Few schools in the twenty-first century are without some method of gathering input from its stakeholders, and the most common form is the satisfaction survey. This format is often a requirement of school improvement planning, and many schools use sophisticated surveys that have been validated by national organizations, which are usually more than happy to analyze the results for a fee. Schools also are much more prone in this generation than the last to take these surveys seriously, to analyze the results internally, and to use the results to drive school improvement planning. I applaud these listening systems as far as they go, but I believe they seldom go far enough.

In Chapter 4, we discussed at length the importance of collaboration and the reality of a collective wisdom that emerges when groups apply their "common" sense to solve a problem. In Chapter 6, we discussed briefly the importance of corrective feedback in improving student achievement and in learning knowledge correctly the first time it is encountered. In the context of a thorough environmental scan designed to provide the wealth of data that we need to make better decisions about our current reality and to respond to demands of the future, listening systems need to be designed to provide both collective wisdom and corrective feedback. They need to do so efficiently, routinely, and not just annually. Can you see how the rearview-mirror effect is indeed alive and well? For these reasons, a single satisfaction survey will not suffice. In fact, several satisfaction surveys, one for teachers, one for parents, and even one for students, will not be adequate if excellence is what we desire.

An effective listening system will allow us to see multiple dimensions and perspectives from "all the angles" and triangulate the information with precision and wisdom. It will launch numerous probes throughout the school year, just as we would ideally have in place a comprehensive assessment system that is monitored and directed by an effective assessment calendar (Exhibit 2.9). Finally, an effective listening system will insist that action be taken on the basis of data derived from it. Many educators resign themselves to satisfaction surveys because they understand that few parents and fewer students know what they really need. The argument goes that if physicians did everything we told them to, they would be taking unnecessary and reckless liberties with our health. The argument continues that educators would be equally unwise to take the advice of those we serve. Students are not customers, after all. They are children who present themselves to us during a period in their lives when they have great potential for growth and inspiration. So, the argument is persuasive, if flawed. Let us return to the medical model once more. While it is true that physicians would be unwise to allow us to self-medicate and self-diagnose, it is also true that physicians have learned to listen well to their patients, involve them in understanding the data, and ask for their feedback frequently, continuously. Listening systems are not to dictate how we as a profession will respond to the needs of our "clients"—our students and their families—but they are a means to collect meaningful data for analysis, just as teacher behaviors are important pieces of data. And like the physician's patient, many of our students and parents have extraordinary insights whereby, if we listen to them, we can avoid performing surgery and get them on the path of educational health and learning.

The data in a day program (Education Northwest, 2001) included a debriefing session with the entire staff and is similar to instructional rounds (City, et al., 2009) based on the medical rounds physicians make. The assessment calendar is recommended to include consistent public communication with all those involved in data management, even when no changes are implemented as a result of the data collected and analyzed. While assessment calendars are common, few call out the important data analysis functions of analysis, decisions, or dissemination of findings to stakeholders. Data Teams, discussed in Chapter 6, insist on wide dissemination of Data Team minutes as a means to hold one another accountable and as a means of creating a history—a narrative—as its own reflective type of data. By conducting the business of public education in public, we introduce the principle of audience that always calls participants to their highest standard. Listening systems, like the assessment calendar, demand a response from those analyzing the data. Educators who communicate the data of listening system probes to all concerned will be seen immediately as transparent, responsive, and inclusive.

Exhibit 8.4 presents a framework for an effective listening system that continues to value satisfaction survey data and supplements it with Web site and electronic feedback systems and with focus groups and interview data (qualitative assessments of values, experiences, and perspectives of constituents). Other listening frameworks are available; my own experience includes an office visit feedback card to monitor the degree to which I actually met the needs of those who took their own time to visit my office.

The purpose of the listening system is to gather data on multiple fronts simultaneously and, at a minimum, build capacity to triangulate data from surveys, upfront via focus groups and interviews, and electronically through Web sites, e-mail, and student information systems that are available and distinct depending on the agency. Appendix F provides a template for readers.

The second feature is the expectation that a rationale is provided that justifies current practice for each component of the listening system. This expectation ensures a means to revisit each component to determine whether it is still useful or it should be changed or subtracted.

A third feature is found in the columns marked P, I, and E. Is the component in the proposal stage, has it been introduced, or is it established? This is an important factor, not because it recognizes the ebb and flow of any service provided but because it requires respondents to consider the quality of implementation and whether more or less time needs to be given to it.

Sets of four questions are posed for every component to ensure that action is taken on behalf of the data collected and analyzed, that accountability is associated with it in terms of authority to commit resources, and that specific accountability provisions are in place in terms of who, when, and how any action will be initiated.

The listening system template (bottom of Exhibit 8.4) offers four concise guidelines. Examine the sample listening system described in Exhibit 8.5 to determine whether Milford School District's system is cyclical, predictable, transparent, and user friendly. Listening systems need to be cyclical to be of the greatest utility and value. By gathering the same type of information at various junctures throughout the year, schools can monitor the ebb and flow of each school year, not only in terms of opinion but also in perspective and meaningful feedback.

If, for example, the teacher found that parent satisfaction peaked every year following parent conferences in November and reached its low point in May, perhaps a problem in communication exists, or even in terms of the teacher's competency, or student achievement. When we gather data is as important to our understanding as what data we gather. Is the listening system predictable? Do stakeholders have confidence that when they provide input, that input will be analyzed, and if warranted, action taken? Does the school or district value this information sufficiently to make it public in some way or report to stakeholders what was done with the data? Finally, is there a flow to the listening system that makes the benefit of information gained worth the effort expended to provide, collect, and respond to the data?

A predictable listening system is also one in which the opportunity to be heard is reliable and consistent for stakeholders. When such a system is in place, professionals have greater confidence in the results and the likelihood is greater that constituent groups will participate again and again. The template assumes that not only parents and students but also staff, teachers, administrators, and patrons will be surveyed. Patrons often represent a retired community that determines whether a bond issue or mill levy passes or fails; they may be alumni or former employees. But in today's society, where parents and grandparents seldom make up 33 percent of the electorate, this is a key group to hear from often.

Transparency in listening systems inspires confidence and builds trust with constituents. It communicates a willingness to listen, courage to share results, and commitment to learn from the feedback the community provides. Such transparency is not just applicable to the school board and superintendent; principals, teachers, and staff can benefit from this characteristic, especially in relationships with respondent groups. Just as an effective assessment calendar includes a written rationale to everyone involved in the process for action taken or the decision to take no action, a quality listening system communicates that educators listened carefully to the input provided.

The final guideline is to ensure that each component is user friendly. A number of validated parent surveys constructed by reputable educational organizations are nonetheless lengthy and laborious. Some survey parents with 60-word questions, and do it again and again over 70 questions. Few respondents will take the time to respond to such a survey, and the results will be representative when only the most supportive or least supportive take the time to complete it. Often, educators will excuse a poor response rate by comparing the results to a political poll and rely on the standard error of measurement. We are not polling strangers, and while the return may be statistically valid, a small response does not offer the rich insights a more user-friendly—and shorter—survey or interview may provide.

Listening systems are essential to effective data analysis. They are not student achievement results, but like teaching strategies, conditions for learning, and administrative structures that correlate with improved student achievement, the data they provide are essential for thorough analysis and a comprehensive environmental scan of our educational communities.

EXHIBIT **8.4** | **Listening Data**

School _____ Principal _____ Date _____ E-mail _____

Types of Data	Parents	Teachers and Administrators	Staff	Students	Patrons	P	I	E	Rationale: Current Practice
Satisfaction Surveys									
What do we do currently with the data?									
Authority to act (commit resources)?									
Who? / When?									
How?									
Focus Groups, Interviews									
What do we do currently with the data?									
Authority to act (commit resources)?									
Who? / When?									
How?									
Web Site Comments									
What do we do currently with the data?									
Authority to act (commit resources)?									
Who? / When?									
How?									

P = proposed   I = introduced   E = established

Guidelines for Listening Systems: **Cyclical**   **Predictable**   **Public (open, transparent)**   **User Friendly**

School _____   Principal _____   Date _____   E-mail _____

EXHIBIT **8.5** | **Sample Listening Data, Milford School District**

Satisfaction Surveys	Parents	Teachers and Administrators	Staff	Students	Patrons	P	I	E	Rationale: Current Practice
What do we do currently with the data?	Look at it; address top concern area as one SIP goal	Gather; tabulate, publish, discuss with faculty; address in SIP	Gather; tabulate, publish report to all staff	Student council coordinates survey; published in school newspaper	Surveys limited to bond issue and mill levy campaigns; election team review			✓	Satisfaction surveys have been in place for 11 years. Few changes implemented as a result; survey results vary little from year to year; emphasis/monitoring on % responding.
Authority to act (commit resources)?	Established through SIP process	Not defined	Not defined	Student council may propose recommended changes to principal through adviser	Primarily to assess level of community support; action related to campaigns	✓			Authority to act has always been assumed. Only parent survey and faculty satisfaction survey result in action, and even then, may be limited to an activity or objective in the SIP; very limited patron and community efforts other than Web site communications.
Who? / When?	SIP leadership team; May of each year	Principal holds key; annually in May	Principal; annually in May	Adviser coordinates, facilitates review; as needed	No other process to act on patron concerns		✓		Administrative function; some cooperation with teacher representatives; rare to collaborate or insist on action to follow. All data examined at end of year with numerous competing priorities.
How?	Team reviews results, discusses outcomes	Presentation at faculty meeting; Q & A is given to clarify and explain status quo; rare to make changes	Written report distributed	Council > adviser > administration	N/A—no process exists outside of efforts to secure votes	✓			Action is generally discussion or completion of a report. Wide variability in terms of structure that connects results to action. Format for action often misses key opportunities.

P = proposed   I = introduced   E = established

Summary of satisfaction listening system:

Satisfaction is the most established listening format for Milford, with routine inclusion in school improvement plans (SIPs) for parents and teachers; student feedback is obscured through organizational layers, little evidence exists for a predictable and viable cycle, and action is taken on the basis of satisfaction data randomly at best.

EXHIBIT **8.5** | **Sample Listening Data, Milford School District** (continued)

School _____   Principal _____   Date _____   E-mail _____

Focus Groups, Interviews	Parents	Teachers and Administrators	Staff	Students	Patrons	P	I	E	Rationale: Current Practice
What do we do currently with the data?	No data	Faculty meeting minutes; no process to gather open-ended data from faculty	No data	Topic-driven focus groups (e.g., dress code, open campus)	Superintendent conducts quarterly town meetings		✓		Few elements in place; need to make sure current data are analyzed and responded to.
Authority to act (commit resources)?	N/A	Not defined	N/A	Not defined	Superintendent has authority, limited by policy	✓			Ambiguous format for taking action; totally situational.
Who? / When?	N/A	No systemic process in place; as needed	N/A	Principal directs actions	Superintendent responds to situations	✓			Little assurance action will follow input.
How?	N/A	Principal assesses need and responds	N/A	Direct, delegate, or consensus	Varied responses to concerns	✓			Administrative prerogative.

P = proposed   I = introduced   E = established

EXHIBIT **8.5** | **Sample Listening Data, Milford School District** (continued)

School _____   Principal _____   Date _____   E-mail _____

Web Site	Parents	Teachers and Administrators	Staff	Students	Patrons	P	I	E	Rationale: Current Practice
What do we do currently with the data?	Complaint review by leadership team; acts on select complaints	Teachers and administrators have individual Web sites to communicate	Discretion to create and respond to Web site	Same chance to respond as parents with school officials	Same chance to respond as parents with school officials	✓			Plan to respond to complaint/concern next year based on technology.
Authority to act (commit resources)?	Leadership team grants authority to act if complaint is viewed as having merit	All have authority to respond to concerns or suggestions within job description or sphere of influence	Staff are expected to respond to all concerns	No format for response to students	No format for response to patrons, except phone policy of 48 hours	✓			No standards in place at current time; action taken varies by admin discretion; reactive.
Who? / When?	Administrators, department chairs, counselors; no response standard	Response based on concern raised and time constraints; no response standard	Staff respond as if phone policy—48 hours	No requirement or time frame standard exists	No requirement or time frame standard exists	✓			No systematic connection from process for input to action taken.
How?	Principal assigns responsibility	Collaboration, modify instruction, materials, time, and opportunity	E-mail, involve others	N/A	N/A	✓			Wide discretion to administrators; no standard for action.

P = proposed   I = introduced   E = established

Summary of focus group/interview and Web site listening system:
Focus groups and Web site listening systems are neither systematic nor reliable; response standards nonexistent; need for standards, processes, accountability. Systems fail to adhere to guidelines, even though capacity exists for transparency and user-friendly technology is available.

Guidelines for Listening Systems: **Cyclical   Predictable   Public (open, transparent)   User Friendly**

Common Core State Standards and the Environmental Scan

One of the most perplexing challenges to states as they submitted applications for the Race to the Top Initiative was the lack of comprehensive data systems around assessments and standards, turnaround efforts, and teacher and leader characteristics in practice. No Child Left Behind compliance data were much more accessible (e.g., system of rewards and sanctions, formal content standards, definition of high-quality teaching) than the granular school-level data about effectiveness or evidence of efforts to respond to close achievement gaps or turn around schools (Goe, Bell, & Little, 2008). Had more states, districts, or schools gathered data about their practices through effective environmental scans, the challenge to meet today's rigorous expectations would have been reduced. The rearview-mirror effect continues to challenge the education community, and it is time to stop separating measures of learning from measures of teaching, and even from leadership strategies that impact policy, resource allocation, and change management. All of these factors contribute to the complex process of education, and the profession is long overdue to get beyond the numbers and institutionalize processes that gather data about our craft that are readily available and critical to more effective analysis. The Common Core State Standards provide a bridge to expand the data set and inquiry used to analyze student achievement with antecedent measures of professional practice. Here are some examples.

Specification of content is a defining element of the Common Core standards as they have been deliberately crafted to create a framework for progressively more rigorous content and common attributes of proficiency that cross content areas. The opportunity to "cross-walk" these outcomes for students with professional practices of teachers is best illustrated by the Common Core itself (Common Core State Standards Initiative, 2010d, appendix A, p. 4):

> With the Common Core State Standards Initiative comes an unprecedented ability for schools, districts, and states to collaborate. While this is certainly the case with respect to assessments and professional development programs, it is also true for strategies to support struggling and accelerated students. The Model Course Pathways in Mathematics are intended to launch the conversation, and give encouragement to all educators to collaborate for the benefit of our states' children.

Strategies, professional development, assessments, and other antecedent conditions and actions taken need to be examined in light of common outcomes across content. For example, three factors of task complexity are described in Standard 10 of the Common Core: qualitative evaluation of the text, quantitative evaluation of the text, and matching the reader to the text and to the task (Common Core State Standards Initiative, 2010a, p. 31). Each element is as relevant to instructional design for diesel mechanics as it is for English literature as it is for constitutional history or biology. In terms of an environmental scan, leaders who promote measures of quality implementation (e.g., text complexity) in all content areas will have data about teaching practices (antecedents) that allow them to astutely triangulate data for patterns and trends and to scale up the most effective practices as part of a cohesive school improvement plan. This example illustrates how pregnant the Common Core standards are in terms of advancing better data analysis that yields the kinds of insights necessary to increase capacity among staff to design truly engaging, powerful interventions that close achievement gaps. The standard for text complexity will guide educators to conduct quality environmental scans regarding instructional planning (were teaching strategies effective in terms of text complexity?), whether students were matched to the task and text selected (listening and feedback systems), and what indicators of quality were evident in the text selection. By examining our practices against the Common Core, teacher teams will more effectively select strategies they will use and more precisely be able to identify why the strategy was selected. Applying the Common Core and examining school practices through the lens of an environmental scan will help practitioners identify replicable best practices and extend a rigorous approach to standards to ensure a consistent and high-quality delivery of instruction. Without the framework an environmental scan provides, much of the context of learning will be lost, and schools will continue to try to slice and dice achievement data to a smaller grain size without taking advantage of the rich data set available around the context of learning to inform next steps and identify scalable, replicable practices.

Summary

Apple Blossom USD was ambitious, proud, and committed to excellence. The district was also shortsighted and failed to assess the weather of educational change coming its way. An environmental scan is designed to lessen risk of that eventuality. It scans the horizon for insights, examining the internal workings of a classroom, school, or district in terms of external changes and internal initiatives. It examines these influences through seven components of every organization, and it drills deeper by using the well-known KWL process to determine what is known and what is needed programmatically, instructionally, and organizationally. The environmental scan example provided in Exhibit 8.2 describes how quality data gathering can help improve the school for all stakeholders and especially improve student achievement. The template helps ensure that the user can launch a broad yet focused effort to improve.

We highlight the need to keep things simple and to periodically examine those practices we are most fond of to determine whether an approach can be abandoned or subtracted. Systems analysis is introduced as a construct to reveal interdependence and to discover unintended consequences. Like listening systems, systems analysis assists us in understanding our environment. We live in an age unique to all of human history in its accelerated pace of change, and we need to understand our circumstances and use the full range of data available to make informed, wise decisions and choices. Chapter 9 examines the challenge of replicating best practices.

Reflection

BIG IDEA: Environmental scanning identifies current needs and anticipates future challenges.

What does the reading strategy KWL have to do with analysis of data?

BIG IDEA: The most effective environmental scans examine organizations on the basis of finance, personnel, special education, textbooks, and logistics.   T   F

Explain why you responded as you did:

Shouldn't we just focus on internal changes in our own organization? Why or why not?

BIG IDEA: A differentiated listening system ensures thorough feedback from all stakeholders.

Describe the key elements in your own words regarding a listening system. What changes do you envision making in your work environment this year?

Replication: Sharing the Wealth

Just do it.

—NIKE

The Nike slogan immediately resonates; it speaks of making the most of our opportunities, and it applies to replication. Teachers and teaching are treasure chests of innovation and inspiration, and we need a means to capture, expand, and apply those practices that work best to as many settings and to reach as many students as possible. Replicating good ideas should be the reason we analyze data in the first place, to extend what works as quickly and efficiently as possible. Replication and subtraction are evidence of a dynamic and effective data management system. If schools fail to replicate best practices or to eliminate practices that are ineffective, where is the improvement?

Foundation for Replication

Ample evidence is provided in the literature and blueprints abound about how to implement and sustain program replications. Very few educational programs are formally adopted or replicated without application of a rigorous validation process, and 24 Comprehensive School Reform Program models have been identified as "research based" innovations, including familiar programs such as Core Knowledge, Direct Instruction, Success for All, Accelerated Schools, Onward to Excellence, High Schools That Work, and the School Development Program (National Clearinghouse for Comprehensive School Reform, 2004). A rigorous evaluation process for professional development insists on the capacity to generalize to new settings (Shaha, et al., 2004). Commercial publishers of textbooks and educational materials, including McGraw-Hill; Addison-Wesley; Silver-Burdett; Sage; and Holt, Rinehart, & Winston, subject themselves to rigorous validation methods.

Successful programs such as those classified as research based by the Comprehensive School Reform Program, part of the No Child Left Behind Act, have a number of characteristics in common. By statute, they must employ the following (No Child Left Behind Act,

2002; American Recovery and Reinvestment Act, 2009):

- A systematic approach to school-wide improvement that incorporates every aspect of a school—from curriculum and instruction to school management
- A program and process designed to enable all students to meet challenging academic content and performance goals
- A framework for using research to move from multiple, fragmented educational programs to a unified plan with a single focus: academic achievement
- A product of the long-term, collaborative efforts of school staff, parents, and district staff

These characteristics are valuable guidelines for replication. They require an effective data system that monitors growth and addresses all the key factors and elements of a school setting, examining the role and function of instructional strategies and other antecedents to design a program to meet challenging academic and performance goals. As described in Chapter 1, the Race to the Top Initiative explicitly requires evidence of a state's capacity to scale up or replicate the most effective practices.

McDonald and Schneider (2007) found that scaling up remains problematic within K–12 education, in part because the "gold standard" of randomized clinical trials is difficult to conduct in the education setting; education and child development are generally complex issues in their own right; and high stakes are associated with educational innovations, which require very rigorous scientific methodology. Lucy Steiner (2000) conducted a meta-analysis of replication in education and identified six elements of successful "scale-up" or replication efforts: program design; buy-in at the school level; support factors, including resources and freedom from restrictive regulations; leadership; quality assurance; and conscious effort to build constituencies that support necessary changes. These elements describe how effective replications warrant understanding of antecedents; collaborative analysis, including the insights gleaned from triangulation; and a clearly delineated accountability structure whereby individuals are held responsible for specific actions at specific times for specific purposes. Educators should be leaders in replicating best practices and taking advantage of the rich incubators of innovation we call schools, but the evidence suggests otherwise.

The "knowing-doing gap" (Reeves, 2004b) is a problem everyone in education can recognize. Graham and colleagues (2003) describe how only 42 percent of teachers, when presented compelling evidence about the power of nonfiction writing with editing and revision to improve achievement in all areas, made any adaptations at all for poor writers. Only 10 percent utilized the strategies of mini-lessons, tutoring, and revised instruction that were presented as the antecedents that lead to improved achievement. As a profession, educators struggle with applying the lessons from the research that shout at us about leveraging numerous antecedents of excellence.

Steiner (2005) refers to replication as "scaling up" in a review that recognizes the problem is not unique to education. Unfortunately, according to Steiner, the problem of replicating good ideas is particularly severe within public education. Several reasons are given to explain this phenomenon. One is the need for large groups of educators to "unlearn" the assumptions that underlie current work, work designed for a different era, when data was a necessary inconvenience, not a central component to reform and school improvement. Linda Darling-Hammond (1997, pp. 199–204) describes schools as bureaucratic structures that have changed very little in the past century. Reeves (2004b) argues that the knowing-doing gap is not the result of indifference, indolence, or a lack of knowledge or even a lack of will. The problem is, we are looking in the wrong place for answers to replication. Replication that is agile enough to help students when they need it is personal. Surowiecki (2004) tells the story about farmers who were convinced a new seed would increase yields dramatically but did nothing to change their planting regimen. Even when their neighbors had success with the new seed, most farmers would only test the seed in a small part of one field. Not until each farmer experienced personal success did anything closely approximating a program adoption take place. The analogy to our classrooms is striking: teachers must first see the benefit that replicating the practice will accrue to their classroom and to their students.

Data analysis is the parent of action research and replication. One reason best practices in schools have not been replicated sufficiently is because few vehicles were available to validate successful programs and because the antecedents for success were, and still are, rarely monitored to produce evidence that warrants replication. This chapter attempts to ensure that replication of best practices becomes the norm for successful practices rather than the exception it has been for so long. We begin by comparing two actual schools of comparable demographics within the same school system, using more than a decade's worth of data depicted in discrepancy charts.

A discrepancy chart establishes a standard of performance and depicts actual performance along a horizontal line. Performances exceeding the standard are represented by bar graph or data points above the line, and those not achieving the standard are represented by data points or bars below the line. Discrepancy charts also depict success in achieving zero tolerance, as in achieving zero expulsions or zero gun incidents at school, or percentage of expenditures against budgets. In this case, we will be comparing actual student performance against predicted performance. Exhibits 9.1 and 9.2 illustrate the difference between achievement test scores for two elementary schools and the predicted score for each. In these data, a value of zero means that the actual score was the same as the predicted score. A positive value means that on average the students in that school scored higher than predicted. Achievement test scores were predicted from cognitive ability and socioeconomic status. The amounts above or below those predicted are expressed in standard deviations, providing actual trend data and school performance against expected performance.

EXHIBIT **9.1** | **Hypothetical Sixth-Grade Text Complexity and Language Conventions, SCHOOL A**

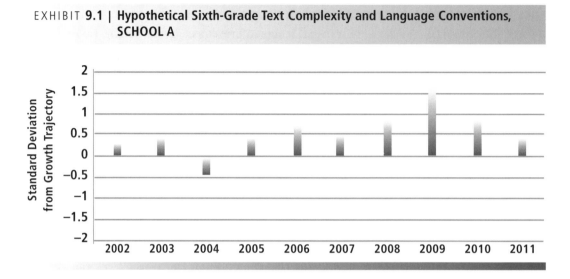

By 2010, students in school A were outperforming their demographics by almost 1.7 standard deviations. Now consider the data for the same time period for school B.

EXHIBIT **9.2** | **Hypothetical Sixth-Grade Text Complexity and Language Conventions, SCHOOL B**

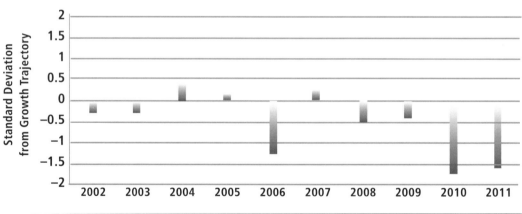

Because both schools have similar demographics in their student body, and because both schools are part of the same school system and enjoy the same resources, reasonable people should agree that school B needs some help, and school A's students have outperformed their demographic counterparts at school B in 9 of 10 years. The real question, however, is, when was the most opportune time to begin looking for replicable practices? In 2004, school B looked like the successful school, at least in terms of gains in text complexity and language conventions. In 2005, differences were negligible, and 2006 was the first year school B showed a serious decline. It would have been easy, in small increments, to explain the differences between these schools and to miss the opportunity to learn from the distinctions that warrant a second look. On the other hand, waiting several years, attuned professionals attentive to the data may have called for a closer look and found those antecedents at school A that could help school B. We need to ask ourselves in this era of standards and accountability whether we have several years to wait. Replication in teaching will not happen by adopting a new program that was proven effective elsewhere, especially when other "proven" practices are not subtracted from a very full plate first. Some educators who are quick to call for pilot programs to scrutinize an innovation for statistically significant differences are perfectly content with the status quo, even though current practice has no more validity or evidence of effectiveness, and sometimes has less. Others are willing to require a supermajority of faculty buy-in before replicating an instructional strategy in the name of collaboration. Unfortunately, neither approach serves improved student achievement well. We need to find ways for practices that are true antecedents of excellence to be replicated in earnest, take stock of lessons learned, and make adjustments to improve student achievement. We need a recipe for replication.

Recipe for Replication

Replication is personal, even when the data seem to indicate otherwise. Recipes, for example, are rapidly disseminated ideas when they are replicated, but they are only replicated when a proficient cook sees and experiences the benefit of that recipe—when he takes a personal interest and recognizes personal value in its ingredients. It is not enough for someone to enjoy the recipe; those who both understand and enjoy the benefits will replicate it. Stephen Covey (1996, p. 60) describes a process he refers to as "third person learning." Using the example of a favorite casserole recipe, the first person shares knowledge of the recipe with a second person by demonstrating the steps of the recipe and its pacing. The second person teaches the new knowledge to a third person, having captured the basic content or ideas and then expanding his understanding by adding the benefit of experience and knowledge, which is applied by sharing examples or modeling the proper demonstration of the recipe and offering corrective feedback as needed. The third person receives added-value knowledge. In other words, recipes are replicated because cooks experience the benefits of a best practice firsthand. Thus, recipes serve as a useful illustration for how to replicate practices at the classroom level. Exhibit 9.3 reminds us of the salient features of "recipe" replication.

It is a fair question for busy professionals to ask how replicating any practice will benefit them, or more accurately, benefit their students. Teachers have every reason to be skeptical; far too many "silver bullets" have been promised in the form of questioning strategies, lesson openings, and summarizing strategies. On the other hand, busy education professionals must understand that teaching and learning are interdependent in the same way that they are collaborative. Interdependence requires a collective responsibility for results, a common accountability for the learning and achievement of every student we have the privilege to serve.

EXHIBIT **9.3 | Informal "Recipe" Replication**

• Benefit is obvious to person(s) planning to replicate.

• Replication is user friendly.

• Replication occurs informally through "third person learning."

• Replication rarely takes hold just from external success stories, research reports, or other data.

• Replication is more likely to take hold if the practice is successfully implemented internally.

• Replication is most likely to take hold if the teacher experiences the benefit of the strategy or innovation.

Remember Mary Ann and Georgia at Maple High School, profiled in Chapter 4? Mary Ann was talented and dedicated but assumed no responsibility for the growth of her peers. Reflect on the previous discussion about Data Teams, where mini-lessons, reflection, and essential questions were put into action. Their closeness to the classroom allowed Data Teams to impact instruction directly with instructional strategies or novel transitions, as long as its activities did not involve changing practices Mary Ann had grown accustomed to. Georgia, on the other hand, needed help and was open to collaboration.

Charlotte Danielson's *Enhancing Professional Practice: A Framework for Teaching* (2007) is a highly regarded and frequently replicated approach to supervising and evaluating teachers. Her four-point rubric characterizes proficient teachers as having relationships with colleagues whereby they support and cooperate with one another. A distinguished designation would include taking a leadership role among colleagues. On this continuum, Mary Ann would be at least proficient and possibly distinguished. However, Georgia needed more from Mary Ann than the opportunity to observe her class, and professionalism should compel us to recognize that our best work only gets better when collaboration is allowed to generate the collective wisdom needed in the complex business of teaching and learning. Exhibit 9.4 offers a number of suggestions.

Early replication signals are the other side of the coin to "canaries in the coal mine." Many times, I hear the statement, "We just implemented that program. Give it time to succeed." How much time? If programs are not seeing progress almost immediately, only three explanations for that lack of progress are possible: (1) teacher training requires more time for the teacher to demonstrate the desired level of proficiency; (2) clarification is needed to make sure the program is implemented with consistency across teachers and settings; or (3) local contextual characteristics are at play that inhibit its success, including student readiness, alignment with other work habits, and alignment with local curriculum expectations. Otherwise, the practice being replicated should demonstrate improvements almost immediately. Because improvement in student achievement on the end-of-course (EOC) or state-level assessment will not be evident, how can improvements occur immediately? "Have you lost your mind?" the reader may be thinking. No, I haven't, and yes, improvements can and should be evident from day one. The indicators that should accompany a process worthy of replication are student (or teacher)

EXHIBIT **9.4** | **Strategies to Promote Replication**

	External (between schools, across districts)	Internal (within schools, departments, grades)
School and District	• Disseminate results of Data Team minutes to like colleagues at other schools via Web sites, e-mail; omit student names and other confidential data. • Quarterly disseminate/present school data charts/graphs of ideas borrowed, ideas given away, and results to other schools. • Develop a Q&A communiqué that invites ideas, strategies, structures to address real student and teacher needs in real time; rotate responsibility for developing answers from school to school. • Establish an electronic "We Made a Difference" data wall. • Define a preponderance of evidence to initiate external, school-to-school or district-wide replication.	• Establish a "We Made a Difference" data wall (electronic and physical) that monitors the number and type of interventions that have been implemented with accompanying results. • Have principal establish expectation to receive weekly reports of "ideas I borrowed, ideas I gave away, and results from ideas." • Add a column to "We Made a Difference" data wall labeled "Learning Opportunities" where results were less than immediate. • Create standing agenda items for meetings: what works well for whom, why, and how do you know? • Define a preponderance of evidence to initiate internal replication.
Classroom	• Identify students whose behavior or performance has turned around: verify with data. • Value observation data as much as possible. • Disseminate classroom practices that save time (Q&A or "We Made a Difference" data wall). • Disseminate classroom practices that students would like repeated (Q&A or "We Made a Difference" data wall). • Disseminate classroom practices that increased collaboration (Q&A or "We Made a Difference" data wall).	• Create and institutionalize "What's Working" meetings with recorders and group responsibility (verify preponderance of evidence, what works well for whom, and why). • Have all teachers submit to principal a list of "ideas I borrowed this week, ideas I gave away each week." • Monitor early replication signals: evidence of changes, enthusiasm, indicators, students outperforming their demographics. • Identify classroom practices that: – save time – students would like repeated – increase collaboration

enthusiasm, high levels of engagement, understanding of what is expected, participation, improvement ideas from students, increased time on task, fun, and all of the indicators of effectiveness teachers keep in their heads every day. The expectations listed in Exhibit 9.4 will require data collection and monitoring of antecedent teacher and student behaviors. If additional record keeping is required to monitor teacher and student antecedents (e.g., what students would like repeated), it is recommended that a structure be included for students in the listening system. The data about saving time and ideas borrowed and given away lend themselves to a listening system. In this way, teachers and teacher teams can structure any data collection in a deliberate, user-friendly, and achievable fashion, complete with time for reflection and for action. The principle of subtraction is critical at this point, but my observation has been that teachers, given the opportunity to improve a process or structure, are more than capable to find ways that save time, assuming they are also given the permission to subtract and become accountable. Exhibit 9.5 identifies eight structural questions to build a foundation for replication.

EXHIBIT **9.5 | Establishing a Foundation for Replication**

1. How would you identify homegrown successes?
2. What is needed in a data system to ensure that such successes are (a) defined, (b) recognized, and (c) validated for replication?
3. What is reasonable to consider as a preponderance of evidence and best practices?
4. Define preponderance of evidence.
5. Define internally a best practice.
6. What are some high-performing schools' practices we want to replicate?
7. What steps are necessary before a decision is made to replicate a practice?
8. Should replicable practices be tested through action research? When? Why?

The lessons of recipe replication are that it is personal and that smart people need to see the benefit. It would behoove those committed to serious reform efforts and breakthrough improvements to structure any effort to replicate around the personal nature of replication.

Where Should We Start?

Strategies to promote replication will generate ideas as varied as students, as varied as the experience and background of teachers, and varied even more because of the context and history of the work habits at each school. The ideas may become as universal as writing every day in every subject and have enormous impact on education for years. The ideas also may become "learning opportunities" that will not be repeated but will inform faculty of a path to avoid in the future. In Exhibit 9.6, 25 such antecedents that have great potential to improve student achievement are listed.

Quick, Get the Camera!

The third-person learning process described earlier offers three basic steps for replication: capture, expand, and apply. As when using a digital camera, first we need to develop a work habit to capture evidence of success—even incremental, qualitative evidence like a smile or a raised hand or on-time attendance for the high school junior who lets everyone in class know every day that she does not like being there. Second, just as digital cameras are, first and fore-

EXHIBIT **9.6** | **Antecedents of Excellence: Replicable Practices Right Now**

Structures, Conditions, and Teacher Behaviors Worth Replicating	Categories of Effective Teaching Strategies
1. More writing, thinking, analysis, and reading, every content area[1]	12. Summarizing and note-taking[8]
2. Collaborative scoring of student work[1]	13. Reinforcing effort and providing recognition[8]
3. Flexible schedules and greater investment of time in basic sources; these are associated with lower failure rates[1]	14. Homework and practice[8]
	15. Nonlinguistic representations[8]
	16. Cooperative learning[8]
4. More frequent feedback, which is associated with improved student work ethic, motivation, and performance[1]	17. Setting objectives and providing feedback[8]
	18. Generating and testing hypotheses[8]
5. Collaboration structures for analysis of data[2]	19. Questions, cues, and advance organizers to increase student cognition and engagement[8]
6. Creation of Data Teams; they increase the presence of effective teaching strategies and increase student achievement[3]	20. Differentiation of instruction[9]
	21. Challenging goals in novel areas[10]
7. Discussion, review, and focus on actual student work; these actions close the learning gap for all cohort groups[4]	22. Feedback about correct responses rather than errors[10]
	23. Evaluating results from graphs[10]
8. Learning logs to collaboratively monitor student progress[5]	24. Explicit monitoring of implementation fidelity[10]
9. Mandatory department teams with responsibility and authority for selecting effective strategies and for development and evaluation of EOCs[6]	25. Spaced practice opportunities rather than immediate mass practice[10]
10. Relentless focus on student achievement; protection of time, and deep professional development[7]	
11. Identification of similarities and differences[8]	

Sources:

[1]Reeves (2000, p. 55).

[2]Surowiecki (2004, p. 39).

[3]Leadership and Learning Center (2010).

[4]See Schlechty (2000, pp. 134–139); Heacox (2002, pp. 27–41); Reeves (2002a, pp. 201–207); Singham (2003).

[5]Schmoker (2001, pp. 13–15).

[6]DuFour, DuFour, and Eaker (2008, pp. 326–327).

[7]National Staff Development Council (2001).

[8]See Marzano, Pickering, and Pollock (2001a, pp. 6–10); Schlechty (2000, pp. 147–153); Reeves (2002a, pp. 201–207); Fredricks, Blumenfeld, and Paris (2004, pp. 59–109); Intrator, S. (2004). The engaged classroom. *Educational Leadership*, September, pp. 20–26.

[9]Heacox (2002, pp. 91–111).

[10]Hattie (2009, pp. 162–227).

most, so easy to use that major film companies are abandoning photographs completely in recognition that the future is digital, data need to be user friendly to reduce its costs. Many benefits can be derived from a robust data system, but as with the Timberline Middle School and Colson Intermediate School District examples, robust data that take too much time to analyze and act on compromise their value. Catching them (both students and teachers) doing something good is a great idea; recording the good they do is better.

Action Research

Action research is simply a proactive hunt for a better way. After analyzing data for patterns, teachers develop hunches about relationships between instructional strategies, antecedent conditions such as materials or programs, and student achievement. Sadly, many of these hunches become either folklore or are lost altogether to the profession simply because we fail to act on them. Witness the story of Flora Flagg, who single-handedly gave the profession a simple and effective tool to engage students in thinking and reasoning every day, in every classroom (personal correspondence with Flora Flagg, November 13, 2004). Ms. Flagg is the Milwaukee principal who introduced the notion of gathering writing samples from each teacher and scoring them herself weekly. The school became a 90/90/90 school, but had this pioneer failed to engage in a form of action research, a relative handful of students would have benefited rather than millions who did.

EXHIBIT **9.7 | Steps of Action Research**

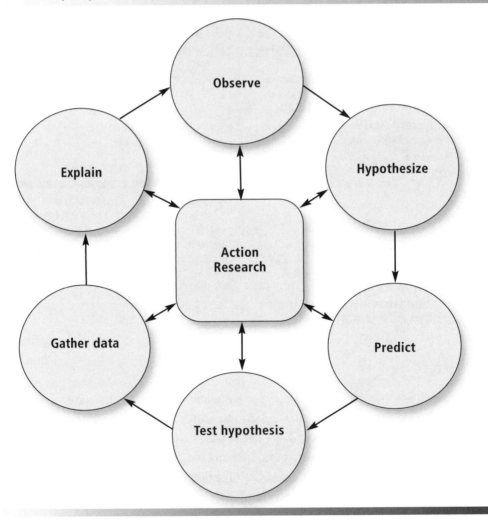

Emily Calhoun (2002) recommends three levels of action research that continue to advocate for action and replication: teacher as individual researcher, collaborative action research, and school-wide action research (our discussion focuses primarily on her first two levels, places where action research is relatively easy to implement). Calhoun (2002, p. 2) defines action research in five steps: (1) select an area to research, (2) collect data, (3) organize data, (4) analyze and interpret data, and (5) take action. The process offered in Exhibit 9.7, a variation on the Calhoun approach to action research, has six steps: (1) observe, (2) hypothesize, (3) predict, (4) test hypothesis, (5) gather data, and (6) explain.

Action research is the kind of analysis warranted when a desire is evident to replicate externally. It is the process of verifying results achieved using the same problems and variables but with variations in terms of whom, when, and where. A general rule of thumb for action research is the following:

Use action research when patterns from the data suggest that a new situation is emerging that needs to be verified, clarified, or discovered.

Action research should not be so rigid that it cannot adjust midcourse if the change is expected to improve student achievement. For instance, if students in the treatment group are experiencing dramatic improvement in their ability to achieve rigorous standards and students in the control group are not, it is advisable to make a midcourse adjustment and include both groups in the treatment. But won't that invalidate the research? Yes, but no more than ceasing to administer placebos to advanced-state cancer patients midstream when the treatment is proving successful for the treatment group. Action research needs to be about action, and while allowing a study to play out for the entire, planned term is preferred, occasions may arise when, as with the cancer patients, we take action on behalf of student achievement.

Replication and Common Core State Standards

The Common Core is designed to provide a clear understanding of student progress from kindergarten through postsecondary levels by a series of explicit, high-quality expectations that represent a deep understanding and application of English language arts and mathematics and their application across a wide range of academic content areas. Because the Common Core delineates text complexity demand standards K–12—writing standards for argument, informational, and narrative writing; discrete mathematical practices; and clearly articulated standards for listening and speaking—it is designed to support frequent action research efforts that advance replication. This section describes how dedicated teachers and a willing principal applied the experience of school A to implement specific Common Core standards through five suggestions to facilitate quality replication.

Respond to Data Patterns

After attending a seminar on writing excellence and the Common Core State Standards, two intermediate teachers agreed to focus on nonfiction writing text complexity, with consistent and challenging editing and revision processes such as explicit corrective feedback for writing conventions and posting of writing standards in both classrooms. When their peers noted how engaged students were; how students from their classrooms were self-editing written work in other classes; and how the quality of written work was neater, more apt to be complete, and more consistent, they asked for assistance in replicating the outcomes. Their first suggestion was to respond to data patterns with action research when those patterns suggest that a new occurrence is taking place that needs to be verified, clarified, or discovered.

Within the first year, four of the nine intermediate teachers had joined the two "pioneers," and achievement for their students was showing less variability and higher performance on EOC assessments; the district writing assessment; and, for those classes, on the state language arts assessment. Now these teachers had the principal's attention, and she wanted to replicate the process school-wide. Primary teachers were resistant, however, citing demands on their time and the need for students to learn to read rather than expect them to read to learn. The principal was convinced that the improved scores in text complexity contributed to the improved reading comprehension scores and vocabulary improvements for intermediate students.

She then brought the idea to conduct the study before the faculty, indicated the value of paying attention to the data, introduced external research that validated the writing emphasis, and stressed the need for progressively more challenging text complexity. The principal closed her presentation by asking for ways to study this strategy to verify whether it could help everyone in the school. Primary teachers took the lead to monitor cohorts of students with low and high reading performance on the state assessment. A third-grade teacher suggested they monitor whether introduction of this focus on nonfiction reading and writing was having a desirable impact on discipline referrals and tardies. Two intermediate classes were selected for the control group, one of which had a teacher volunteer interested in possible differences but with a very busy personal schedule the coming year due to preparing for her daughter's wedding and caring for her elderly father. This teacher volunteer knew she could continue doing a great job with her current duties but was not sure she could give the new approach the focus it might deserve. The second classroom selected was not as clean as a control group, because the volunteer teacher was scheduled to receive a student teacher in the second semester. Nonetheless, the entire faculty agreed that if the treatment group included teachers other than those who brought the innovation to the school, everyone could have confidence that the results were meaningful, especially if the differences were significant.

Determine the Number of Variables

The faculty completed a detailed Hishakawa fishbone chart to isolate those variables they believed would be most important to monitor and agreed to study the following independent variables or antecedents:

1) Daily nonfiction writing across core areas for the treatment group targeted at text complexity; nonfiction to be used only as one of several language arts genres with the control group, and no effort was to be made to institutionalize it across the core subjects.

2) Use of discrete editing and revision of writing assignments in all four core subjects with a minimal standard for conventions incorporating complete sentences and tiered word levels (Common Core State Standards Initiative, 2010b, p. 33) and use of writing assessments at least weekly.

The variables dependent on those antecedents were limited to (1) EOC assessments, because all students took the same assessments and every grade used them in all four core areas, and (2) the number of discipline referrals and tardies. The entire staff at school A realized that the study had some limitations and that other factors may influence the results, but with effective facilitation by the principal, every teacher supported the study and agreed to modify their work if the results warranted.

Keep It Short and Simple

The third suggestion for the school was to "keep it short and simple" (KISS). The KISS approach was well received, as the faculty recognized from the selection of variables how easily the study could become complicated. They decided to use pre/post measures on the dependent variable state assessment scores on text complexity and language conventions and to monitor changes in reading comprehension. Independent variables would be monitored for implementation according to a 10-point checklist developed by the school innovators, and all involved agreed that those implementing the changes needed access to them and to receive sufficient training from them prior to the start of the school year. Because this study involved only four teachers, the principal would also monitor progress with the same observation checklist and data would be tabulated and monitored monthly (see Exhibit 9.6, item 24). The behavior data were considered the easiest to gather, as the discipline incidents and tardies prior to the intervention were already in the school database. After some discussion, the faculty agreed to measure improvement on this variable rather than raw score or percentage of classroom referrals.

Select Analysis Tools

The principal recommended using two analysis tools to help depict progress, or lack thereof, throughout the year at faculty meetings; the team selected a 2×2 matrix and a scatter diagram to track the data. These tools would reveal three basic constructs behind statistical analysis: measure of central tendency (examination of means, modes, medians), measure of relationship, and analysis of differences (including analysis of variance). All nine intermediate teachers requested that the principal involve the district assessment coordinator by asking her to run the statistics at the end of the study and report back to the faculty. In this way, all involved were satisfied that the action research study was solid, balanced, and fair and that results would be both reliable and valid.

Select Proven Antecedents

The final suggestion was to select from those antecedents that have been proven to make a difference to date (e.g., Exhibit 9.6), especially with an initial study. The team selected the three-part model for measuring text complexity in the Common Core: qualitative, quantitative, and reader and task considerations to build capacity in writing and identify an emerging best practice at school. The result was a credible, in-house action research study where professional educators relied as much on their own professional judgment and common sense as on any formula for research. When the faculty agreed that the conditions for the study were solid, balanced, and fair, reliability and validity issues were already addressed. Reliability (confidence in multiple administrations of the program across classrooms, grades, and time periods) and validity (confidence that the measures selected accurately reflect desired changes) can be derived through simple statistical means, but reliability and validity for practitioners boils down to the level of confidence teachers have in the study or report. This scenario, using the Common Core State Standards, illustrates how committed teams of teachers need not wait to replicate practices they recognize as effective. The Common Core provides conceptual frameworks that lend themselves to credible action research and a geometric rise in replicable practices.

Summary

Replication may be the best indicator of a high-quality, effective system of data analysis. It represents efforts by educators to multiply what works and epitomizes continuous improvement. It is intensely personal and will seldom occur at the classroom level in earnest if teachers do not experience the benefit of adopting the practice firsthand. Replication has traditionally been associated with large-scale change efforts, programmatic changes, and even professional development models. It needs to become much more pervasive and much more automatic to build the capacity we need to respond to student needs, and several suggestions are provided in the chapter to facilitate a functional and dynamic system for replication. "What's Working?" meetings and "We Made a Difference" data walls can go a long way toward facilitating those work habits that result in everyday replication that is as common as sharing a favorite recipe. Appendix A provides a scoring guide to monitor and measure one's familiarity and application with replication and action research (see section 6 of the appendix).

Reflection

BIG IDEA: Replication is simply making sure what works well for a few students is available to as many students as possible.

What elements need to be defined to establish a foundation for replication?

BIG IDEA: Replication is like a recipe: personal, immediate, and social.

Why do educators have such a difficult time replicating best practices? What strategies are needed to make replication a central component of your data analysis system?

Discuss with a colleague the relative advantages of replicating "proven" practices as opposed to a great idea that emerges at your school. (Hint: there is no right answer.)

CHAPTER 10

The Teacher as Expert

Our remedies oft in ourselves do lie.
—WILLIAM SHAKESPEARE (1564–1616)

CASE STUDY

"In general, less variance in a range trading in the higher score possibilities produces the highest F score. Multiple regression, on the other hand, studies the magnitude of the effects of multiple independent variables on one dependent variable using principles of correlation and regression. Analysis of variance, abbreviated as ANOVA, looks for deviations from the mean, while regression analysis looks for relationship. Both examine the interaction of the variables, and respective contributions to the treatment variable(s)." The instructor, Dr. Corwin, noticed two students in the back of the classroom who were not paying attention.

Todd and Liz were attending the seminar to increase their expertise in data analysis. Liz had always been interested in data, evidenced by the faculty's reliance on her to create all the charts and graphs the past two years. Todd taught math at the middle school, and colleagues brought data problems to him, expecting his math background to carry the day with data.

"Does content validity measure the subject content that's intended, as long as it is corroborated by face validity and sampling integrity?" Liz whispered. "I think construct validity is similar, but it is the degree to which a test measures a trait like honesty or intelligence that can't be measured precisely as opposed to subject content or areas of knowledge. Todd, is that right?"

"I think so. Try this one. I'm constructing my final exam with 10 multiple-choice items per standard, and since we are addressing all six math standards, I'll need 60 items plus a written component where students describe how to solve a problem in algebra, geometry, and measurement. I'm thinking about splitting the 10 questions between best answer from alternatives and questions requiring a one-correct-answer response. What do you think?"

Dr. Corwin interrupted their conversation at this point and caught Liz by surprise with a question: "Liz, assume you are designing a research project. Describe the threat a pre-test poses to external validity."

"If students respond differently to the treatment as a result of pre-test learning, external validity can be compromised, I think."

"All right," Dr. Corwin replied, albeit slightly disappointed. He continued with the lecture. "Is there a volunteer who can describe the four characteristics of normal distributions?" Both Todd and Liz began to page through their notes, relieved.

Returning to teaching in August, these teachers were certainly better equipped to understand educational research, testing, and basic data analysis. Unfortunately, they had forgotten as much as they remembered from their summer data analysis class. The content seemed to have little relevance to the challenges they faced, with all the expectations for results. They appreciated having a greater capacity to read the results of the district norm-referenced test, but they were hardly experts in data analysis.

Few teachers enter the profession to become either famous or wealthy, and my own observations have been of a profession that is so self-effacing that it fails to recognize the complexity of its craft or the skill and expertise teachers demonstrate every day. After all, the need for and expectation to make decisions based on data is a relatively new phenomenon in education, one that current accountability systems have elevated in importance. Data continues to be associated more with Statistics 101 than practical management of teaching practices to improve student achievement. Data analysis continues to conjure up thoughts of root canals or fingernails on a chalkboard. Educators, from the boardroom to the classroom, are reluctant to view themselves as experts, deferring instead to "number crunchers" and policy wonks who deal with large data sets and macro-trends. It is time to celebrate the fact that educators in the field are the best equipped to make decisions about curriculum content, assessment design, and instructional delivery, especially when collaborative processes provide the benefit of multiple viewpoints and interpretations. It is time to celebrate the teacher as expert in data analysis, and this book is an initial effort to assist educators in finding out what they already know about the data of teaching and learning.

David Berliner has been a staunch defender of the U.S. system of public education, and an even stronger advocate of its teachers. Berliner (1994) studied expertise across professions and identifies three ways in which experts differ from novices: experts bring knowledge to bear more effectively on problems than do novices, experts solve problems more efficiently and accomplish more in less time than do novices, and experts are more likely to arrive at novel and appropriate solutions to problems than are novices. Knowledge, efficiency, and insight are the primary features that distinguish the expert teacher from the novice.

The purpose of this book is to provide practitioners the skill and understanding to make insightful decisions based on the data available to them. While districts and schools across the United States have multiple measures of student achievement, few monitor the antecedent data that contribute to that achievement. Those who understand the pitfalls of traditional data analysis like the rearview-mirror effect, the challenge of having too much data, and the need for subtraction are much more likely to be empowered to apply their talents and contextual understanding, as experts, to avoid the experiences depicted by the scenarios highlighted throughout the book.

In Chapter 2, we found that data analysis must be as deliberate as lesson planning, that data collection, analysis, reflection, and a continuous improvement cycle are critical to the capacity to make sound decisions about data. A data calendar was introduced as a structure to ensure that teams of educators take time to examine data, "unwrap" assessments to align purpose to standards, and ensure that emphasis for each assessment is well placed and measured. A proven improvement cycle for data analysis offered insights into the need for discrete and focused processes that probe to determine when to intervene, adjust, and generally make midcourse corrections with data.

Chapter 3 introduced the concept of antecedents of excellence: those behaviors, strategies, structures, and learning conditions that can be correlated with improved student achievement. The Leadership and Learning (L^2) Matrix, developed by Dr. Douglas Reeves, was included to reveal the power in leveraging antecedents to produce improved student achievement as well as the vulnerability of educators who fail to apply antecedents deliberately and strategically. A checklist for a standards-based classroom was analyzed to illustrate the distinctions between antecedents, and key questions added value for those faced with decisions about how to allocate resources. Finally, a Hishakawa fishbone chart was modified with guidelines to help identify those causes and antecedents that produce positive results and those that lead to consequences we wish to eliminate or reduce. Educators empowered by an understanding of antecedents, infused with the ability to select strategically from a robust antecedent repertoire, and afforded the knowledge to determine the relationship between cause and effect—characteristics of experts in other professions—can more effectively overcome problems than those who lack such skills and abilities.

Antecedent structures that capitalize on the power of collaboration were described in Chapter 4, with methods provided to develop team thinking and candor. Nine explicit methods were recommended to integrate collaboration into decision making. Collaboration helps educators like Liz and Todd solve problems more efficiently, accomplish more in less time, and arrive at novel and appropriate solutions to problems as experts.

Accountability was reviewed in Chapter 5 to underscore how responsibility for results must also be accompanied by the authority to take action and commit resources and a comparable authority to eliminate practices and obstacles to improvement. Ten actions of accountability, common barriers to them, and remedies to equip educators to become accountable were delineated. Educators who solve problems efficiently reflect the ability of experts, and Chapter 5 offered several concrete strategies and structures for that purpose.

Chapter 6 described the need for early warning indicators that compel us to act on behalf of students and improved achievement. Data Teams, data in a day, scoring guides, performance tasks in performance assessments, and corrective feedback were presented as "canaries in the coal mine," effective indicators that enable expert data analysts to respond with agility as needs warrant.

Readers were introduced in Chapter 7 to triangulation as a means to apply the principles of accountability, collaboration, and antecedents to effective data analysis. Several examples were provided, including the use of a wagon wheel data analysis tool. The wagon wheel empowers those who use it to effectively conduct multivariate analysis of distinct variables to reveal patterns and trends that would otherwise remain veiled or unclear. Experts are more likely to arrive at novel and appropriate solutions to problems, and triangulation provides insights and tools that allow teachers and administrators in the field the same capacity to find creative solutions to the challenges before them.

Environmental scanning was discussed in Chapter 8 to enable readers to plan a thorough and comprehensive analysis of those organizational factors that impact every organization. The framework builds on instructional strategies that are well known and commonly applied by teachers, and an extensive environmental scan example in Exhibit 8.2 illustrated how the process can offer educators strategic reform efforts that get at the heart of how things work in schools. The need for a comprehensive listening system added practical ways to bring knowledge to bear more effectively on problems than available to those whose approach to data analysis is dominated by attention to results alone.

The discussion of replication in Chapter 9 provided readers with strategies to multiply practices that work quickly; approaches to selectively identify practices that warrant replication; and methods to build a structure to ensure that replication is valued, promoted, and monitored. A practical teacher-to-teacher view of replication was introduced to jump-start action research and relentlessly pursue replication of local teaching practices as a matter of equity, fairness, and even social justice.

Berliner's definition of expertise identifies insights, knowledge, and efficiency as measures of expertise in a particular discipline, implying the need to replicate and adapt strategies that work in as many applications as possible. His study and others represent expertise as continually unfolding, strengthened by practice and experience, but differentiated by insights, knowledge, and efficiency.

The premise of *Beyond the Numbers* is that teachers and hands-on principals possess right now the expertise to make good decisions on the basis of sound data. We need to move beyond the numbers of test scores and introduce the insights of experts working together in collaboration to discover solutions that make a difference. Educators are savvy learners with extensive experience and expertise, making hundreds of decisions every day. Multidimensionality and simultaneity are realities for educators at all levels, and when teams give their best effort to reflection with a commitment to act on lessons they learn from the data, the potential for creativity and improvement is enormous.

Summary:
Creating a Culture of Expertise in Data Analysis

Teachers like Todd and Liz learned in their seminar that they were short on facts and formulas and therefore unqualified to serve as experts in data analysis. The reality is that teachers committed to leveraging antecedents, embracing collaboration that is long on candor and respect, and demonstrating accountability by acting on what is learned are experts in every sense of the word. When professionals apply their insights to triangulate complex issues with divergent data, apply fast-track multivariate analyses without the need for statistical tests, and conduct in-depth and focused environmental scans, they are operating as experts. As actions are systematically driven by their collective wisdom, educators will reclaim the initiative to perform data analysis from policymakers and politicians. It is hoped that *Beyond the Numbers* and its companion handbook, *Show Me the Proof!,* will dramatically improve data analysis in schools by providing a standards-based framework for data analysis, practical strategies and processes to build capacity, and specific tools to usher in successful replications and improved student achievement.

Beyond the Numbers and the
Common Core State Standards

The first edition of *Beyond the Numbers* did not have the benefit of explicit standards from which to draw in the design of discrete measures of achievement or measures of professional practice that are available from the Common Core State Standards today. As a result, today's practitioners not only have dramatically increased capacity through technology for data repositories and subsequent analysis but they also have a wealth of content to guide the design of insightful data frameworks. The Common Core is a ready partner with educators to identify salient data for achievement and antecedent professional practice measures prior to local studies and action research. The beneficiaries are the students of tomorrow, as the Common Core facilitates development of experts at all levels across the profession who will choose to go beyond the numbers on behalf of their students.

REFERENCES

Ainsworth, L. (2003). *Unwrapping the standards.* Denver, CO: Advanced Learning Press.

Ainsworth, L., & Christinson, J. (2000). *Five easy steps to a balanced math program.* Denver, CO: Advanced Learning Press.

Allensworth, E., & Easton, J. (2007). *Freshman grades, attendance striking predictors of later graduation for Chicago high school students.* Chicago: Consortium on School Research, University of Chicago.

American Recovery and Reinvestment Act of 2009, Pub. L. No. 115-5, Educational Recovery Act Race to the Top Initiative, CFDA No. 8395A (2009).

Analysis. (2010). In *Merriam-Webster's online dictionary.* Retrieved from http://www.merriam-webster.com/dictionary/analysis

Anderson, B., & Fagerhaug, T. (2000). *Root cause analysis: Simplified tools and techniques.* Milwaukee, WI: ASQ Quality Press.

Berliner, D. (1994). Expertise: The wonder of exemplary performances creating powerful thinking in teachers and students. In J. N. Mangieri & C. C. Block (Eds.), *Creating Powerful thinking in students and teachers.* New York: Holt, Reinhart & Winston.

Bernhardt, V. (2000). New routes open when one type of data crosses another. *Journal of Staff Development, 21*(1), 34.

Blume, H. (2010, September 13). Rising test scores allow 5 local schools to thwart outside takeover. *Los Angeles Times*, p. 1.

Calhoun, E. F. (2002). Action research for school improvement. *Educational Leadership, 59*(6), 18–24.

Carr, E., & Ogle, D. (1987). K-W-L plus: A strategy for comprehension and summarization. *Journal of Reading, 30*, 626–631.

City, E., Elmore, R., Fiarman, S. E., & Teitel, L. (2009). *Instructional rounds in education: A network approach to improving teaching and learning.* Cambridge, MA: Harvard Education Press.

Collins, J. (2001). *Good to great: Why some companies make the leap…and others don't.* New York: HarperCollins.

Common Core State Standards Initiative. (2010a). *Common Core State Standards for English language arts & literacy in history/social studies, science, and technical subjects.* Washington, DC: National Governors Association & Council of Chief State School Officers.

Common Core State Standards Initiative. (2010b). *Common Core State Standards for English language arts & literacy in history/social studies, science, and technical subjects, appendix A.* Washington, DC: National Governors Association & Council of Chief State School Officers.

Common Core State Standards Initiative. (2010c). *Common Core State Standards for English language arts & literacy in history/social studies, science, and technical subjects, appendix B.* Washington, DC: National Governors Association & Council of Chief State School Officers.

Common Core State Standards Initiative. (2010d). *Common Core State Standards for mathematics.* Washington, DC: National Governors Association & Council of Chief State School Officers.

Commonwealth of Virginia. (2003). *Virginia reads: Every minute counts: Virginia's reading first program.* Richmond, VA: Author. Retrieved from http://www.doe.virginia.gov/ federal_programs/ esea/title1/part_b/reading_first/va_reads_every_minute.pdf

Concerning Ensuring Quality Instruction through Educator Effectiveness (EqUITEE), Colo. Rev. Stat. 22-9-102 (2010).

Consortium on Chicago School Research. (2010). *About CCSR.* Chicago: Author. Retrieved from http://ccsr.uchicago.edu/content/page.php?cat=1

Costa, A., & Garmston, R. (1997). *Cognitive coaching: A foundation for renaissance schools* (3rd ed.). Norwood, MA: Christopher-Gordon.

Covey, Stephen. (1996). *The seven habits of highly effective people.* New York: Simon & Schuster.

Danielson, C. (2007). *Enhancing professional practice: A framework for teaching* (2nd ed.). Alexandria, VA: ASCD.

Darling-Hammond, Linda. (1997). *The right to learn: A blueprint for creating schools that work.* San Francisco: Jossey-Bass.

Denver Public Schools. (2010). *Research brief: Predictors of success.* Denver, CO: Author.

DuFour, R., DuFour, R., & Eaker, R. (2008). *Revisiting professional learning communities at work: New insights for improving schools.* Bloomington, IN: Solution Tree.

Education Northwest. (2001). *Data in a day: Listening to student voices. A self-study toolkit.* Portland, OR: Author. Retrieved from http://www.nwrel.org/scpd/scc/studentvoices/diad.shtml

Education Week (2010). *Quality counts 2010: Fresh course, swift current—momentum and challenges in the new surge toward common standards.* Bethesda, MD: Editorial Projects in Education.

Elmore, R. F. (2007). *School reform from the inside out* (4th ed.). Cambridge, MA: Harvard Education Press.

Evans, R. (2001). *The human side of school change* (2nd ed.). San Francisco: Jossey-Bass.

Fredricks, J. A., Blumenfeld, P. B., & Paris, A. (2004). School engagement: Potential of the concept, state of the evidence. *Review of Educational Research, 74*(1), 59–109.

Fullan, M. (2008). *The six secrets of change.* San Francisco: Jossey-Bass.

Gewertz, C. (2010). More states leaning toward online assessments, study finds. Alexandria, VA: *Education Week Curriculum Matters Blog.* Retrieved from http://blogs.edweek.org/edweek/curriculum/2010/04/more_states_leaning_toward_onl.html?qs=more+states+leaning+toward+online+assessments

Goe, L., Bell, C., & Little, O. (2008). *Approaches to evaluating teacher effectiveness: A research synthesis.* Washington, DC: National Comprehensive Center for Teacher Quality.

Graham, S., Harris, K. R., Fink-Chorzempa, B., & MacArthur, C. (2003). Primary grade teachers' instructional adaptations for struggling writers: A national survey. *Journal of Educational Psychology, 13*(June), 279.

Grissom, J. A., & Loeb, S. (2009). Triangulating principal effectiveness: How perspectives of parents, teachers, and assistant principals identify the central importance of managerial skills (National Center for Analysis of Longitudinal Data in Education Research [CALDER] Working Paper No. 35). Washington, DC: Urban Institute.

Hattie, J. (2009). *Visible learning: A synthesis of over 800 meta-analyses relating to student achievement.* New York: Routledge.

Heacox, D. (2002). *Differentiating instruction in the regular classroom.* Minneapolis, MN: Free Spirit.

Hinkle, V. A., Hinkle, K. T., &. Monetti, D. M. (2009). *What a difference data-in-a-day makes.* Valdosta, GA: Valdosta State University. Retrieved from http://www.community worksinstitute.org/exemplars/exemphghed/datainaday.html

Hord, S. M. (1997). Professional learning communities: What are they and why are they important? *Issues…about Change, 6,* 6–18.

Kerlinger, F. N. (1986). *Foundations of behavioral research* (3rd ed., 449–467). New York: Holt, Rinehart, and Winston.

Killion, J., & Bellamy, G. T. (2000). On the job: Data analysts focus school improvement efforts. *Journal of Staff Development, 21,* 27–32.

Kober, N., Chudowsky, N., Chudowsky, V., & Dietz, S. (2010a). *A call to action to raise achievement for African American students* (Student Achievement Policy Brief No. 1). Washington, DC: Center on Education Policy.

Kober, N., Chudowsky, N., Chudowsky, V., & Dietz, S. (2010b). *Improving achievement for the growing Latino population is critical to the nation's future* (Student Achievement Policy Brief No. 3). Washington, DC: Center on Education Policy.

Kober, N., Chudowsky, N., Chudowsky, V., & Dietz, S. (2010c). *Policy implications of trends for Asian American students* (Student Achievement Policy Brief No. 2). Washington, DC: Center on Education Policy.

Kros, J. (2007). *Spreadsheet modeling for business decisions.* New York: McGraw-Hill.

Langer, G. M., Colton, A. B., & Goff, L. S. (2003). *Collaborative analysis of student work* (p. 13). Alexandria, VA: ASCD.

Leadership and Learning Center, The. (2010). *Data Teams* (3rd ed.). Englewood, CO: Author.

Lencioni, P. M. (2004). *Death by meeting.* San Francisco: Jossey-Bass.

Lyster, R. (1998). Recasts, repetition and ambiguity in L2 classroom discourse. *Studies in Second Language Acquisition, 20,* 51–81.

Mackey, A., Gass, S., & McDonough, K. (2000). How do learners perceive interactional feedback? *Studies in Second Language Acquisition, 22,* 471–497.

Marzano, R. J. (2007). *The art and science of teaching.* Alexandria, VA : ASCD.

Marzano, R. J., Pickering, D. J., & Pollock, J. E. (2001a). *Classroom instruction that works: Research-based strategies for increasing student achievement.* Alexandria, VA: ASCD.

Marzano, R. J., Pickering, D. J., & Pollock, J. E. (2001b). *A handbook for classroom instruction that works.* Alexandria, VA: ASCD.

McDonald, S. K., & Schneider, B. L. (Eds.). (2007). *Scale-up in education: Issues in practice* (Vol. II). Lanham, MD: Rowman & Littlefield.

Montgomery County Schools. (2010). *Seven keys to college readiness: A pathway for students to follow that will increase their chances of being ready for and successful in college.* Rockville, MD: Author. Retrieved from http://www.montgomeryschoolsmd.org/info/keys/

Murphy, C. U., & Lick, D. W. (2005). *Whole-faculty study groups: Creating professional learning communities that target student learning* (3rd ed.). Thousand Oaks, CA: Corwin Press.

National Clearinghouse for Comprehensive School Reform. (2004). *Catalog of school reform models, 2004.* Washington, DC: Center for Comprehensive School Reform and Improvement. Retrieved from http://www.nwrel.org/scpd/catalog/index.shtml

National Staff Development Council. (2001). *NSDC's standards for staff development.* Oxford, OH: Author.

No Child Left Behind Act of 2001, Pub. L No. 107–110 (2002).

Popham, W. J. (2003). *Test better, teach better: The instructional role of assessment.* Alexandria, VA: ASCD.

Raymond, M. E. (2003, December 3). Track the relationship between teachers and their students. *The Charlotte Observer/Hoover Institution,* p. 1.

Reeves, D. B. (2000). *Accountability in action*. Alexandria, VA: ASCD.

Reeves, D. B. (2002a). *The daily disciplines of leadership* (14–16, 60, 201–210). San Francisco: Jossey-Bass.

Reeves, D. B. (2002b). *Holistic accountability*. Thousand Oaks, CA: Corwin Press.

Reeves, D. B. (2004a). *Accountability in action* (2nd ed., chap. 19). Denver, CO: Advanced Learning Press.

Reeves, D. B. (2004b). *Making standards work* (3rd ed.). Denver, CO: Advanced Learning Press.

Reeves, D. B. (2007). *Ahead of the curve*. Bloomington, IN: Solution Tree.

Richardson, J. (2000, October/November). The numbers game: Measure progress by analyzing data. *Tools for Schools*. Oxford, OH: National Staff Development Council. Retrieved from http://www.learningforward.org/news/tools/tools10-00rich.cfm

Sanders, W. L. (1998, December). Value-added assessment: A method for measuring the effects of the system, school and teacher on the rate of student academic progress. *The School Administrator, Web Edition*. Retrieved from https://www.boarddocs.com/mo/sdclay/Board.nsf/a8f91a9c9696786e8725731b0060d1e7/cb4491fc57ec27df852570d1007c9f7e/$FILE/ValueAddedAssmnt.pdf

Schlechty, P. (2000). *Shaking up the school house: How to support and sustain educational innovation*. San Francisco: Jossey-Bass.

Schmoker, M. (2001). *The results fieldbook: Practical strategies from dramatically improved schools*. Alexandria, VA: ASCD.

Schmoker, M. (2006). *Results now: How we can achieve unprecedented improvements in teaching and learning*. Alexandria, VA: ASCD.

Senge, P. (2000). *Schools that learn*. New York: Doubleday.

Shaha, S. H., Lewis, V. K., O'Donnell, T. J., & Brown, D. H. (2004). An approach to verifying program impact on teachers and students. *Journal of Research in Professional Learning, 1*, 1–18.

Shipley, J. (2001). *Orientation to performance excellence* (2nd ed.). Seminole, FL: Jim Shipley & Associates.

Singham, M. (2003). The achievement gap: Myths and reality. *Phi Delta Kappan, 84*(8), 586–591.

Steiner, L. (2000). *A review of the research literature on scaling-up in education: The problem of scaling-up in education*. Chicago: North Central Regional Educational Laboratory.

Steiner, L. M. (2005). *School restructuring options under No Child Left Behind: What works when? State takeovers of individual schools*. Washington, DC: Center for Comprehensive School Reform and Improvement.

Surowiecki, J. (2004). *The wisdom of crowds: Why the many are smarter than the few and how collective wisdom shapes business, economies, societies and nation.* New York: Doubleday.

U.S. Department of Education. (2010). *Race to the Top Application for Initial Funding*, CFDA No. 84.395A.

van Barneveld, C. (2008, August). Using data to improve student achievement. *WHAT WORKS? Research into Practice* (Research Monograph No. 15). Toronto, ON: The Literacy and Numeracy Secretariat.

Wade, H. H. (2001). *Data inquiry and analysis for educational reform* (ERIC Digest 153-December). Eugene: University of Oregon Clearinghouse on Educational Management.

Wenglinsky, H. (2002). How schools matter: The link between teacher classroom practices and student academic performance. *Education Policy Analysis Archives*, *10*(12), 6–31.

White. S. (2005). *Show me the proof! Tools and strategies to make data work for you.* Englewood, CO: Advanced Learning Press.

White, S. (2007). Data on purpose: Due diligence to increase student achievement. In D. Reeves (Ed.), *Ahead of the curve* (chap. 10). Bloomington, IN: Solution Tree.

White, S. (2009). *Leadership Maps.* Englewood, CO: Lead and Learn Press.

ANOVA Analysis of variance. A method for dividing the variance observed in experimental data into different parts, where each part is assignable to a difference between representative samples based on central tendency deviations.

AYP Adequate yearly progress. A term created for Title I schools to monitor improvement gains and extended in the No Child Left Behind Act of 2001 as a measure of improvement gains for all sub-groups; although states develop their own standards, this component serves as a linchpin of accountability in the landmark legislation.

BOE Board of education. The governing board for almost 15,000 school districts throughout the United States; its members are referred to as directors or trustees in some states.

CEU Continuing education unit.

CRT Criterion-referenced tests. Measure discrete knowledge and skills.

DDDM Data-driven decision making.

EOC End-of-course assessments. Also known as common assessments.

ES Elementary school.

ESA English skills acquisition. Levels in acquiring proficiency in English.

ESL English as a second language.

F ratio Part of the ANOVA statistical test. Named after Ronald Fischer, the inventor of the analysis, the F ratio divides the variance between each group by the variance within each group studied (V_b / V_w) to yield a ratio that is used to determine the significance level for the analysis.

FTE Full-time equivalent. Usually reserved to discussions of employees or students.

GE Indicates the year and month of school for which a student's score is typical. A GE of 6.2, for example, indicates that the student is achieving at a level that is typical of students who had completed the second month of grade 6 at the time the test was standardized. Interpret GEs with caution. A student in grade 3 may attain a GE of 6.2, but the score does not mean that the student is capable of doing sixth-grade work, only that the student is scoring well above average for grade 3.

HS   High school.

IQ   Intelligent quotient. A scaled score with 100 representing the population average in terms of the ability to solve verbal, mathematical, and spatial problems.

ISD   Independent school district.

KISS   Keep it short and simple. Great advice for just about everything.

KWL   A three-part summarizing reading strategy used across subjects and ages of learners: (1) What do I know about a topic? (2) What do I want to learn about that topic? (3) What have I learned about the topic?

MS   Middle school.

NAEP   National Assessment of Educational Progress. A comprehensive assessment authorized by the U.S. Congress to gather samples of student performance on standards in the United States for comparison purposes with students from other nations, track longitudinal trends, and monitor basic skills in core content areas.

NCE   Normal curve equivalent. Equal-interval scores used to compare achievement across subject areas over time. They provide information that is more precise regarding raw score performance than the national percentile score but, absent sub-scale information, offer little to help in diagnosing student performance or designing interventions.

NCLB   No Child Left Behind Act of 2001 (P.L. 107-110).

NP   National percentile. A scaled score that indicates what percentage of participants scored below the individual score reported; a common measure often misinterpreted, as the percentile differences are not equal interval in terms of raw score. National percentiles compare the achievement of students in a local group with that of students in the nation as a whole.

NRT   Norm-referenced test. The traditional standardized test that measures students' performance against that of their peers rather than against standards or criteria.

p value   The value of probability that the results obtained reflect differences attributable to chance or differences between groups that indicated a significance attributed to the independent variables (causes of desired effects, antecedents); p values of less than 0.05 for given samples indicate that the likelihood that the differences were attributable to chance are less than 5 chances out of 100; hence, a p value or level of significance of 0.05 or 0.001 is usually predetermined in most educational research efforts as an acceptable level of certainty.

PDSA   Plan-Do-Study-Act. One form of a continuous improvement cycle.

r value The product moment correlation coefficient, or Pearson *r*, that tells us how similar the rank orders of two different measures are; *r* values range from a perfect positive relationship of +1.00 to a perfect negative relationship of −1.00. Both are very unlikely but could exist in rare circumstances such as the relationship between senior grade point average and SAT scores or the negative relationship between grades and behavior referrals. Pearson's *r* is very common, and scattergram charts typically depict the outcome of *r* value calculations.

Rdg Reading.

SAT Formerly known as Scholastic Aptitude Test. One of two major norm-referenced college entrance exams designed to sort and select students through rankings.

SFETT San Fernando Education Technology Team. An instructional technology effort that has changed work habits dramatically and, in doing so, increased graduation, college entrance, and access to employment in a low-income area of Los Angeles.

SIP School improvement plan.

SMART A proven approach to goal development, ensuring that goals are specific, measurable, achievable, relevant, and timely. The Center for Performance Assessment adds the letter B, as in baseline, and B-SMART goals.

SS Social studies.

SWOT Strengths, weakness, opportunities, threats. An assessment method used to examine organizational environments and organizational health.

USD Unified school district. A term used to describe a K–12 or pre-K–12 school system where elementary and secondary grades are operated by the same organization.

WISC-IV The fourth iteration of the Wechsler Intelligence Scale for Children, a popular and well-respected IQ assessment for school-aged children.

Wrtg Writing.

APPENDIX A: **Scoring Matrix for Analysis of Data**

Dimension	Meeting the Standard	Progressing toward the Standard	Not Meeting the Standard
1.0 MANAGEMENT OF DATA			
1.1 Data Collection	The educator makes informed decisions at all levels based on formative assessments of prior learning, embedded assessments during instruction, and summative assessments of results following instruction. Data collection demonstrates understanding of **antecedent** data, including administrative **structures and conditions** and **cause data** (teacher behaviors that engage students in thinking and learning). Results **(effects)** data include student performance; pre/post data; use of longitudinal cohort data for patterns and trends; embedded performance assessment data; and common assessments by department, grade, or discipline. Data provide evidence of antecedents and instructional strategies, and data collection minimizes interruption of instruction, with data collected limited to critical variables that lend themselves to triangulation.	The educator ensures that teachers and support staff collect and monitor data associated with goals and that data are maintained for both summative and formative purposes; emphasis is primarily on collection of results (effects) data, with limited evidence of cause data measures or programmatic and administrative antecedents (conditions and structures that correlate with excellence in student achievement). Educator attempts to schedule data collection so it does not interrupt instruction.	The educator's data collection system is limited to external requirements for compliance in annual student assessment results. Attempts to link cause and effect; institute continuous assessment measures before, during, and after learning; or address timing issues of data collection are not evident.
1.2 Improvement Cycles	The educator employs improvement cycles for **all major programs** and unit teams. Cycles ensure that plans are informed by data, implemented to address gaps and opportunities, analyzed, and routinely and systematically revised for improvement (e.g., 7-step data-driven decision making [DDDM], Plan-Do-Study-Act).	The educator is beginning to apply an improvement cycle to assess student achievement across state or local requirements (e.g., seat time, Carnegie units, state assessment). Application to adult practices or administrative and programmatic structures has yet to be attempted.	The educator reacts to state or local requirements for data and does not employ improvement cycles that link data to planning and implementation.

APPENDIX A: Scoring Matrix for Analysis of Data

Dimension	Meeting the Standard	Progressing toward the Standard	Not Meeting the Standard
		1.0 MANAGEMENT OF DATA continued	
1.3 **Analysis** **Reflection/Action**	The educator examines test scores for trends within subjects, relationship to grades and state assessments, internal consistency across subjects, unanticipated gains, and outlier performers who score well above and well below standard. Data are routinely triangulated with antecedent, collaboration, and accountability data to reveal insights not available from examining single data points. The educator has formed teams and meeting times to examine data for improved student achievement. The educator sets aside specific times and formats to ensure that collaborative analysis takes place; that quality data tools are applied to facilitate that analysis; that insights from reflection are recorded; and that action is planned, implemented, and monitored on the basis of the analysis.	The educator has formed teams and meeting times to examine data for improved student achievement. The educator examines test scores for trends within subjects, for relationship to grades and state assessments, for internal consistency across subjects, and to identify students with unanticipated gains.	Data are collected and recorded but seldom analyzed to improve student achievement.
		2.0 ANTECEDENTS OF EXCELLENCE	
2.1 **Cause Data and** **Instructional Strategies**	The educator provides evidence of specific antecedents used in classrooms or school to increase student achievement effects (results) through teacher behaviors in the classroom (causes) and systematic teaching strategies. The educator modifies and adjusts antecedent cause data (teaching behaviors and practices) and shares with colleagues current research findings describing causes that produce the greatest gains in student achievement for all sub-groups; effective cause strategies are implemented in classrooms or the school, and Hishakawa fishbone is frequently used to examine current data, determine root causes, and take action through effective intervention plans.	The educator recognizes effective teaching strategies that impact student thinking and reasoning as causes that lead to achievement effects (results) and is fluent with current research about those causes most apt to produce the greatest gains in student achievement for all sub-groups. The educator recognizes that cause/effect data represent strong correlation data, not actual causes. The educator is beginning to identify antecedents to improve student achievement based on available data.	The educator is not able to identify antecedents or leverage them to increase student achievement.

APPENDIX A: **Scoring Matrix for Analysis of Data**

Dimension	Meeting the Standard	Progressing toward the Standard	Not Meeting the Standard
		2.0 ANTECEDENTS OF EXCELLENCE continued	
2.2 Administrative Structures & Conditions	The educator leverages a wide range of antecedent conditions and structures to increase student achievement and monitors their impact with user-friendly data. The leader is adept at creating antecedents that increase student achievement, leveraging time, settings, and resources to align and focus efforts (e.g., technological capacity, time and opportunity issues, staff training, levels of implementation in specific teaching strategies, attendance).	The educator recognizes antecedents in terms of time, technology, training, logistics, and level of implementation and applies them periodically to improve student achievement based on external research findings and antecedents employed in neighboring or comparable schools.	The educator does not view administrative structures of time, technology, textbooks, or training as possible antecedents for excellence that can be modified for improved student achievement.
		3.0 COLLABORATION AROUND STUDENT WORK	
3.1 Planning to Execution	The educator ensures ongoing, reflective, and meaningful collaboration that captures the best thinking of staff to improve student achievement through a variety of methods, such as (1) **action planning**, including all steps of a continuous improvement cycle; (2) **lesson logs** shared and distributed by departments or grade-level teams; (3) **common assessments** created, evaluated, and revised by teacher teams; (4) **instructional calendars** that align curriculum and instruction with regent examinations; (5) **development of Data Teams** that monitor outlier student performance and close learning gaps; or (6) establishment of a clearly defined **program evaluation** process. Teacher-developed measures of collaboration complement those initiated by individual educator.	The educator promotes collaboration around student work by examining student work at faculty meetings and asking staff to identify solutions to patterns of lagging student achievement and strategies to replicate evidence of dramatically improving student achievement. The educator promotes collaborative data analysis by establishing one or more ongoing method to examine student performance and implement strategies to improve that performance: (1) **lesson logs** shared and distributed by departments or grade-level teams; (2) **common assessments** created, evaluated, and revised by teacher teams, or (3) **instructional calendars** that align curriculum and instruction with regent examinations.	The educator looks for the path of least resistance in developing data monitoring systems; he frequently avoids collaboration beyond initial consensus to adopt a program or strategy; reflection is nonexistent.

APPENDIX A: **Scoring Matrix for Analysis of Data**

Dimension	Meeting the Standard	Progressing toward the Standard	Not Meeting the Standard
	3.0 COLLABORATION AROUND STUDENT WORK continued		
3.2 Team Thinking	Solutions generated by others are valued, especially when generated from within educator's support group. The leader ensures that team thinking permeates the data analysis process by requiring that (1) all team members proactively analyze data for discussion in advance of meetings; (2) team processes routinely identify improvements; (3) training is provided and encouraged in mental models, team learning, and cognitive coaching; and (4) training updates are provided to all teams in data analysis tools.	The educator promotes team thinking in data analysis by providing and encouraging (1) training in mental models, team learning, and cognitive coaching and (2) training in data analysis tools for interested team members.	The educator's systematic plan to improve the quality of collaborative thinking in examining student work is not evident.
3.3 Integration into Decision Making	The educator integrates collaboration in data analysis into all key decisions through collaborative processes that benefit from the best thinking of classroom teachers. Evidence is demonstrated through a variety of means, such as (1) recommendations reviewed only when submitted with peers; (2) collaborative schedules that provide common planning, teaming; (3) teacher teams examine student work and leader requests analysis and recommendations for specific students; (4) assessment calendars required of all department/grade-level teams; (5) early release times for collaboration around student work; (6) time and effort reallocated to respond to urgent challenges through collaboration that develops powerful instructional strategies. **Assessment calendars establish times for collaboration in analysis, reflection, action planning, and implementation.**	The educator attempts to integrate collaboration in data analysis into decision making by one or more of the following: (1) request recommendations be submitted with support by two other peers; (2) establish school schedules with common planning, teaming; or (3) provide data to teacher teams (flexible grouping) and request analysis and recommendations for specific students.	The educator views decisions regarding data analysis to be the prerogative of administration or as isolated acts of leadership separate from lessons revealed by data.

APPENDIX A: **Scoring Matrix for Analysis of Data**

4.0 ACCOUNTABILITY

Dimension	Meeting the Standard	Progressing toward the Standard	Not Meeting the Standard
4.1 Authority to Act	The educator establishes written policies within his direct control and influence that provide teachers and other staff the authority to implement changes designed to improve student achievement based on preponderance of evidence revealed from data available at any given time; preponderance of evidence is determined through triangulation of data and thoughtful collaboration around actual student performance.	The educator advocates for written policies within his direct control and influence that provide teachers and other staff the authority to implement changes designed to improve student achievement; data provide some evidence to assist teachers and staff in making changes designed to improve student achievement; triangulation and thoughtful collaboration around student performance occur sporadically among teachers and staff.	The educator defers to popular opinion in making changes, with little evidence of efforts to extend authority for program or instructional changes to teachers or staff.
4.2 Accountability Structures	The educator integrates accountability into all major decisions by delineating explicit responsibilities for teams and individuals and establishing user-friendly timelines for data, and establishes multiple feedback systems, such as assessment calendars or formal listening systems for student, teacher, parent, and staff stakeholder groups, grade-level/department teams, or Data Teams.	The educator has developed accountability methods that specify responsibilities for teams and individuals, establish timelines for data collection/ disaggregation, and provide at least one formal and responsive feedback system to improve student achievement.	Focus is on compliance with external requirements established by supervisor or institutional policy; little evidence exists to demonstrate a commitment or plan to add value with accountability systems.
4.3 Accountability Reports	The educator publicly displays and communicates results of ongoing monitor accountability measures for Tier 1 data (system-wide indicators), Tier 2 data (school-based indicators), and Tier 3 data (narrative description of school successes and challenges), and he supplements measures at all levels with performance indicators that add value and focus efforts to improve student achievement.	The educator communicates results of ongoing monitor accountability measures that exceed Tier 1 (district-wide indicators) requirements, and he supplements such measures with a number of performance indicators that add value and focus efforts to improve student achievement.	The educator communicates only those results required by external requirements (Tier 1 or compliance measures), and evidence is not available indicating plans to develop, monitor, or communicate Tier 2 or Tier 3 data to staff, parents, students, or patrons.

APPENDIX A: **Scoring Matrix for Analysis of Data**

Dimension	Meeting the Standard	Progressing toward the Standard	Not Meeting the Standard
		4.0 ACCOUNTABILITY continued	
4.4 **Permission to Subtract**	The leader establishes written policies within his direct control and influence that provide teachers and other staff permission to eliminate, reduce, or omit historical practices or instructional strategies that inhibit improved student achievement based on a preponderance of evidence revealed from data **available** at any given time; preponderance of evidence is determined through deliberate triangulation of data and thoughtful collaboration around actual student performance.	The leader has developed a policy providing teachers and staff permission to eliminate, reduce, or omit historical practices or instructional strategies that inhibit improved student achievement but has yet to establish written policies within his direct control and influence to that effect, or developed a system to monitor implementation of the policy. Data provide some evidence of assistance to teachers and staff in eliminating obsolete, redundant, or neutral practices that do not contribute to improved student achievement; triangulation and thoughtful collaboration around student performance occur sporadically among teachers and staff.	The leader is reluctant to share the authority to eliminate, reduce, or omit existing practices with staff and is unable to identify current instructional strategies or antecedents (conditions and structures) that inhibit improved student achievement for groups or individuals.
4.5 **Responsibility for Results**	Performance goals are met for student achievement that meets AYP requirements and closes the learning gap for all sub-groups. Sustained record of improved student achievement on multiple indicators of student success can be verified.Explicit use of previous and interim data indicates a focus on improving performance. Efforts to assist students who demonstrate proficiency to move to the advanced or exemplary level are evident, and new challenges are met by identification of needs from existing data, creation of timely and effective interventions with monitoring data, and selection of meaningful and insightful results indicators.	Staff reports they should be responsible for student achievement results but have limited understanding of the factors (antecedents) that affect student achievement. There is evidence of improvement for one or more sub-groups but insufficient evidence of changes in antecedent measures of teaching, curriculum, and leadership to create the improvements necessary to achieve student performance goals for all sub-groups.	Indifferent to the data, tendency to blame students, families, and external characteristics. Staff and leaders do not believe that student achievement can improve through their efforts. No evidence of decisive action to change time, teacher assignment, curriculum, leadership practices, or other variables of achievement.

APPENDIX A: **Scoring Matrix for Analysis of Data**

Dimension	Meeting the Standard	Progressing toward the Standard	Not Meeting the Standard
5.0 TRIANGULATION			
5.1 Triangulation	The educator applies at least two data tools to every triangulation, triangulating student achievement data effectively with supporting student achievement data, **antecedent** (conditions and structure) data, **accountability** (responsibilities; reporting; specific, measurable, achievable, relevant, and timely [SMART] measures) data, or **collaboration** (various team formats, lesson logs, instructional calendars, etc.) data. Educator monitors staff triangulation of achievement data to ensure inclusion of related and unrelated data points (e.g., instructional strategies, allocation of time, professional development, side-by-side curriculum analysis, standards, assessments).	The educator applies at least one data tool to every triangulation effort and is beginning to triangulate student achievement data with antecedents, collaboration data, or accountability structures (**principles of DDDM**).	The educator is unaware of the principle of triangulation of data, focusing his efforts on compliance with district and state reports.
5.2 Low Inference Insights	Educator leverages triangulation to engage teachers in self-discovery of insights, new learning, and recommendations for changes in the educational process. Educator triangulates data effectively with each point serving as a check on the other dimension, with the desired outcome the realization of new insights from the various data points (and types) that is not available from examining one type of data or one perspective in isolation.	The educator understands that triangulation requires teams to make assumptions, draw inferences, and come to conclusions without total certainty. The educator recognizes that triangulation necessitates discovery of a center point from other, often unrelated, data, and the educator triangulates student assessment data with antecedents and cause data wherever possible.	Educator is directive in interactions with teachers and does not engage teachers in triangulation of data.

APPENDIX A: **Scoring Matrix for Analysis of Data**

Dimension	Meeting the Standard	Progressing toward the Standard	Not Meeting the Standard
		5.0 TRIANGULATION continued	
5.3 **Triangulation** **Conversations**	The educator models triangulation in formal and informal settings and asks teachers to add value to their analysis of all data by triangulating data with colleagues. Triangulation is an expected exercise for all grade, department, and Data Team meetings, and the leader routinely includes cause data and administrative antecedents in triangulation. Educator applies triangulation to encourage innovative teaching strategies and facilitate new approaches to instruction through action research. Data are specifically analyzed to engage staff in conversations about assessments.	The educator uses the triangulation process to coach teachers in making assumptions, drawing inferences, and developing hunches that can help identify replicable practices, verified through action research.	The educator views data as numbers and does not engage faculty or staff in making inferences or reaching for assumptions, believing that none of the school staff is a statistician and should not claim to be.
		6.0 REPLICATION	
6.1 **Replication**	The educator has a system in place to identify homegrown successes that includes a common definition, a process to recognize successes, and a method to validate and replicate the successful practice. The educator has defined a preponderance of evidence as sufficient data to answer the questions, **What works well for whom, why, and how do you know?**	The educator promotes replication of best practices from current educational research and has a system in place to recognize teachers for improved student achievement. At least one replication is discussed, and teachers are encouraged to observe each other for best practices.	The educator resists efforts to formally replicate practices, viewing the process as divisive and as singling out one teacher over another.

APPENDIX A: **Scoring Matrix for Analysis of Data**

Dimension	Meeting the Standard	Progressing toward the Standard	Not Meeting the Standard
		6.0 REPLICATION continued	
6.2 **Decision to Replicate**	The educator follows up on hunches associated with data patterns by initiating a process for replication with teachers when student performance patterns correlate with specific strategies or antecedent structures and conditions for learning. The educator employs a specific decision-making process at key intervals with affected teachers to determine how, when, and whether to replicate a practice.	The educator communicates frequently with teachers to identify patterns and trends in student performance that correlate with specific instructional strategies or the presence of antecedent structures and conditions for learning. The leader initiates a discussion about possible replication with affected teachers and staff.	The educator views differences in classroom performance as inherent differences in teaching personality and student demographics.
6.3 **Action Research**	The educator is fluent with the six steps of action research and is quick to translate hunches from patterns into action research hypothesis, engaging teachers and staff in a common action research approach, characterized by: • Simple relationship design between one independent variable (cause data) and one dependent variable (effect) or 2 × 2 variable matrix if necessary • Simple pre-post assessments • Use of same course/grade classrooms as control group • Recommended use of meta-analysis categories of effective teaching strategies as independent variables • Data collection embedded into instruction • Prescribed time period, format	The educator is fluent with the six steps of action research: 1. Observe 2. Hypothesize 3. Predict 4. Test hypothesis 5. Gather data 6. Explain The educator examines data for patterns and trends associated with specific classrooms and instructional strategies.	The educator shows no interest in action research, viewing the time and effort required to implement it as disruptive to the learning process.

Common Questions about Data Analysis

Classroom- and School-Level Assessment Concerns

1. **How can we best use test data to capture common assessment data?**

    Common end-of-course (EOC) assessment data provide the capacity to find patterns related to sub-group performance differences, teacher strategies, curriculum alignment, and time and opportunity to develop proficiency. Other formative assessments offer insights into skills, concepts, and content knowledge. More formal summative assessments are excellent measures to monitor patterns and trends and determine the degree of alignment with curriculum, pacing, and standards. These data should be particularly powerful for teacher teams in that they allow the teams to glimpse inside their classrooms and determine what is working, what is not, and why.

    The data will immediately reveal differences among groups, among classrooms, and within the curriculum. These differences and patterns will provide the basis for modifying instruction, focusing curriculum, and adjusting time and opportunity issues.

    Presentation ideas: Tell this story in two parts: (1) findings, patterns, and differences and (2) lessons, modifications, and planned adjustments. Common EOC assessments offer the most agile form of district assessments for modifying professional practice. One or two graphs or charts for part 1 of the presentation and one or two for part 2 should be instructive to any audience and play well within a three- to five-minute board of education (BOE) presentation.

    Recommended tools: Wagon wheel/relations diagram to identify such patterns by teacher and by curriculum unit for sub-groups.

Questions Regarding Annual State Tests (Both Norm-Referenced Tests and Criterion-Referenced Tests)

2. **How can we best use test data to capture norm-referenced data?**

    Norm-referenced data offer five basic benefits:

    1) Norm-referenced tests (NRTs) allow us to identify patterns and gaps by subject and sub-scales that reflect local emphasis on curriculum and instruction for all students.

    2) Norm-referenced tests also provide a vehicle to examine the degree to which students are achieving within their expected abilities (NRT relationship between cognitive ability scores on some state assessments).

    3) By triangulating NRT data with criterion-referenced tests (CRTs), EOC, state assess-

ments, safety-net performance assessments, and writing assessments, one can determine the degree to which these tests corroborate one another and identify the types of assessments where groups of students excel and where performance differs.

4) The NRT data primarily compare our students and our curriculum preparation by subject and sub-scale with performance of students across the United States. That comparison alone offers insights into how well local schools are preparing students to compete in a larger arena with their peers.

5) Norm-referenced tests are always indicators of the range of student responses and offer local districts a picture of the degree of variance in student performance. Norm-referenced tests can be used to monitor that range over time and develop interventions to reduce the variance and close the gap.

Caveat: NRT averages mask gaps within subjects and between sub-groups. Norm-referenced tests also rank students and do little to determine proficiency or provide meaningful comparisons outside their respective NRT sampling pool. Norm-referenced tests always have 50 percent scoring above the norm and 50 percent below, although reducing the variance in benefit 5 can provide a strong external measure of success.

Presentation ideas: Present NRT scores in the context of one of many *valid* assessments rather than the primary measure of achievement or student ability. Describe briefly how NRTs differ from CRTs and standards-based assessments, and frame NRTs in terms of the value they offer *you* locally, stressing your intent to *close the gap* by reducing variance over time.
Recommended slides: (1) bell curve with desire to reduce variance; (2) patterns suggesting strengths and weaknesses of current curriculum; (3) chart/table comparison with other assessments; (4) caveats, especially masking, inability to measure proficiency in terms of knowledge and application; and (5) trend data for local performance by sub-group on the NRT. If combined with other assessments in presentation, choose one or two slides from these five. Stand-alone should allow for a BOE presentation of five minutes or less.

3. **I'd also like to know more about interpreting ability scores, for example, when they show we are working above anticipated abilities and achieving beyond predicted levels of performance.**
Ability scores are scaled in a similar way to traditional intelligence quotient (IQ) tests but are not IQ scores. They reflect only the ranked performance on a scale where 50 percent of students score below the scale of 100 and 50 percent score above. Standard deviations have been calibrated at 16 points, again reflective of many IQ tests (e.g., Wechsler Intelligence Scale for Children, Fourth Edition), but ability scores should not be substituted for the individually administered cognitive IQ exams. The value of the ability score is its thumbnail look at cognitive ability and the comparisons one might draw in terms of students exceeding expected performance. Comparing a cognitive ability score to the norm curve equivalent (NCE) scores provides a convenient correlation for this issue.

3a. How can we reflect this achievement in our success stories?

Presentation ideas: Present patterns comparing cognitive ability measures where scores "beat the odds" or where ability scores mirror actual performance. Limit to one or two slides.

4. How can we best use test data to capture criterion-referenced data?

Criterion-referenced test data offer important information about student performance against certain criteria or standards. Like a quality performance assessment addressing a safety-net standard, CRTs allow us to determine whether students have met the criterion, with this caveat: unlike a performance assessment, we may have to assume that performance on a select response CRT actually reflects the student's knowledge of the criterion and his ability to demonstrate and apply that knowledge with the appropriate skill in various applications. Benefits of CRTs include the following:

1) Test data reflect student proficiency in terms of knowledge of the criterion.
2) Criterion-referenced test data give detailed information about how well a student has performed on each educational goal or outcome included on that test. For instance, a CRT score might describe which arithmetic operations a student can perform or the level of reading difficulty he can comprehend.
3) As long as the content of the test matches the content that is considered important to learn, the CRT gives the student, the teacher, and the parent more information about how much of the valued content has been learned than an NRT does.
4) All students can "pass" a CRT test, while only 50 percent can meet or exceed the mean NRT score.
5) Most state academic content standard assessments are CRT tests in that "cut" scores are identified to indicate a level of proficiency.

5. How can we best use test data to capture NCE scores, national percentiles, and scale scores?

a. **Normal curve equivalent** scores are equal-interval scores used to compare achievement across subject areas over time. They provide information that is more precise regarding raw score performance than does the national percentile (NP) score but, absent sub-scale information, offer little to help in diagnosing student performance or designing interventions.

b. **National percentile** represents the percentage of students in the norm group whose scores fall below a given level. A student whose NP is 65 scored higher than 65 percent of students in the norm group. National percentiles compare the achievement of students in a local group with that of students in the nation as a whole.

c. **Grade equivalent (GE)** indicates the year and month of school for which a student's score is typical. A GE of 6.2 indicates that the student is achieving at a level that is typical of students who had completed the second month of grade 6 at the time the test was standardized. Interpret GEs with caution. A student in grade 3 may attain a GE of

6.2—this does not mean that the student is capable of doing sixth-grade work, only that the student is scoring well above average for grade 3.

d.   **Scale scores** are similar to NCE scores in that they provide a common scale to compare variability in student performance from grade to grade or subject to subject. On the National Assessment of Educational Progress, scale scores are used almost exclusively to ascertain the degree to which performance is improving and to determine whether the variability in scores is tightening. Scale scores on the state assessment can provide similar helpful information.

Presentation ideas: Present patterns in terms of scale scores. While school and district averages may move only slightly, scale score results can indicate movement toward higher achievement by indicating reduced variance in scores and consistency across subjects. Scale scores also can help drill down to areas of need where discrepancies are evident. For BOE presentations, omit or use one slide to tell the above story in one or two minutes.

6.   **How can we best use test data to capture quartile growth?**
    Examining test results in light of students most apt to move up to the next quartile helps reveal how relatively easy it is to make significant growth when we concentrate on individual students with names and faces. A second benefit of examining performance by quartiles is that it is a quick and easy way to identify how cohorts compare from grade to grade or school to school to determine how effective curriculum is by grade and how effective teaching practices are by school.

7.   **How can we best use test data to develop fall to spring comparisons?**
    Fall and spring data points are wonderful opportunities to update data walls, celebrate improvements, and revise goals. This question underscores the importance of maintaining and growing a comprehensive and multifaceted assessment battery because cohort survival changes occur between fall and spring and because the snapshot exams within the testing window will always be influenced by illness and other personal factors. Performance assessments that are embedded and address Power Standards with leverage are essential components of any assessment battery.
    Fall to spring should always anticipate gains, and the test data can be used to inform curriculum planning, especially instructional calendars that emphasize safety-net standards at specific junctures within a school or department during prescribed months or weeks.

Presentation Concerns

8.   **I think we still need some data-driven decision-making skills in presentation graphics and longitudinal data interpretation.**
    Training in presentation graphics such as command of Excel and application with PowerPoint is always valuable. The ability to interpret longitudinal data improves as more data

points are added. This may seem self-evident, but one problem with longitudinal data is the need to start over as data sets change. Find a quality measure, something you are confident will be just as important a decade from now as it is today, and stay with it (antecedents as well as results indicators). Advanced data-driven decision making (DDDM) will include practice in Microsoft Excel at higher levels and general principles of presentations, including colors, clutter, charts, graphs, and data scales.

9. **I would like information on the most effective way to scale graphs. Some of the differences on data points may have been exaggerated by using too small a scale on the y-axis.**

This is a common complaint and legitimate criticism of data presented for almost every purpose. If the gains are minimal, conventional wisdom suggests that we shrink the y-axis scale; if scores have shown significant decline, we enlarge the y-axis scale to minimize that decline. To stop this practice, we need common standards for presenting data graphically just as we promote common EOC assessments for students. I would suggest the y-axis always span the range of possible outcomes. If percentile scores are compared, a scale from 0 to 100 is warranted. If raw scores or scale scores are used, every possible score should be accommodated by the y-axis. Some educators improve even on this basic expectation for presenting data by using logarithmic scales that increase geometrically as the number value increases. In other words, the y-axis distance between 1 and 10 is equivalent to the distance between 10 and 100, which is equivalent to the distance between 100 and 1,000. Microsoft Excel accommodates this format, a scale widely used in medicine, agriculture, and finance for its accuracy in establishing trend lines for growth and contraction. This tool is addressed in a brief exercise within advanced DDDM.

10. **I would like to look at some nontraditional ways of displaying large numbers of data points. Usually large amounts of data are summed or averaged in order to be displayed. Unfortunately, this also results in loss of data. Are there other ways we've not seen to display all the pertinent information?**

The Indiana Academic Content Standards Web site, http://www.doe.in.gov/, examines data in several different ways. One of the most useful methods is its "drilldown" graphs, which examine by sub-group and test the difference between a school's average score and the minimum passing score for that standard. A school's performance (average skill score) is compared to the passing skill score. With the zero line representing the passing skill score, the graph displays how far above or below the school performed on a specific standard.

Other methods for examining issues include a wagon wheel, which offers graphical representations to compare performance of several entities (classrooms, students, schools) across multiple variables (up to eight). Its primary purposes are to (1) determine which issue is most critical and (2) compare performance across multiple dimensions. An equally powerful tool is simply to graph the range of student performances on particular assessments, an important measure because we always will want to reduce the variability in student performance and at the same time see achievement increase. These two measures and others provide insightful ways of displaying data without resorting to totals or averages in such a way as to mask important patterns and discoveries. They provide interesting alternatives to traditional line and bar graphs of average scores for presentations.

11. **What data can you compare, and how do you accurately represent data when interpreting and sharing with others?**

Comparisons are useful with almost all data when a benchmark exists for excellence or high performance given similar demographics and resources. Comparing apples with oranges is such a common metaphor that the phrase is used for almost any comparison, but the lesson is a valid one. Comparing a high-performing school with schools that are performing below standard seldom yields meaningful information for improvement. Comparing one's school with the most successful school in the district or state by sub-groups and sub-scales on specific tests, on the other hand, can yield important information when we drill down to identify antecedents (adult behaviors) that led to higher achievement. Certainly, assessment data lends itself to comparisons, while data processes and antecedent data are better assessed by examining the integrity of internal factors, such as redundancy, duplication of effort, consistency, and timeliness in delivery of the process. The previous question inquired about alternative ways to gather and represent data in presentations. Data are best represented when a number of guiding principles are applied, including the following:

a. **Describe data in its context** by separating anecdotal information in your presentation and labeling it as such (anecdotal data are extremely important to tell the story, but if they cannot be presented in terms of data, present them separately).

b. **Describe data with integrity**, using scales representing the full range of possible responses or scores (0–100 for percentiles or percentages, etc.).

c. **Interpret data conservatively and avoid conjecture**; let the data tell the story. Explaining differences in terms of "a different group of kids this year" insults your audience. Offering subsequent graphs and charts to describe those differences with deeper analysis (e.g., correlations for certain sub-groups based on teaching methods, attendance, behavior) strengthens the story you are telling and adds credibility.

d. **Never present data that are dependent on anecdotal narrative to tell the story.** If the data do not reveal patterns or trends, let them tell the message of the null hypothesis (assumption that changes will be miniscule). Lessons can be learned when no changes are evident, especially lessons for examining at deeper levels, identifying alternative measures.

e. **Use graphic organizers liberally** to interpret data and share with others. Graphic organizers are "thinking tools" that lend themselves to group processing and data analysis.

f. Remember the axiom: **data should make visible what is otherwise invisible.**

g. **Know your data so well** that you can tell the "story behind the numbers" without apology, conjecture, or embellishment.

12. **How do we improve the process of communicating data? It is the prelude to determining its meaning for future action.**

    This question gets at the heart of effective data analysis: pervasive, ubiquitous, user-friendly communication of data that promotes a data-driven culture. How is that accomplished? All data systems, whether classroom, school, or district, need to include the following:

    a. Scheduled dates and times for collection, aggregation, and disaggregation of data

    b. Required time for analysis, reflection, and recommendations for changes

    c. Mandatory decision to proceed with no changes or to implement recommendations with a written rationale for the decision

    d. Dissemination of decision driven by the data to all affected parties, including parents and the public

    District and school data are different from classroom data in that district data are almost exclusively results or effects data; schools engage and monitor both cause and effect measures, and classrooms engage in antecedent and causal factor data as well.

13. **Principals need to learn how to present data well, so it tells the true picture. What guidelines can you offer to assist in this process?**

    This question is an excellent illustration of the desire of many educators to add precision to our craft, especially when we present findings to a broader audience. The seven guidelines provided for question 11 above address the telling of the "true picture" by insisting on a common scale or principle for y-axis scales and other principles. Present only what is important and adhere to Schmoker's axiom to "make visible the invisible." Four additional recommendations for presentations include the following:

    a. **Present the story in terms of comparisons, relationships, or trends.** Without these connections, data has very little meaning.

    b. **Limit presentation slides to seven lines of type and no more than three comparisons** per chart or table (2×2 matrices have only two dimensions per axis).

    c. **Avoid charts and tables with more than seven variables.** Eight or more variables result in cluttered presentations and are difficult to interpret.

    d. **Let the data breathe and speak.** Never use color or templates that draw attention away from the message of the data presented.

Analysis Concerns

14. **How can I better read the sub-skills portion of our data to know what is the most important skill to focus on? What should I do to get the "best bang for our buck and time"?**

    Sub-skills data tell a story about strengths and weaknesses, both of which can inform decisions and help prioritize skills to focus on. In math, the building-block skills of basic operations may be compelling enough to stay with that instructional focus even though students may show a weakness in statistics or geometry. In language arts, a reading sub-skill weakness in sentence fluency can influence how you design and monitor the writing process and how writing is infused in all other content areas. As a general rule of thumb, however, ask the following questions:

- How do the sub-skills interact?
- Are some sub-skills prerequisite to proficiency in another content strand (e.g., text complexity in reading or algebraic reasoning in mathematics)?
- Is there a sub-skill that offers greater leverage opportunities?
- Do students consistently show higher performance in one sub-skill than another?
- Have classroom teachers conducted a side-by-side analysis of curriculum with test data?
- Have you analyzed where time and resources are allocated in the subject area tested?

You will determine what is most important by examining the number of classrooms and students with the same common pattern, applying the power of the research regarding effective teaching strategies to deepen areas of strengths, and reallocating time to make sure sufficient attention is given to areas of general weakness. Sub-skill performance data for each school will be analyzed in advanced DDDM using several new tools, including the wagon wheel.

15. **Schools are still comparing state assessment scores among noncohort groups. Because we are held accountable each year for state assessment results, what can be done to help us focus on longitudinal progress of cohort groups?**

Comparison of different groups of students from year to year is a legitimate and pervasive criticism of standardized testing from educators. Maintaining this practice is built on the assumption that while students will differ, the cohort as a whole will be representative of the previous year's cohort (same neighborhoods; same racial, economic, ethnic, and educational backgrounds). Hence, the assumption persists that improved scores indicate improved practices while declining scores indicate less than stellar teaching practices. In fact, with very large schools and large samples (e.g., 100 or more per grade), the data will reflect many common characteristics from year to year. This analysis satisfies the null hypothesis, and given a sufficient sample size, we have every right to expect similar results. The problem, of course, is that similar results are no longer acceptable. The very reason that annual comparisons have so little value for analyzing individual student performance is what makes them so useful in analyzing curriculum. If sub-scales indicate strong number sense and geometry skills accompanied by weak performance in measurement and problem solving, we can confidently attribute the pattern to the emphasis we place on various aspects of the curriculum, not student differences.

The No Child Left Behind Act's emphasis on all sub-groups showing sustained improvement in reaching proficiency is consistent with standards-based education. The act's requirement for annual testing, grades 3 through 10, will soon push states to begin reporting by cohort, even though historical practice examines the test (third-grade reading, fourth-grade math, fifth-grade writing, etc.).

What can be done? Begin today to track performance by cohorts and to take advantage of the rich data that effort will provide about teaching quality articulation across levels; and the need to vary time, interventions, and opportunity to ensure that all students achieve proficiency. Longitudinal measures shift the focus from specific tests to the ability of the district or school to show continuous improvement. Do not forget to include antecedents that correlate positively with excellence as measures and a liberal proportion of cause data. The result will be a data framework that will allow us to see clearly what is occurring with any learning gaps by cohort groups, and to monitor individual performance.

Caveat: Be careful in selecting indicators for longitudinal tracking, as far too often in public education, the target shifts with new tests that require at least a trend line distinguishing prior test results from current results. This question underscores once again the need for a comprehensive, multifaceted assessment program that includes embedded performance assessments, common EOC assessments, assessments for Power Standards, CRTs, writing assessments, and NRTs or the blended efforts in most state assessments that attempt to measure performance against fixed criteria (standards) using a multiple choice, select response framework common to NRTs with shifting cut scores based on percentiles rather than adhering strictly to a proficiency standard.

Presentation ideas: Compare prior year performance on specific assessments for the most recent two to three years to describe the annual testing paradigm still in place. Point out with a second slide key patterns that emerged in sub-scale scores with a description of plans to address the discrepancies and bolster the curriculum. Finally, present with one or two slides the longitudinal gains made by cohorts referenced in slide 1. Again, this analysis could be completed for most BOEs in three to five minutes, excluding questions.

16. **How do we determine the most critical data and conduct comparative analysis of criterion-referenced assessments (CRAs), common formative assessments (CFAs), and standardized test data?**
    Many schools and school systems examine their state assessment data to identify the area of greatest weakness and proceed to name that weakness as their top priority for the coming year. Frequently, school improvement plans establish annual goals on the same basis, only to shift emphasis the following year when scores for a different cohort of students improve in one area and lag in another. So, the question itself is critical. How do we develop priorities based on the data, including not only classroom assessments, EOC assessments, and state assessments but also lessons from the research?
    Several tools lend themselves to this process, including the Hishakawa fishbone, where we analyze data in terms of cause and effect. Use of a decision-making matrix with weighted factors is a useful tool to establish priorities based on current realities. A less well known process, which is equally collaborative and enlists our best thinking, is the use of the critical incident process, which examines events related to the data to help us understand with greater precision how to

solve the problem indicated by the data. Low scores in reading are not a problem but an indicator. Critical incident analysis allows us to take the data, reveal the root cause of low performance, and prioritize what will be done differently to achieve a different result. For example, assume the assessment data consistently point out that students struggle with the writing process, as measured by a holistic analytic writing process or 6+ trait rubrics. The critical incident process shifts our thinking from the effect data (resulting writing scores) to their causes, asking questions like, "Which aspect of the writing process is most difficult to handle? Is there a point in the process, in the use of prompts, in submission of final products where students are most apt to shut down, express resistance, or generally perform below their ability? Critical incident analysis examines root causes for very specific data deficits, linking our allocation of time, resources, and teaching strategies to develop priorities that lead to action.

Finally, a process of triangulation used widely in construction and by mariners is a helpful tool in determining the most critical point to start from diverse assessment data. Most educators are faced with multiple forms of data, all administered at different junctures and ranging from classroom performance assessments to EOC assessments, unit tests, projects, CRTs, state assessments, and independent NRTs such as SAT or ACT scores. We need to be able to triangulate with confidence, and advanced DDDM provides exercises to apply these tools and procedures to go deeper with greater precision and focus.

17. How do we process through the drill-down data by sub-skills and by break out groups (identifying needs)?

Another insightful question. The seven-step DDDM process takes us to the point where we not only identify needs by sub-skills for sub-groups but begin to identify effective teaching strategies to address the needs of very diverse learners. The Advanced Data Analysis seminar, offered by The Leadership and Learning Center, illuminates the lessons from DDDM by providing numerous analysis tools and the ability to triangulate (see question 16) data from multiple sources.

I would also suggest adopting a list of common expected teacher behaviors to ensure that school leaders and classroom teachers have a deep understanding of expectations from the state assessment, content standards, district curriculum, and each of their students (transformational schools). Here are a few standard expected behaviors:

- Teachers know what concepts and skills are tested on district/state assessments for their particular grade level.
- Teachers know the district standards and English language development (ELD) standards for each grade level.
- Teachers have studied a side-by-side content analysis of standards, assessments curriculum, and textbooks.
- Teachers at each grade level schedule what they are going to teach each month based on the assessments and standards.
- Teachers have selected target students by name to whom they give extra attention and help based on assessment data.

• The principal knows—at least monthly—which students have recently reached grade level.

Transformational schools identify many other behaviors, but the key point is to be explicit enough about professional expectations that each teacher knows as much as they possibly can about their own curriculum, assessments, standards, and teaching materials.

18. **How do we select approaches to address weaknesses once drill-down data have been analyzed?**

This question underscores the need for advanced data analysis by pointing out the importance of establishing strategic priorities based on best practices in teaching strategies and data analysis. It is critical to sustain key principles from DDDM in all we do, especially reliance on the power of collaboration, use of antecedents in planning and execution, and accountability. In the Advanced Data Analysis seminar, The Center employs a framework to remind us to address each of these issues in selecting from a wide variety of approaches in a data-driven environment where questioning and positing hypotheses is the rule rather than the exception.

Data Systems Concerns

19. **Can you suggest books/resources for teacher-leaders responsible for promoting data-driven decision making at the school level?**

Schmoker's *Results Now* (2006) and *Results Fieldbook* (2001) continue to offer exceptional insights into managing data. In addition, other authors such as Guskey, Reeves, and Popham offer excellent resources in the journal *Educational Leadership* and in Dr. Reeves' books *Holistic Accountability* (2002b) and *Accountability in Action* (2004a). *Ahead of the Curve*, also by Reeves (2007), is an excellent resource, as is *Spreadsheet Modeling for Business Decisions*, by John Kros (2007), to assist teacher-leaders who are serious about making the data work for the school in becoming fluent with Excel and its many functions. You learn to not only "crunch numbers" but also analyze to the third or fourth probe or "drill" levels.

20. **How do we organize and track consistent data? Each year we add new data sources, such as STAR or Acuity. Which do we keep, and which do we eliminate?**

A very important element of the Advanced Data Analysis seminar is a section on managing the data calendar. This task is no less critical for schools and classrooms than for the central office, and all need a process to spread out important data points; reduce the crunch in December, April, and June (or any other months that may serve as data bottlenecks); and ensure that data are verified, collected, examined, analyzed, evaluated, and acted upon to improve decision making. A wide number of vendor products have opened up opportunities for data analysis and research through powerful data management software platforms. Many have test-builder capacity so schools and teachers can create and monitor online assessments that can be administered quickly with excellent reporting capability. The questioner raises compelling concerns that are also central to our seminar approach in Advanced Data Analysis: How do we eliminate anything, and what process will allow us to routinely make good decisions about aggregating certain data and eliminating other data? Who has the authority to give permission to eliminate certain data points, and how can that authority be established within a comprehensive school system? For all of these concerns, a concise and helpful process is provided all participants in Advanced Data Analysis.

Concerns about DDDM for Instructional Improvement

21. **What is the most effective way to correlate the successful strategies with the improvements? Are we as successful as we might be in determining our antecedents of success?**

In the Advanced Data Analysis seminar, The Leadership and Learning Center takes great care to make sure the key principles in data-driven decision making are extended and refined. Strategies that are highly correlated with effective teaching are infused with these principles in such a way as to deepen participant application of both data-driven decision making and effective teaching strategy seminars while participants learn new tools to apply local data in their own districts, schools, and classrooms. An extensive hypothesis matrix provides each participant with a process to incorporate the principles of data-driven decision making with the most effective teaching strategies for applying data analysis to close the learning gap and improve student achievement for all with confidence. This matrix addresses the first half of this question to ensure that participants are careful to include antecedents for success, collaboration, and accountability in each effort to address needs revealed by thoughtful and focused data analysis. As educators, we seldom are as successful as we might be, but The Leadership and Learning Center offers practical tools that advance our efforts to a new level of precision, clarity, and focus in data analysis that works.

APPENDIX C: **Template for Triangulation of Data**

```
          ┌─────────────────────────┐
          │ Instructional Strategies│
          │   and Teacher Routines  │
          │   (antecedent causes)   │
          └─────────────────────────┘
```

Instructional Strategies and Teacher Routines (antecedent causes)

Collaboration Measures (antecedent causes)

Accountability Measures (antecedent causes)

Student Achievement (Effects Data)

What do we know from these data (patterns, trends, similarities, differences, outliers)? _____

_____

_____

What do we want to find out? (decide on purpose of analysis)_____

_____

_____

What do we need to learn, and how will we know we learned it? (choose analysis method) _____

_____

_____

Purpose of Analysis

Analysis Method Selected

Tools

APPENDIX D: **Template for Wagon Wheel Tool for Data Analysis**

Steps in using the wagon wheel:

1. Assign key variables to each spoke on the wheel (8).
2. Collect data across key variables.
3. Establish a scale for each spoke, with the highest performance on the outer rim of the circle. Label individual spokes with their own scale.
4. Plot performance data along spokes, color coding to distinguish units being compared (classrooms, schools, departments, grade levels, budgets, even certification areas).
5. Connect the lines for each unit if comparisons are made between units.
6. Identify the pattern of performance against selected performance standards.

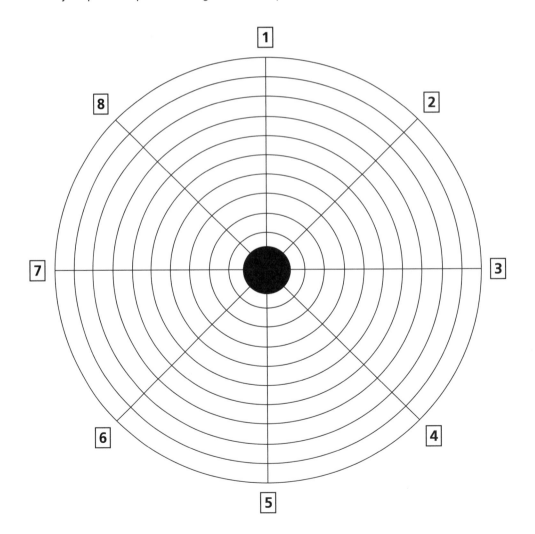

Wagon Wheel Tool for Data Analysis

School: _____ Date: _____

Department/Team: _____

Team Members: _____

_____

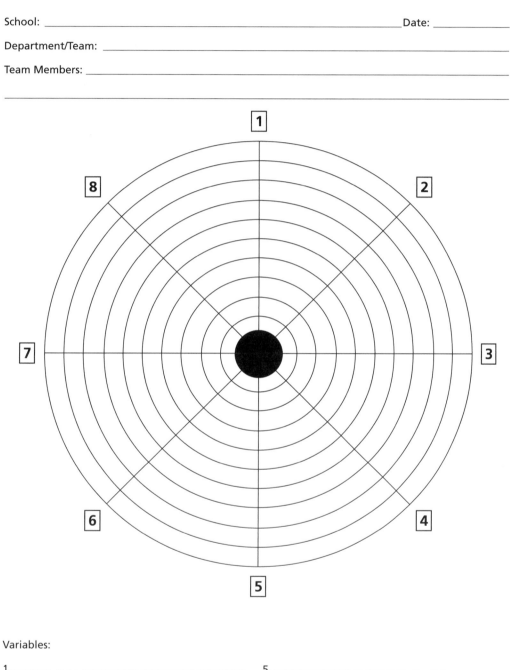

Variables:

1. _____   5. _____

2. _____   6. _____

3. _____   7. _____

4. _____   8. _____

APPENDIX E: **The Hishakawa Fishbone:
A Cause-and-Effect Diagram**

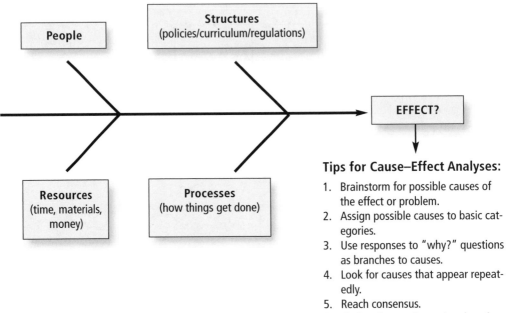

Tips for Cause–Effect Analyses:

1. Brainstorm for possible causes of the effect or problem.
2. Assign possible causes to basic categories.
3. Use responses to "why?" questions as branches to causes.
4. Look for causes that appear repeatedly.
5. Reach consensus.
6. Gather data to determine the relative impact of causes.
7. Develop an action plan to address the cause at its "Root."

APPENDIX F: Listening System Template, Part I: Stakeholder Satisfaction

School _____ Principal _____ Date _____ E-mail _____

Stakeholder Surveys	Parents	Teachers and Administrators	Staff	Students	Patrons	P	I	E	Rationale: Current Practice
What do we do currently with the data?									
Authority to act (commit resources)?									
Who? / When?									
How?									
Summary of stakeholder satisfaction listening system:									

P = proposed   I = introduced   E = established

Guidelines for Listening Systems: **Cyclical   Predictable   Public (open, transparent)   User Friendly**

APPENDIX F: **Listening System Template, Part II: Focus Groups and Structured Interviews**

School _____ Principal _____ Date _____ E-mail _____

Focus Groups and Structured Interviews	Parents	Teachers and Administrators	Staff	Students	Patrons	P	I	E	Rationale: Current Practice
What do we do currently with the data?									
Authority to act (commit resources)?									
Who? / When?									
How?									

Summary of focus group and structured interview listening systems:

P = proposed   I = introduced   E = established

Guidelines for Listening Systems: **Cyclical   Predictable   Public (open, transparent)   User Friendly**

APPENDIX F: Listening System Template, Part III: Web Site

School _____ Principal _____ Date _____ E-mail _____

Web Site Listening	Parents	Teachers and Administrators	Staff	Students	Patrons	P	I	E	Rationale: Current Practice
What do we do currently with the data?									
Authority to act (commit resources)?									
Who? / When?									
How?									
Summary of Web site listening system:									

P = proposed   I = introduced   E = established

Guidelines for Listening Systems: **Cyclical   Predictable   Public (open, transparent)   User Friendly**

APPENDIX G: **Critical Incident Report**

Critical incident reporting is an informal analysis tool that helps teams understand the most troublesome symptoms in a problematic situation. Even the most careful triangulation of data can fail to reveal patterns that prevent schools and classrooms from moving ahead. Critical incident reporting is fundamentally a group process to systematically and fairly articulate emerging or persistent problems that influence the quality of efforts to improve student achievement. It is also a prequel for other tools, such as the cause and effect fishbone diagram or relations diagram. It works like this:

1. Assemble a group of participant stakeholders, making sure to represent every department, grade level, or classification of employee who may be impacted by the problem or the challenge to dramatically improve performance or raise student achievement.

2. Ask each participant to respond in writing to one or two predefined questions with as many specifics as possible. Scaffold your request to elicit an incident that:

Was most difficult to handle? OR Repeated itself unnecessarily?	Cost the most? OR Wasted the most time or effort?
What Incident?	
Was the most difficult assignment to complete? OR Embarrassed the school?	Required the most re-work? OR Inhibited student achievement?

3. Select a set of questions that get at the crux of issues that have been resistant to change, slow to improve relative to other district or school efforts, or keep people from performing at their highest level.

4. Collect the responses and create an affinity chart on which major categories of responses are grouped by responses and presented graphically for discussion.

5. Through consensus or use of a decision-making matrix, distill the responses down until you identify the most critical incident and use it as a starting point to identify possible causes and antecedents (Hishakawa fishbone diagram).

Critical incident reporting provides "soft" data, not unlike narratives that supplement district or state accountability reports and give the "story behind the numbers." It has the capacity to clarify a particular challenge, and it is an excellent opportunity to model transparency and a safe learning environment. It is recommended as a "fast track" tool to identify relatively easy improvements to implement and to ensure that observations and perceptions are part of a comprehensive data system.

APPENDIX H: **A Data Road Map**

The data plan road map is designed to reveal issues where improvement has been lacking, growth has been stagnant, and efforts have failed to produce results. **Drive carefully.**

1. Intersections

1. _____

2. _____

3. _____

Identify at least three sets of data you will triangulate with your peers to make visible the invisible in your organization. Connect these intersections with arrows to indicate possible ways to triangulate the data.

1. _____

2. _____

3. _____

Student Achievement (effects)

1. _____

2. _____

3. _____

1. _____

2. _____

3. _____

Insights for Action?

1. _____

2. _____

3. _____

2. Data Driving Habits

What needs to change?	What needs to increase?	What needs to improve?	What data do you need to create?

3. Rearview-Mirror Effect

Halogen headlights: proactive strategies

1. _____

_____ (will begin __/__/201_)

2. _____

_____ (will begin __/__/201_)

3. _____

_____ (will begin __/__/201_)

4. _____

_____ (will begin __/__/201_)

Canaries for your classroom

1. _____

    _____ (will begin __/__/201_)

2. _____

    _____ (will begin __/__/201_)

3. _____

    _____ (will begin __/__/201_)

4. _____

    _____ (will begin __/__/201_)

Canaries for your school

1. _____

    _____ (will begin __/__/201_)

2. _____

    _____ (will begin __/__/201_)

3. _____

    _____ (will begin __/__/201_)

4. _____

    _____ (will begin __/__/201_)

Canaries for your district

1. _____

    _____ (will begin __/__/201_)

2. _____

    _____ (will begin __/__/201_)

3. _____

    _____ (will begin __/__/201_)

4. _____

    _____ (will begin __/__/201_)

4. Stoplights (feedback systems)

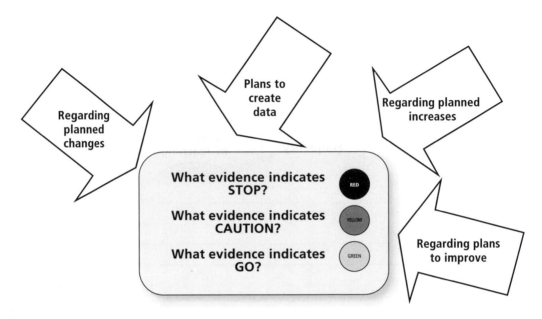

5. Detours and Road Closures

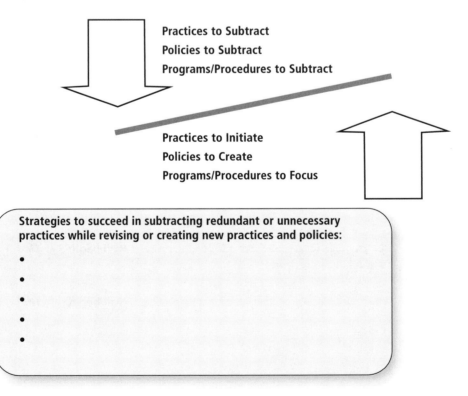

6. Use your digital camera (user-friendly embedded data)

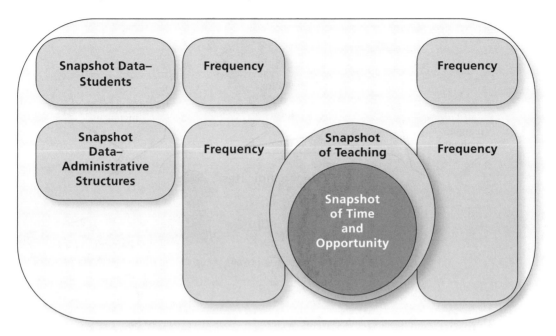

Time-referenced artifacts are excellent measures of gains in classrooms and schools. Literal snapshots can provide meaningful data at any time.

Possible snapshots of student data, teaching, administrative structures, and time/opportunity:
1. _____
2. _____
3. _____
4. _____
5. _____
6. _____
7. _____
8. _____
9. _____
10. _____
11. _____
12. _____

7. Data in action—explicit changes in driving data

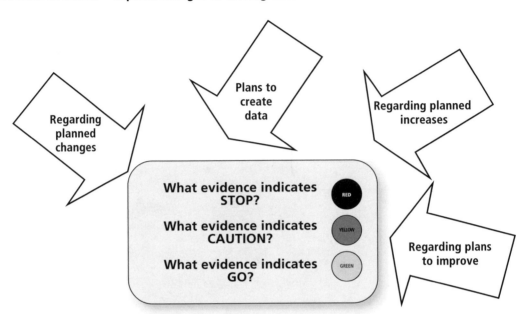

Regarding planned changes

Plans to create data

Regarding planned increases

What evidence indicates STOP?   RED

What evidence indicates CAUTION?   YELLOW

What evidence indicates GO?   GREEN

Regarding plans to improve

Identify the routines and behaviors that need to change, those that need to be increased, strategies to improve the quality of others, and new measures of teacher performance. Then, answer the stoplight questions to chart the most effective path to success.

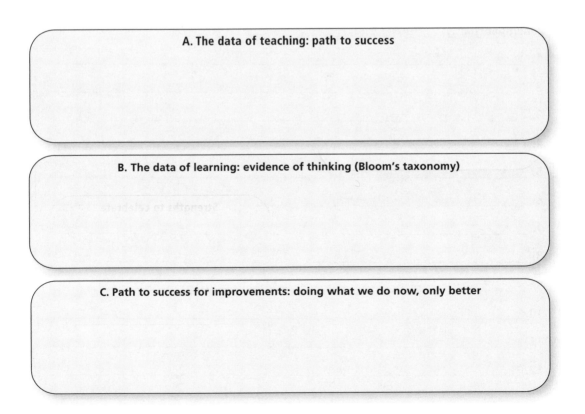

A. The data of teaching: path to success

B. The data of learning: evidence of thinking (Bloom's taxonomy)

C. Path to success for improvements: doing what we do now, only better

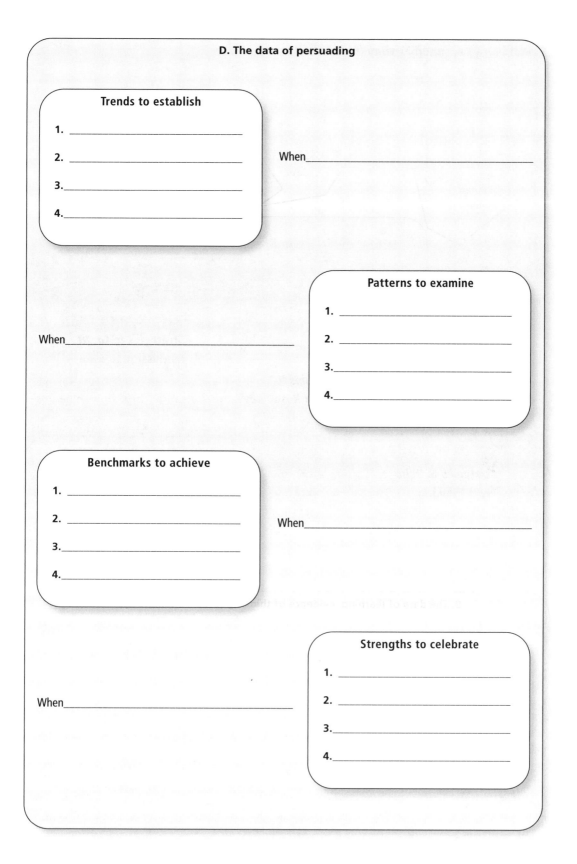

D. The data of persuading

Trends to establish

1. _____

2. _____

3. _____

4. _____

When_____

Patterns to examine

1. _____

2. _____

3. _____

4. _____

When_____

Benchmarks to achieve

1. _____

2. _____

3. _____

4. _____

When_____

Strengths to celebrate

1. _____

2. _____

3. _____

4. _____

When_____

8. Building your superhighway (leadership)

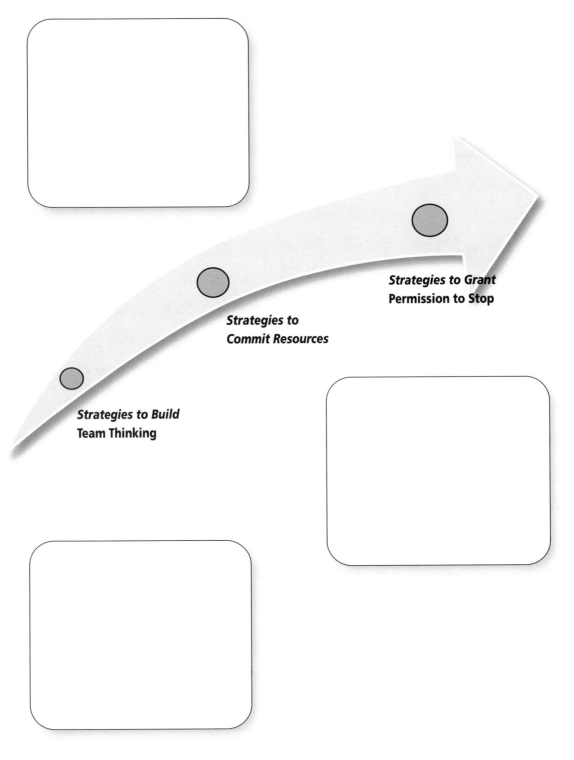

**Strategies to Build
Team Thinking**

**Strategies to
Commit Resources**

**Strategies to Grant
Permission to Stop**

The Data Road Map Summary

School _____ School Year _____

Data Team _____

	Implementation Timeline		
	Start	**Evaluate**	**Complete**

Intersections

| Triangulation | Triangulation | Triangulation | Triangulation |

Data driving habits

| To Change | To Increase | To Improve | To Create |

Rearview-mirror effects

| Improve the Headlights | Canaries for the Classroom | Canaries for the School | Canaries for the System |

Traffic signals and signs

| Feedback System Changes | | Listening System Changes | |

Detours and road closures

| Practices to Subtract | Policies to Subtract | Structures to Subtract | |

Use your digital camera: catch the scenery

| Student Data | Adult Data | Structure Data | Time & Opportunity Data |

Data in action

| Teaching | Learning | Improving | Persuading |

Building your superhighway (leadership)

| Team Thinking | Agility in Committing Resources | Permission to Stop | |

Summary _____

_____

_____

_____